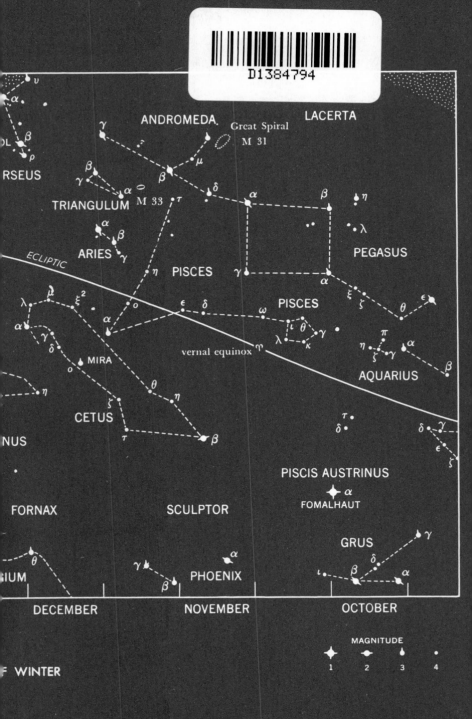

# SPLENDOR IN THE SKY

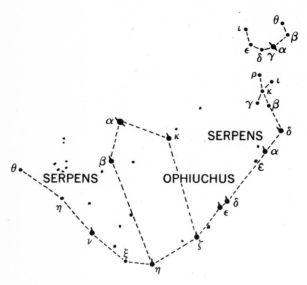

# Splendor

WITH PAINTINGS BY ROBERT E. RIDLEY

# GERALD  S.  HAWKINS

*Associate Professor of Astronomy,*
*Boston University*
*Director Boston University Observatory*
*Research Associate Harvard College Observatory*

# *in the Sky*

HARPER & BROTHERS, PUBLISHERS  *New York*

*Library of Congress catalog card number: 61-10222*

*This book is dedicated to
my reader.*

# ILLUSTRATION CREDITS

The author wishes to thank the following people and organizations for supplying illustrative material for this book: Robert Edwyn Ridley, illustrations prepared especially for the book, Plates 1, 4, 7, 8, 9, 10, 12, 14, 15, 16, 17, and Figures 1, 2, 3, 5, 6, 7, 8, 9, 10, 11, 12, 13, 14, 15, 19, 20, 21, 22, 23, 24, 25, 26, 27, 28, 29, 30, 31, 33, 34, 36, 37; Alexia Hayes for Figure 32 prepared from a contemporary print especially for this book; Adelaide H. Crowne, Figure 38; Stanley R. Larson, Magnuson and Vincent, Cambridge, Massachusetts, Figure 4 and endpaper maps drawn for this book; John A. Farrell, Plate 28; Dr. Curtis L. Hemenway, Dudley Observatory, Albany, New York, Plate 25; Dr. G. H. Herbig, Lick Observatory, Mt. Hamilton, California, Plate 26; Dr. John S. Rinehart, Colorado School of Mines, Plates 29, 30 (Smithsonian Institution photographs); photographs from the Mount Wilson and Palomar Observatories, Plates 3, 21, 22, 18, 35, 33, 34, 36; Lick Observatory photographs, Plates 11, 13, 23, 24, 26; by courtesy of Harvard College Observatory, Plates 19, 20; United States Weather Bureau, Plates 5, 6 (number 6 by E. Fontsere); Official United States Navy photograph, Plate 37; National Aeronautics and Space Administration photographs, Plates 31, 32; Sacramento Peak Observatory, U. S. Geophysical Research Directorate, AFCRC, Plates 19, 20; United Press International, Ed Fitzgerald, Plate 2; Macmillan and Company, London, *Stargazing* by Norman Lockyer, Figure 16, 18; The Clarendon Press, Oxford, Handbook of Astronomy, Vol. II, by George F. Chambers, Figure 17; D. Appleton and Company, New York, *Popular Astronomy,* by Camille Flammarion, by courtesy of Appleton-Century-Crofts, Inc., Figure 18; by courtesy of Sky and Telescope, Cambridge, Massachusetts, Plates 23, 24, 28; *The New York Times,* Figure 35.

# CONTENTS

# PLATES

# PREFACE

FOR MANY YEARS I HAVE BEEN INVOLVED IN A PROGRAM OF "Observatory Open Nights." People come to the observatory to look through the telescopes at the showpieces of the universe—the moon and planets and star clusters. For the astronomer, it is a rewarding experience to hear the gasp of amazement when somebody looks through a telescope for the first time. The question-and-answer period which usually follows an open night once again shows the enthusiasm that there is for the sky. There is never sufficient time to answer all the questions, even if a complete answer were always available.

Experiences such as these have encouraged me to write this book, which attempts to cover a wide range of interest, from the planets to the stars and the galaxies beyond. It is a book which attempts to emphasize the depth of astronomy, showing that recent innovations in space science have roots which go deep into the past. A person whose interest in astronomy is first kindled by the idea of space travel and satellites will soon find the trail of knowledge leading back to the Middle Ages when the first vague understanding of planetary laws began. A person who is attracted by the brilliancy of Venus as an evening star will turn his interest to the pattern among the stars, the constellations designed by the Babylonians in prehistory. A person who scans with a telescope the craters of the moon will become acquainted with the names of ancient philosophers such as Aristotle, Plato, and Archimedes.

In any outline of astronomy it is difficult to avoid a bias in the interpretation of the facts. Science contains many rival theories which are vehemently supported by their protagonists and rashly denounced by their opposers. I have tried to avoid such controversy but in many areas the evidence seems, to my mind, to favor a certain theory. The particular theory has therefore been described in what might be construed as a biased manner. For example, I belong to the group of scientists who believe that craters on the moon were formed by meteorite bombardment rather than volcanic eruptions; that comets are icy conglomerates and not clouds of dust; that the planets condensed from a solar nebula and were not formed by a collision process, and that the universe of galaxies is not expanding from a single primeval atom which appeared in the remote past.

There are also differing viewpoints in the interpretation of historical events. In many instances new information comes to light which changes our outlook. Sometimes there is a reappraisal of the character of a person or his motivations. In this regard I have taken account of the more recent discoveries relating to the life of Kepler. There is a growing body of opinion which elevates Johannes Kepler above his contemporaries of the Renaissance period. This viewpoint necessarily lowers, to some extent, our estimation of Copernicus and Tycho, and tends to show Galileo not as a brilliant scientist but more as an eloquent philosopher.

In presenting this story of science I have been greatly helped by the illustrations supplied by Mt. Palomar and Mt. Wilson, Yerkes, Lick, and other observatories. The art work of Robert E. Ridley has added immeasurably to the clarity of the book, and Professor Charlotte Lindgren has helped editorially. The original motivation arose from a suggestion by Mrs. T. Carter Harrison, who continued as an efficient literary agent with the right comments at the right time. Dr. Robert S. Cohen, chairman of the Physics Department, Boston University, was kind enough to read and suggest corrections to the manuscript. I am indebted to Mrs. Edith Homer for the preparation of the final manuscript. Harold E. Grove has helped editorially, and Seamus Byrne is responsible for the imaginative layout.

My wife, Dorothy, has given continued assistance and encouragement during each stage of the book's development. In particular Dorothy aided with research references, proof reading, and in the typing of early drafts.

To these and others whom I have not mentioned but who have contributed to the book in many ways I offer my grateful appreciation and thanks. Any errors that remain are my own responsibility, but I hope there are few if any obscurities left in the book to cause puzzlement to my reader.

G. S. Hawkins

Cambridge, Massachusetts
January 1961.

# PART 1

# THE SHEPHERDS' VIEW

e stone of Denderah showing the
nstellations as they were known
re than two thousand years ago.
m an old French print, drawn
m the slab which was moved
m the Temple of Isis in Egypt to
ris in 1820. (*Sky and Telescope*)

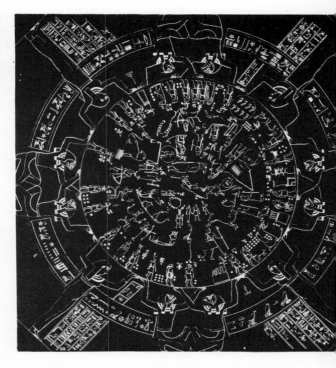

# CHAPTER 1

# STARGAZING

ANTARES

SCORPIUS

THE SPREAD OF CIVILIZATION ACROSS THE EARTH BROUGHT A MESSAGE of encouragement to mankind. The primitive beginning in the dank caves eventually gave way to a more secure life based upon the growing of crops, which in turn led to the development of an organized society. Today, the few isolated tribes who live by hunting are regarded by sociologists as a curious link with the past.

For perhaps a million years Homo sapiens has been on the Earth in a form not much superior to the animals. The first awakening seems to have taken place in the Middle East—Persia, Turkey and present-day Iraq. We know that primitive man could make stone implements and light fires because we find the evidence today; we know he must have spoken or communicated with his fellow men because the art of working stone spread rapidly, but he could not write, and he took no interest in the universe. The cave paintings all show an obsession with the hunt, but nowhere do we see pictures of the sun, moon, or stars.

The big step forward came when man looked away from the Earth. At the time of Noah and the Flood, which probably dates back to 4000 B.C., men must have begun to recognize the pattern of the stars for we find references to the constellations in the very earliest clay tablets of the Babylonians. Later, astronomy was to be intimately connected with Greek literature and philosophy, religion and the Renaissance. Even the promise of tomorrow is coupled with the stars and planets. Yet we have tended to lose contact with the splendor of the sky, the source of inspiration in antiquity. Because of civilization we find ourselves living in cities where night is turned into day by the glare of electric lights. We look upward only when there is a noisy jet or a vapor trail.

The shepherds between the valleys of the Tigris and Euphrates must have known the sky very well. They considered the Earth to be a flat disk which ended just beyond the horizon, while over their heads stretched the celestial sphere, the dome of the heavens. Their imaginations shaped a few stars into the form of the herdsman Boötes, with the sun, moon, and stars as his flock of sheep. They noticed that the stars turned once around the pole every twenty-four hours, and Orion would rise in the east to make a long sweep across the sky before setting in the West. The five planets were wandering sheep that moved slowly amongst the other stars, presenting an ever-changing picture. Sometimes a comet would appear, or a shower of shooting stars would fall. Sometimes a nova would flare into view to change the shape of a constellation. There was much to see during the course of the long night, and the shepherds had time enough for contemplation under the canopy of stars.

But the pattern of the constellations was not designed by the shepherds. Some higher authority must have been responsible, otherwise we would not find such universal agreement on the constellations. The pattern was fixed according to some well-developed religion or mythology. The Egyptians copied the patterns from the Babylonians, the

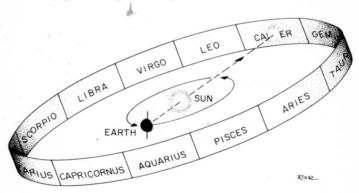

**Fig. 1.   Apparent path of the sun around the zodiac**

Greeks copied the Egyptians, and we copied the Greeks. The same constellations have been handed down with little change for five thousand years, but we are puzzled by our inheritance for the meaning of the ancient cult is lost. There was, for some reason, a desire to duplicate things. There are two serpents, two slayers of serpents, two fish, two streams, and the double figure of Gemini the twins. Sometimes the stars lend themselves naturally to the figure, but more often the stars are a misfit, as with Pegasus the upside-down horse, and Ursa Minor the little bear. The designer wanted these figures in the sky even though the stars suggested other, more striking, patterns.

At a very early time, the high priests, or whoever designed the patterns, marked out the belt of the zodiac. This is the band in which the planets, sun, and moon are always found. The sun moves along the middle of the belt, its path marked by the ecliptic. The zodiac, stretching entirely around the sky, is divided into the twelve signs so familiar to us because of astrology. They are set out in order in the diagram, and the stars which make the various figures can be identified in the end paper charts. Taurus the bull and Scorpio the scorpion were probably the first constellations of the zodiac to be named. The stars lend themselves very well to these figures. Scorpio, its heart marked by the red star Antares, has a raised tail ready to sting. It is easy to discern the horns of the bull and the right eye, marked by a bright orange star called by the Arabs Aldebaran. Around 3000 B.C., Taurus and Scorpio were at the equinoctial points; they were overhead at the equator. You will notice that Taurus was in a different position in the zodiac in the year 1000 B.C. and 1000 A.D., for each constellation moves one space along the ecliptic every two thousand years. This slow drifting toward the left is caused by the precession of the Earth's axis, and it is very important to remember it when we probe the meaning of the ancient constellations.

By watching the sunrise, a person could tell the position of the sun in the zodiac. Spring, or the vernal equinox, was marked by Taurus five thousand years ago. This signified the beginning of the year as the sun was sent on its way around the zodiac by a gentle prod from the horns. At midsummer the sun had reached the highest point in the ecliptic, the constellation Leo the Lion, a figure which personifies tropical heat. In the fall, the sun moved lower in the sky, and the autumnal equinox was symbolized by Scorpio clasping the sun with its claws. In the middle of winter, the sun reached Aquarius the water carrier, a man who poured rain on the Earth.

Some archeologists believed that the ancient cult used only six constellations, probably Taurus, Gemini, Leo, Scorpio, Capricornus, and Aquarius. A change was needed by the year 1000 B.C., because precession had moved Taurus away from the vernal equinox. Spring was now occurring when the sun was in the hind quarter of the bull, and autumn began when the sun was at the tip of the scorpion's claws. Aries the ram and Libra the scales were probably marked out at this time to show the equinoxes more clearly. Cancer and Capricornus

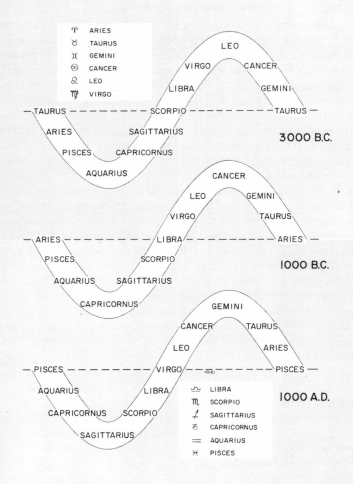

Fig. 2. The zodiac in history

were at the high and low points of the ecliptic. The Greek astronomers adopted the zodiac of 1000 B.C., and we followed the Greeks. That is why today we talk of the Tropic of Cancer and Capricorn even though the tropics are now marked by the constellations of Gemini and Sagittarius. '

The early stargazers recognized that some stars were brighter than others. These differences were described more exactly by the Greeks, who divided the stars into six categories of brightness. The brightest stars in the sky were of first magnitude, the medium-bright stars were second magnitude, and stars of average brightness were third magnitude. At the lower end of the scale, the stars which could only just be seen with the naked eye were placed in the group of sixth magnitude. There were therefore five intervals between the brightest and the faintest stars. We have adopted the notion of magnitude in modern astronomy, and with precise instruments we can measure brightness with an accuracy of 1 per cent. Nowadays the word "magnitude" carries a more precise meaning, a difference of five magnitudes, for example, means that one star is exactly one hundred times brighter than the other. Antares in Scorpio, Aldebaran in Taurus, and Pollux in Gemini are stars of the first magnitude. The stars in the Big Dipper are magnitude $+2$, and the fainter stars in the Pleiades are magnitude $+5$. A few stars are more than one hundred times brighter than the faint sixth-magnitude stars, and astronomers have been forced to extend the old magnitude scale. Vega, in the constellation of Lyra, and Arcturus, in Boötes, are 0-magnitude stars—one magnitude brighter than Antares. Sirius is brighter than Vega, and to express this fact its magnitude is less than 0. Sirius therefore has a negative magnitude, $-1.4$. Vega is one hundred times brighter than a star of fifth magnitude, and Sirius is one hundred times brighter than a star of magnitude $+3.6$. The full moon has a magnitude of $-13$, and the sun $-27$. The sun is fourteen magnitudes brighter than the moon and so sunlight is nearly one million times more intense than moonlight.

With modern technology we can create again some of the atmosphere of ancient stargazing by means of a planetarium, where star images are projected onto a dome-shaped ceiling which represents the vault of the heavens. The stars can be arranged for any position on the surface of the Earth, for any time of the night. As the audience settles down for the show the lights are dimmed to bring out the stars as they appear in the hazy glare of the city. A further decrease of the illumination takes the audience into the darkness of the countryside where more than two thousand stars can be seen.

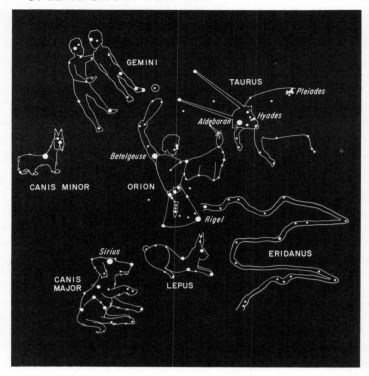

Fig. 3.    The winter sky

The projector can also take us backwards in time, precessing the constellations until they shine as they did in 3000 B.C. It can also speed up events, making twenty-four hours pass by in a minute. Then we get a vivid impression of the celestial sphere spinning around the poles, with each star making a diurnal circle, small if the star is near the pole, and large if it is near the equator. It is easy to see how people were led to believe in the rotation of the sky instead of the rotation of the Earth. A star on the celestial equator rises at the due east point on the horizon, reaches its highest elevation when it is south, and sets exactly in the west. Stars above the equator rise in the northeast portion of the horizon, and stars below the equator rise in the southeast. The stars near the celestial pole never rise or set. They make a circular path which does not cut the horizon. The circumpolar stars of the Northern Hemisphere are shown in Figure 4. The familiar constellation of the Big Dipper is circumpolar for the northern part of the United States.

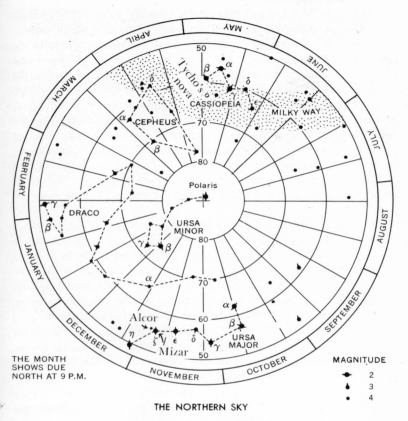

THE MONTH
SHOWS DUE
NORTH AT 9 P.M.

MAGNITUDE
2
3
4

THE NORTHERN SKY

Fig. 4.  Stars in the northern sky

The zodiac follows a band that is tilted at an angle to the celestial
equator. When the planets are speeded up we can see them moving
along the zodiac in an easterly direction from Aries to Taurus and
Gemini. Mercury and Venus stay near the sun because they are inner
planets, but the outer planets, Mars, Jupiter, and Saturn, make a wide
sweep round the entire circumference of the zodiac. Sometimes a
planet falters, then reverses its direction of motion for several weeks
before it regains the eastward drift. Under these conditions the planet
is showing retrograde motion, a great puzzle for the ancient astronomers yet readily explained by Copernicus and the astronomers who
followed him.

If you wish to do a little stargazing you can find your way with the
help of the end paper. If you start your observing on a summer evening

at 9.00 P.M. in the middle of July, you will see the group of stars which form Scorpio above the southern horizon. Antares, with an orange hue, will be the first star to show itself as the sun is setting, and to the right of Antares you will see the three stars that mark the head and shoulders of the scorpion. High to the left of Scorpio is Aquila the eagle, marked by the bright star Altair, and above Aquila the northern cross of Cygnus the swan. If you begin your stargazing in the winter at 9.00 P.M. in February, you will see Orion in the south. For the northern United States Orion appears halfway up the sky, but for southern states, such as Florida and southern California, Orion seems to be almost overhead. This constellation is one of the easiest to find because the stars mark out so clearly the figure of a man with a well-proportioned waist and a diamond-studded sword hanging from his belt.

The winter provides us with quite a picture gallery. Orion is standing on the banks of the river Eridanus, which winds its way down toward the Southwest. He is menacing Taurus with a club in his right hand, but he never quite reaches the bull as he moves toward the west because both constellations are fixed on the celestial sphere. The horns of the bull are as large as Orion himself, and leave no doubt that Taurus could throw the hunter high in the air if Orion came too close. On the same banks of the river as Orion, and crouching for protection at his feet we see a hare marked by the constellation Lepus. Following behind Orion are his two hunting dogs, the bright stars Sirius and Procyon. High overhead we find Gemini, the heavenly twins known as Castor and Pollux. This constellation does not seem to fit in with the picture of the hunt, though perhaps we can imagine it to signify the sky. The Pleiades are a group of seven stars, one of them rather faint, carried on the back of Taurus. They have the popular name of the seven sisters, though they were regarded by the Greeks as seven white doves.

There is a great deal of such mythology written in the sky. It began in pre-Babylonian times, and has been embellished by the poets of Egypt, Greece, and Rome. As an example let us consider some of the stories associated with the winter constellations.

According to the Greeks, there was once a beautiful maiden Europa who was admired by all men who saw her. The gods also noticed her, and Jupiter, the king of the gods, fell in love with her. He seduced her by taking the form of a snow-white bull and swam with her on his back to an island. Once ashore, Jupiter threw off the form of the bull which was hung in the sky to commemorate the exploit. The continent of Europe inherited the name of the maiden.

According to the Latin poet Ovid, Orion was a great hunter who bragged too much. The gods decided to punish him by sending a scorpion to bite his foot. Orion and the scorpion were then placed in the sky opposite each other as an example to all boasters. As the scorpion rises in the east, Orion sets like a coward in the west, only daring to rise again when the scorpion itself is setting. As a subplot, Orion is supposed to be making advances on the seven sisters of the Pleiades, but Taurus is standing there to protect them. Merope, daughter of the King of Chios, is one of the Pleiades, and Orion had at one time tried to elope with her after the King forbade the marriage. The plan was discovered, and Orion was drugged, blinded, and left by the seashore. A one-eyed cyclops, however, helped him regain his sight.

Orion signaled the storms of winter by supposedly causing a disturbance of the water as he dropped into the sea in the cold November mornings.The Pleiades also were used by the Greeks and Phoenicians to mark the opening of the navigation season, rising at dawn in late April when the gales of spring were over. In October the Pleiades rose in the early evening, just as the sun was setting. At this time they heralded the return of the bad weather. It was prudent to sail when the Pleiades were not visible in the night sky. Most other cultures have shared the Phoenician fear of the Pleiades. They have always been associated with bad weather, rain or flood, and death. The "sweet influences of the Pleiades" mentioned in the Book of Job referred to the coming of summer when the Pleiades had moved out of the night sky; their influence was most sweet when they were out of sight. When the Pleiades came into view in November, the druids of Britain let loose a night of terror which is reenacted today by children on Hallowe'en. It is strange to think of a perfectly normal galactic star cluster like the Pleiades creating such a wealth of mythology.

CANCER

CHAPTER 2

# EARTH AND SOLAR SYSTEM

INSTEAD OF THE FIVE PLANETS OF ANCIENT TIMES WE NOW RECOGNIZE nine planets which move around the sun in almost circular orbits. Within the orbit of the Earth are the two inner planets, Mercury and Venus. Beyond the orbit of the Earth we find the six outer planets, Mars, Jupiter, Saturn, Uranus, Neptune, and Pluto. The planets are also subdivided according to size. Mercury, Venus, the Earth, and Mars make up the group of terrestrial planets, while the other planets, except Pluto, are known as the major planets. If we go by the recent measurements of size, Pluto is a terrestrial planet, but in mass and internal constitution it may resemble the major planets more closely. Between the orbits of Mars and Jupiter there are over forty thousand objects, which, although they revolve around the sun, do not merit the name of planet. A few of them are spherical in shape; Ceres, for example, appears as a minute round disk in the telescope and is 480 miles in diameter. Most of the fragments are no more than a mile or so across, and are rough, irregular chunks of stone and iron. These fragments have been given various names—planetoids, minor planets, little planets, but the term generally used is "asteroid." Unfortunately this is a misnomer for it means "in the shape of a star." Although from a distance, shining in the light of the sun, they do resemble stars, there is a marked physical difference. Stars are incandescent balls of gas, whereas planets are cool, solid objects which do not emit a light of their own. The solar system also contains a large number of smaller objects which do not move in circular paths like planets. There are millions of comets following elongated orbits around the sun, evaporating in the solar heat to form long tails of gas. There are billions[1] of meteors; some ejected by comets, and some produced by collisions between asteroids. They appear as shooting stars when they are destroyed in the Earth's atmosphere. Clouds of charged particles, protons, electrons, and other ions which have been expelled from the sun permeate the entire solar system.

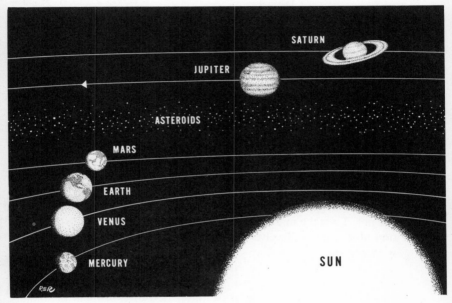

Fig. 5.   The planets move around the sun

The Earth moves once around the sun in 365 1/4 days, or more precisely 365.2422 days. The length of the day is 24 hours, the time taken for the Earth to spin once on its axis when viewed from the sun. It would have been a lucky coincidence if there had been an exact number of days in the year. As it was, the odd quarter of a day caused a problem to the calendar makers of the ancient world, and it took at least one thousand years to put matters right.

If the quarter of a day is neglected, then the calendar falls out of step with the seasons. Every four years, spring comes one day later and in a hundred years the error has amounted to almost four weeks. A solar calendar is difficult to regulate, but a lunar calendar is even more difficult. The moon takes 29.53 days on the average to pass once

[1] In this book the American billion—equal to one thousand million—is used.

around the Earth. If the year is divided up into 12 months controlled by the moon, then the year contains 354 days, an error of 11 1/4 days per year. The seasons arrive a whole month later after only three years have elapsed.

TABLE 1. THE PLANETS

| Planet | Diameter miles | Magnitude | Discoverer | Number of moons |
|---|---|---|---|---|
| ☿ Mercury | 2,900 | −1.9 | Antiquity | None |
| ♀ Venus | 7,600 | −4.4 | Antiquity | None |
| ⊕ Earth | 7,913 | — | Antiquity | 1 |
| ♂ Mars | 4,200 | −2.8 | Antiquity | 2 |
| (Asteroids) | (less than 500) | (less than 5) | Piazzi | None |
| ♃ Jupiter | 86,800 | −2.5 | Antiquity | 12 |
| ♄ Saturn | 71,500 | −0.4 | Antiquity | 9 |
| ♅ Uranus | 29,400 | +5.7 | Herschel | 5 |
| ♆ Neptune | 28,000 | +7.6 | Adams-Leverrier | 2 |
| ♇ Pluto | 3,600(?) | +14.9 | Tombaugh | None |

We have adopted the calendar system of the Romans which began at the supposed founding of Rome in the year 753 B.C. Although the Egyptians knew with fair precision the length of the year, the Romans did not. To make matters worse, they based their calendar on the motion of the moon. Twelve lunar months were used, and every year or so, when the seasons were coming late, an extra month was inserted. This extra month caused hardship, especially when it was used malevolently by politicians. It was sometimes added without warning to lengthen the tax year, to increase the period of enlistment of soldiers, and to postpone the election of new magistrates.

By the time of Julius Caesar the situation was intolerable. The first day of spring was occurring in June, and the population never knew when an extra month would occur. In the year 46 B.C., Julius Caesar called the astronomer Sosigenes over from Alexandria, and during the "last year of confusion," brought into use the Julian calendar. Following the Egyptians, the length of the year was increased to 365 1/4 days by adding 11 extra days to the old lunar calendar. The seventh month was named July in honor of the dictator, with 31 days. The eighth month was named August, during the reign of his successor, Augustus Caesar. At that time August had only 30 days in the month so a day was taken from February to equalize July and August.

It is of course impossible to add one-quarter of a day to the calendar each year. Sosigenes added one extra day every four years which has the same effect over a long period of time. Leap years occur when the year is divisible by four—such as 1960, 1964, 1968—and the extra day is inserted as February 29. But Sosigenes' year was still only an approximation; it was 11 minutes and 14 seconds longer than the true value. This small discrepancy gradually became important, and by the sixteenth century the first day of spring had advanced to March 11, two weeks ahead of the position decreed by Julius Caesar. Pope Gregory XIII, aided by the astronomer Clavius, made the final reform. Three leap years were omitted every 400 years. This was accomplished by making the year at the turn of the century a leap year only if it were divisible by 400, such as the years 1600, 2000, 2400. The Gregorian calendar gives a very good approximation to the true length of the year. It is only 26 seconds too long. By A.D. 4900, our calendar will have accumulated an error of about one day.

The improved calendar of Pope Gregory was adopted almost immediately by the Catholic world but its reception in Protestant countries was lukewarm. For nearly 200 years the Protestants clung to the calendar of Julius Caesar, referring to the dates as "old style." During the period of disagreement it was possible to sail from France on January 4, 1600, and arrive in England on December 25, 1599. There was general confusion in birthdays, legal matters, treaties, and commerce. England and the American colonies finally changed over to the "new style" calendar in 1752. By this time the error amounted to eleven days, and it was necessary to follow September 2 by September 14 to bring the Julian calendar into agreement with the Gregorian. Even then the change-over did not take place smoothly: riots occurred in London with the mob shouting "Give us back our eleven days!"

Both Caesar and Pope Gregory abandoned the notion of a month regulated by the phases of the moon. The new and full phases of the moon, produced as the moon circles the Earth in its orbit, can occur on any day of the month. Sunlight illuminates only one-half of the moon and when this hemisphere is toward us the moon is at the full phase. From the Earth, the moon appears to travel around the zodiac along a path that is slightly inclined to the ecliptic. The tilt is due to the inclination of the moon's orbit. If the inclination were zero the moon would move exactly along the ecliptic and would pass in front of the sun once during each revolution.

It is interesting to follow the moon from night to night as it moves among the constellations. In two nights it moves through one sign of the zodiac, and during this interval there is a noticeable change of phase. When the moon is in the constellation in which the sun is located, the Earth, moon, and sun are in line, and we on the Earth look at the shaded hemisphere of the moon. Astronomically speaking the moon is at the new phase, but in everyday language we follow the Babylonians and call the first thin crescent at sunset the "new moon." If you could visit the moon at this time, the sun would be below the horizon and it would be night. The fully illuminated Earth would be shining in a dark sky, casting a pale earthshine on the surface. This glow can somtimes be seen from the Earth, and then we talk of "the old moon in the new moon's arm."

Seven days later the moon will have traveled three constellations toward the east and the sunlight will be falling on it from the side. The moon has traveled one-quarter of the distance around its orbit, and the phase is "first quarter." After fourteen and a half days, the moon has reached the constellation opposite to the sun. Once again the sun, Earth, and moon are in line, but now the moon is full. If we could look at the Earth from the moon at this time, we would see the nighttime hemisphere; the Earth would be at the "new phase." Seven days later the moon has traveled three-quarters of the distance around the orbit, and is once again seen in a half-illuminated condition at the phase of "last quarter."

Because the orbit is tilted, the new moon usually passes a little above or below the sun. The moon only crosses the path of the sun, the ecliptic, at two points called the "nodes." The Babylonians and Greeks knew that an eclipse took place when the moon crossed the ecliptic, a word clearly associated with eclipse. They could calculate the day and hour when the moon was due to enter the danger zone, but they did not understand the reason for the eclipse. Most primitive societies were terrified by the phenomenon, imagining the sun or moon to be attacked by a demon.

When a full moon takes place with the moon exactly on the ecliptic, then the Earth obstructs the light of the sun. The shadow of the Earth is about 5,700 miles in diameter at the distance of the moon, and the moon takes a maximum of three hours and forty minutes to pass completely through the shadow. Eclipses of the moon usually take place twice a year, five or six months apart. As totality approaches, the moon moves further into the curved edge of the Earth's shadow. The sunlight is obscured and the moon appears to be swallowed in the darkness, but it does not disappear completely. During the total phase, the moon shines very faintly with a copper color, or,

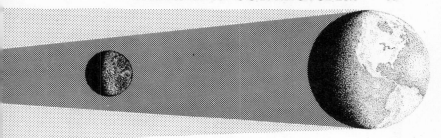

Fig. 6.  An eclipse of the moon -

sometimes, a blood-red hue. Poets have often referred to this coloration as a portent of disaster. The moon is shining by sunlight that
has passed through the atmosphere of the Earth. Refraction bends
the pale light into the dark shadow cone. The dust in the atmosphere
of the Earth scatters away the blue light, letting only the red rays
pass through. Because of the dust we see a red sun at sunset and a red
moon during total eclipse.

No two eclipses are alike. The color and brightness of the totally
eclipsed moon depend to a great extent on the conditions in the
atmosphere of the Earth. If there is a large amount of dust in the
atmosphere, the eclipsed moon glows with a very deep red. If the
weather is stormy, storm clouds fill the twilight zone and sunlight is
obstructed. Then only a small amount of light is scattered to the
moon by the atmosphere of the Earth, and the eclipse is very dark.
On rare occasions the moon disappears completely during a total
eclipse.

When the moon moves around to the opposite node, the sun
itself is eclipsed. A dark, cone-shaped shadow, the "umbra," stretches
behind the moon, producing a small black spot on the surfaces of the
Earth. Only people within the spot see a total solar eclipse, whereas
a lunar eclipse can be seen, weather permitting, by all people on
the hemisphere facing the moon. In a fixed location at least one
eclipse of the moon occurs each year, but the average time between
total eclipses of the sun is three hundred years. To be sure of seeing
a particular solar eclipse a person must travel to the area where the
shadow falls.

The black spot is one hundred miles or so across. Its exact size
and position can be computed beforehand for each eclipse. Theodore
Oppolzer calculated the circumstances of eclipses from 1208 B.C. to
2161 A.D. This work gives us prior notice of eclipses in the future and

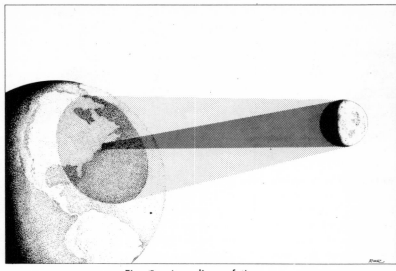

Fig. 7.  An eclipse of the sun

has also been of great help to historians in determining the exact date of events in the past. For example Herodotus, in the classics, gives an account of a battle between the Medes and the Lydians. The battle reached its climax around the time of noon, when suddenly day was turned into night. The clamor died down as the two armies gazed in wonder at the eclipse. When the sun reappeared, a truce was declared, and the two nations enjoyed peace for fifteen years. The date of the eclipse was May 28, 585 B.C., during the life of the Greek scholar, Thales of Miletus.

Eclipses vary considerably; sometimes the shadow cone sweeps rapidly across the polar regions, at other times it moves more slowly across the tropics. The black spot moves along the "path of totality" from the sunrise edge of the Earth to the sunset edge in about four hours. Sometimes the end of the umbral cone does not quite reach the surface of the Earth because the moon is too far away. A total eclipse cannot take place under these circumstances, but people directly below the point of the shadow see an annular eclipse. The moon's disk is too small to cover the sun completely, and a narrow ring of light is seen as the sun shines around the edge. The moon travels at 2,100 miles per hour in its orbit, and the shadow sweeps eastward across the Earth at the same speed. Now the Earth is spinning on its axis in the same direction as the shadow, and a town on the equator is being carried toward the east at 1,060 miles per hour. At latitude 40° the speed is 812 miles per hour, and at the poles the speed of rotation is 0. The latitude therefore influences the duration of totality. The most favorable eclipse occurs when the sun is overhead at noon and the moon is close to the Earth. Even then the total eclipse lasts scarcely more than 7 minutes and 30 seconds.

Although the high priests of antiquity did not understand the cause of eclipses they could predict them with fair accuracy, using their tables of lunar motion. After a long period of observation they must have noticed a pattern in the eclipse sequence. Eclipses of the moon begin to repeat themselves after 223 lunar months,  an inter-

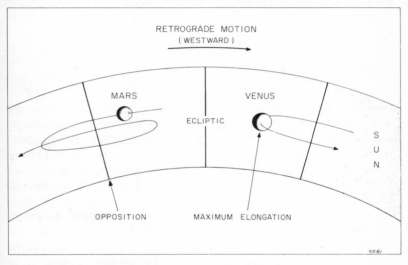

Fig. 8.   Movements of Mars and Venus

val of 18 years 11 1/3 days which today we call the "saros." After this interval, the nodes of the moon's orbit have passed once around the ecliptic and are back again in the signs of the zodiac from which they started. The distances between the Earth, moon, and sun are also close to the original values. If an eclipse occurs on a certain date at sunset, then this eclipse will be repeated in the same constellation and with the same duration one saros later. A small correction is needed for the odd one-third of a day; the eclipse will occur eight hours after sunset instead of at sunset as in the previous saros.

Most of the early civilizations could predict the movement of the planets among the signs of the zodiac. The priests of Maya were particularly skillful in describing the movement of Mercury and Venus. The two inner planets revolve around the sun faster than the Earth does, and they therefore overtake the Earth periodically. When viewed from the Earth, Mercury and Venus swing eastward along the zodiac to the point of maximum elongation, where they shine in the sunset sky as evening stars. Then the planet appears to turn, moving in a westerly direction back toward the sun. The planet overtakes the Earth when it passes close by the sun in the zodiac at inferior conjunction. It moves further to the west to a second point of maximum elongation where it appears as a bright star in the morning sky. As it circles around the sun, the planet is once more aligned with the sun at superior conjunction when it is on the far side of the orbit.

The outer planets behave quite differently. They do not appear to swing from side to side around the sun, but make a complete circuit around the zodiac. Outer planets, such as Mars and Jupiter, make only one conjunction with the sun, when the planet is on the far side of its orbit. The position of inferior conjunction is replaced by the position of opposition, when the planet is on the opposite side of the zodiac to the sun. The planet retrogrades at this time, moving westward in the zodiac in the direction Gemini, Taurus, Aries. This apparent reversal of direction is caused by the motion of the Earth which is nearer to the sun and moving faster. The Earth overtakes the outer planet which therefore appears to lag behind. In the same way an automobile in the slow lane of a turnpike gives us the impression of moving in reverse as it is glimpsed through the side window.

Mars becomes a spectacular object at opposition, rising at sunset and passing due south at midnight. At opposition Mars is closest to the Earth, outshining even Sirius in its brilliance, and dominating the night sky. In the olden days, an opposition of Mars chilled the hearts of men with its forebodings of war and death. Nowadays an opposition of Mars is welcomed for it gives astronomers an opportunity to scrutinize the surface of the planet.

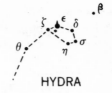

HYDRA

CHAPTER 3

# MYSTERY AND TERROR

WHEN THE MEDE AND LYDIAN WARRIORS PUT ASIDE THEIR WEAPONS in 585 B.C. they did so in terror. A total eclipse of the sun is impressive when you know the cause, but without this knowledge the spectacle becomes terrifying. What has caused the sun to withhold its light and warmth? Will it reappear? Is this the end of the world? Primitive tribes still go wild during totality, beating their chests, tearing their hair, and making noises to chase away the shadow. In ancient China there was a definite ritual for a total eclipse of the sun in which gongs were sounded and firecrackers were exploded. The descendants of the Medes and Lydians seem to have inherited the abhorrence of an eclipse, for Arab assistants hired by a twentieth century eclipse expedition ran away and hid from the shadow.

The fate of primitive man was intimately connected with the sky. Sandstorms and drought parched his crops and killed his cattle. Thunderbolts and lightning struck him down; wind, rain, and floods could destroy his home. It was not surprising to find him looking to the stars and planets for warning of coming disasters. People were superstitious about any happening in the sky. Usually they were pessimistic, expecting dire events to follow. Comets, as they passed around the sun, were unwelcome visitors because they foretold the death of a king or the collapse of a nation. Every hundred years or so an intense meteor storm took place, filling the sky with streaks of light as though the stars were falling from the firmament. This was often regarded as the coming of the end of the world. When the ghostly light of the Aurora Borealis flickered across the northern sky, people imagined all sorts of things—celestial warriors in combat, swords of fire, and a visitation by the spirits of the dead. Even the regular movement of the sun could cause alarm—the beginning of a calendar cycle was dreaded by the Mayans. The farmer's calendar of Maya was 260 days long, whereas the more accurate calendar of the high priests was 365 days long. The two calendars came into agreement every 52 "astronomical" years, or 73 "farmers'" years, when the sun was almost in the same position of the zodiac (except for the effect of precession and the cumulative error of the quarter day). On New Year's Eve, at the beginning of the cycle, the Aztecs expected the destruction of their civilization. During this night of fear they evacuated ancient Mexico City and waited in the surrounding hills. At dawn, when the sun rose, there was great rejoicing for the gods had given the world another 52 years of existence.

Solar eclipses were less fearsome when, by about 400 B.C., the cause was understood. For example, the Greek fleet was embarking in the port of Athens on August 3, 431 B.C. when a total eclipse took place. The Grecian hero Pericles, who was in command, restored the morale of his men by a clever demonstration. He took his cloak and covered the eyes of the pilot of the galley, asking him if he found anything terrible in the darkness and whether he interpreted it as a bad omen. The pilot answered "No," and Pericles then ridiculed the hysteria by saying, "Where is the difference, then, between this and the other, except something bigger than my cloak causes the difference?"

But eclipses of the moon were not so easily explained. Some eighteen years later the Greek army was attacking the town of Syracuse in Sicily, and the Greeks were hard pressed. Reinforcements were brought in by Nicias and Demosthenes, but they arrived too late to turn the battle. The army was safely on board the galleys and about to evacuate when the moon faded to the dull red color of a total eclipse. Nicias shared the terror of his army. The astrologers in the fleet pronounced the eclipse a bad omen, and advised Nicias to postpone the evacuation by twenty-seven days. This superstition led to the downfall of the Greeks, for during the waiting period the Syracusian army was able to destroy the fleet. Many Greeks died in the bloodshed, and the two commanders, Nicias and Demosthenes, were captured and executed.

There must be a great deal of magic that has been forgotten in the course of time. In the flat area of Salisbury Plain in England we find Stonehenge, a weird ring of stone arches. Archaeologists have estimated an age of four thousand years for the structure, and this was recently confirmed by carbon dating. Atmospheric carbon contains a minute proportion of radioactive atoms which are produced by cosmic ray bombardment. In the atmosphere the proportion of radiocarbon is maintained, being continually replenished, but in a solid object the process stops. At the base of one of the stone pillars some old wooden posts were found which were placed there to prevent the block of stone from slipping whilst it was being erected. The tree extracted carbon from the atmosphere during its growth, and this carbon became part of the wood. Over the years the radiocarbon has decayed, and the amount left in the stump tells us the age of the wood. On one or two of the stone blocks the builders of Stonehenge had carved pictures, thirty ax heads of Bronze Age Britain and one hilted dagger of Grecian design. Apart from these facts, we know very little about the builders of Stonehenge or their purpose.

Astronomers have noticed one strange fact about the monument— it points toward the sunrise on Midsummer Day. On June 21 a person standing in the center of Stonehenge will see the sun rising over the pointed "heel stone." Precession does not change the position of sunrise to any great extent. Although at midsummer the sun is now in the constellation Gemini instead of Leo, its distance from the east point on the horizon is still very much the same.

Stonehenge probably was built to mark midsummer, for if the axis of the temple had been chosen at random the probability of selecting this point by accident would be less than one in five hundred. Now if the builders of Stonehenge had wished simply to mark the sunrise they needed no more than two stones. Yet hundreds of tons of volcanic rock were carved and placed in position, some of the material coming from Wales, a hundred miles away. Great care was taken in assembling the stone archways, each slab being carved to form a secure joint. To complete the temple, large pits, trenches, and embankments were made in the surrounding chalk. A large section of the population of southern England must have been engaged in the project. Stonehenge is therefore much more than a whim of a few people. It must have been the focal point for ancient Britains, and it is not difficult to imagine a crowd of several thousand gathering for the ritual of the midsummer sunrise. Writers of the seventeenth century suggested pagan ceremonies conducted by the high priests of the druids, but we have no proof. Indeed, some archaeologists doubt whether the druid cult was established in Britain at this time. The stone blocks are mute, but perhaps some day, by a chance discovery, we will learn their secrets.

The Egyptian temples and monuments are also aligned with the heavens. The great pyramid near Cairo is built with its sides running exactly north, south, east, and west. Such alignment could hardly occur by chance, but the purpose of the builder is a mystery to us. At first sight, the many temples in the valley of the Nile appear to be built in a haphazard fashion, with the central pathway pointing in no particular direction. Careful inspection, however, shows that a large number of the temples were built to point toward the rising and setting of a certain star. Some temples point to the bright Southern Hemisphere star, Canopus, some point to Sirius, while others point to the sun at midsummer or midwinter. There is no mention of astronomical observations in the hieroglyphic writings, nor did the Egyptians show any interest in the theory of the universe, but several archaeologists believe that the temples were of practical value —at least to the priests. The temples were a cultural center, a repository of wealth, and also an accurate clock. Seasonal flooding of the Nile was very important to Egyptians, since a new layer of fertile soil was deposited on the fields. Although the flooding was irregular when measured against the erroneous calendar of the peasants, the high priests had no difficulty in predicting it. They knew that the water began to rise at midsummer, and this date was marked by the temples of the sun and Sirius. Sirius rose at dawn at the time of midsummer and the priests could see the star as they stood at the altar and looked along the colonnade of pillars. As a final check, the priests could use the sun, for on Midsummer Day it was farthest north, setting between the central pillars of the solar temples. A successful flood warning earned them respect for the ensuing year.

The temple at Karnak is one of the largest temples oriented toward the sun. It is a composite structure, several temples joined together to form a building over one-quarter of a mile in length. In the center of the temple, the Pharaoh Seti I built a hall containing 136 giant pillars, each one gilded and beautifully painted. Behind the hall was the inner sanctum visited only by the high priests and the Pharaoh. The central passageway of the temple was kept completely clear for several hundred yards, presumably to enable the high priests to watch the sunset as Midsummer Day drew near. The power of the priests was enormous; in some dynasties they had more wealth and influence than the Pharaoh himself. Some writers have accused them of intimidating the public by deceit. On Midsummer Eve the doors of the inner sanctum were open for a brief instant, allowing the sunset to flash on a figure of the god moved by strings and supplied with a human voice.

Certainly the priests of Amen-Ra encouraged the name of "the mysterious city" for Karnak, as they busied themselves with the ritual in the temple and walked with shaven heads through the sun-baked streets. But such intrigue was inevitable in any culture where the king ruled with absolute authority and was answerable only to the gods in the sky.

A few people still have a superstitious outlook today. After World War II we were swamped with reports of "flying saucers." When most reports were examined, the "flying saucer" was found to be a planet such as Venus, a meteor, or a weather balloon. A few of the more spectacular reports were deliberate hoaxes perpetrated on scientists and the general public. The propaganda value of Sputnik I was unexpected. In many respects the launching was a normal scientific advancement with the broad results quite predictable yet there was surprise, bewilderment, and fear. In many newspapers the Russian moon made headline news for a period of two weeks, almost a record for a single event.

As an astronomer I am often asked "Do you believe in the power of astrology?" I reply by asking the person a counter-question "Do you believe in fairies?" The stars and planets are material objects, and to assign them power over human destinies is nothing but a superstition. The movement of planets around the zodiac depends upon the choice of viewpoint. We happen to see the panorama from a somewhat inconspicuous planet, the Earth, but the astronaut, moving between the planets, sees quite a different picture. A conjunction between two planets is no more significant than the alignment of two trees as you pass them in a car. Yet the cold facts have not been fully accepted, and there is still an audience for our present-day wizards, witches, and astrologers.

Astrology was developed several thousand years ago to predict the destiny of a nation and to read from the sky whether or not the king was held in favor by the gods. Thus the astrologers and soothsayers used to be important people since they could to some extent influence the government. Their position was also dangerous, because if their prediction did not come true they were liable to imprisonment, torture, or death. Most astrologers kept alive, of course, by being vague or cleverly ambiguous. The "science" of astrology was built upon coincidence. If wars occurred sometimes when Mars was in opposition, then Mars at opposition was a forerunner of war; if a great king was born when Jupiter and Saturn were in conjunction in Sagittarius, then another great king would be born when the conjunction occurred again. This remarkable process of putting one and one together to make three still persists today.

A person's life is supposed by astrologers to be spelled out for him by his horoscope—the position of the sun, moon, and planets in the zodiac at the instant of his birth. The planets are divided into those of evil influence, and those of good. Mercury, for example, denotes brain power, while Saturn is associated with slothfulness. The planets are supposed to combine their influences according to their aspect, or separation in the zodiac. For example, three planets in Trine, equally spaced around the zodiac, are extremely lucky. The sign of the zodiac rising at the time of birth is called the sign in the ascendant, and the cardinal signs of Aries, Cancer, Libra, and Capricornus are the most important. The signs of the zodiac are also linked in groups of three, or trigons, with different "influences":

The Trigons of the Soothsayers

| Aries | | | Gemini | | |
|-------|---|-------|--------|---|------|
| Leo | } | Fiery | Libra | } | Airy |
| Sagittarius | | | Aquarius | | |
| Taurus | | | Cancer | | |
| Virgo | } | Earthy | Scorpio | } | Watery |
| Capricornus | | | Pisces | | |

Great importance is attached to the "fiery trigon," especially the leading sign Aries. A person born between March 21 and April 20 is fortunate enough to have the sun in Aries in his horoscope. These people, according to most astrologers, "are usually very executive, earnest, and determined. They are leaders, and dominate those about them." As we would expect by the laws of chance, about one dictator out of twelve is born under Aries; Adolf Hitler is an example. According to another astrologer, the best wives are born when the moon and Jupiter are in a favorable aspect, especially if Jupiter is in Leo, the sign that rules the heart.

With a little ingenuity, horoscopes can be cast for any day of our life besides the day of our birth. We have only to assume that the position of the sun at our birth can be imprinted on the zodiac and cast our horoscopes accordingly. For example, if our birthday is in April we can imagine a lucky period to occur whenever Jupiter is in the sign of Aries, or at the Trine positions of Leo and Sagittarius. In fact there seem to be no limits set to our fancy.[1]

[1] *A Primer of Natal Astrology for Beginners, How to Cast the Horoscope and Read Its Happy Auguries or Portents,* by George Wilde, Rexo Publishing Company,

Though it seems strange to us today, astrology was important in the medieval age and some serious scientists of earlier times, like Tycho Brahe and Kepler, were very much involved in it.

is an example of a concise astrology "textbook." According to Mr. Wilde, all forms of life—men, dogs, and mules—are subject to the cosmic law of the sky: "Actual life is subject to planetary authority and though the cosmic law is as inexplicable as gravitation it is no less potential!" (The exclamation mark is my own.) His concluding words are prophetic: "Doubtless the day will come when only men whose stars are propitious will be selected to fill positions of power, of rulership and of momentous importance where failure means unmitigated disaster. The man whose stars are brooding will cease to occupy positions in which any act of his can bring misfortune to others; thus mischances will never come, since ill-starred men will be relegated to a sphere of action which carries no responsibility of calamitous consequences." But somehow I feel that if this comes to pass we will have returned to the era of the druids and the high priests of Amen-Ra.

CHAPTER **4**

# GREEK SCHOLARS

ONLY THE GREEKS, A SMALL SECTION OF THE ANCIENT WORLD, thought deeply about the universe. The advancement of knowledge was slow because education was reserved for the privileged upper classes; because communication was difficult; because books were rare and expensive; and, above all, because the mind of man was paralyzed by superstition. We do not know how many irreplaceable books were destroyed when the mob burned down the library at Alexandria in 389 A.D. Some historians claim that the library had fallen into disrepair; many books had already been lost or stolen, and the mob did no more than finish the destruction. Other historians see in the ashes of Alexandria an estrangement from the past which will never be overcome. Certainly many books of the ancient philosophers are missing; their ideas on science come to us at second hand, by legend, myth, and hearsay. Judging from the references in existing relics, at least nine-tenths of the ancient books are missing and we shall never know their true content. The most extensive astronomical writing we have is the textbook by Ptolemy, *The Almagest.* Before him, we have the encyclopedic works of Aristotle and the remarks of Plato.

Thales of Miletus is one of the earliest philosophers we recognize, but we are not sure how much of his work was original, nor how much has been erroneously ascribed to him by later authors. He is credited with the prediction of a solar eclipse in the year 585 B.C., but this is almost certainly apocryphal since the necessary theory was not available to him. He measured the angular diameter of the sun as one-sixtieth of a sign of the zodiac, or one-half a degree. A local potentate praised him very highly for this and offered him a reward for revealing such valuable information about the universe. Although

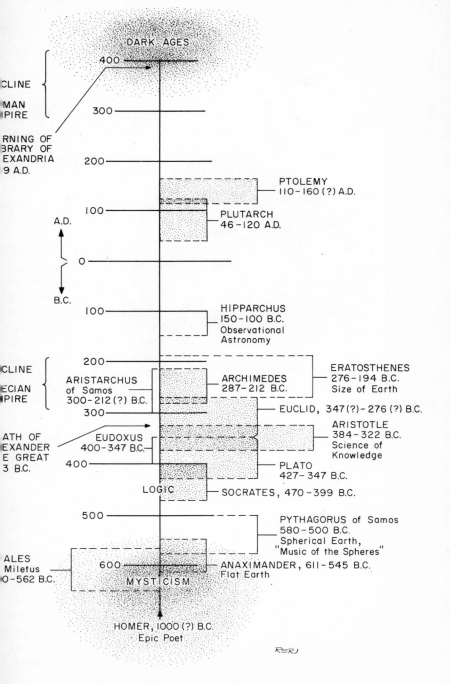

DARK AGES

400

CLINE
MAN
PIRE

300

RNING OF
BRARY OF
EXANDRIA
9 A.D.

200

PTOLEMY
110-160 (?) A.D.

100

A.D.

PLUTARCH
46-120 A.D.

0

B.C.

100

HIPPARCHUS
150-100 B.C.
Observational
Astronomy

200

CLINE
ECIAN
PIRE

ARISTARCHUS
of Samos
300-212(?) B.C.

ARCHIMEDES
287-212 B.C.

ERATOSTHENES
276-194 B.C.
Size of Earth

300

EUCLID, 347(?)-276 (?) B.C.

ATH OF
EXANDER
E GREAT
3 B.C.

EUDOXUS
400-347 B.C.

ARISTOTLE
384-322 B.C.
Science of
Knowledge

400

PLATO
427-347 B.C.

LOGIC

SOCRATES, 470-399 B.C.

500

PYTHAGORUS of Samos
580-500 B.C.
Spherical Earth,
"Music of the Spheres"

ALES
Miletus
0-562 B.C.

600

ANAXIMANDER, 611-545 B.C.
Flat Earth

MYSTICISM

HOMER, 1000 (?) B.C.
Epic Poet

R=RJ

Fig. 9.   Philosophers of the Mediterranean

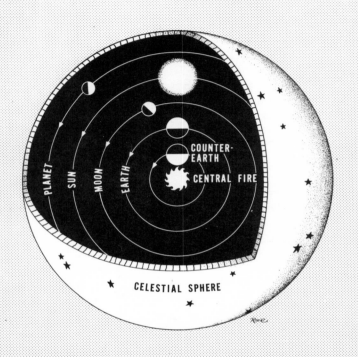

Fig. 10.  The Pythagorean system

knowledge was at a premium, Thales refused the reward. For him, the prestige of the discovery was enough.

Anaximander, an associate of Thales', produced some rather odd ideas about the celestial sphere. People had talked of stars being hung from the celestial sphere by cords, or being fixed to the inside of the sphere like studs, but Anaximander invoked a universal fire. The celestial sphere was solid but pierced with holes through which the fire was seen, producing the sensation of stars, the sun, and the moon. He must have realized that the sun and moon travel over the background of the stars, for he proposed solar and lunar "tubes" moving within the celestial sphere. Eclipses occurred when the aperture in the side of the tube was covered up. Pythagoras set up a rival school of thought to that of Thales. Like Thales, he soon became a symbolic figure, and it is difficult to decide how much of the theory of the Pythagoreans was originally due to him. The Pythagoreans formed what amounted to a secret society, being careful not to spread their ideas to people who were not members of the cult. Philolaus was supposed to have broken the silence by writing an account of the Pythagorean doctrine, but his original manuscript has never been found. Indeed some historians suggest that Philolaus was a fictitious character invented by Plato to represent the Pythagoreans.

In their system of the world, the Pythagoreans supposed everything to revolve around a central fire. By intuition they had broken away from the flat Earth concept which was quite a step forward. The stars are hung on a sphere, they argued, so the Earth itself must be also a sphere. In their philosophy the celestial sphere was fixed, but the Earth traveled round a circular orbit once every twenty-four hours. The back of the Earth always faced the central fire, and people in Greece faced outward toward the sky. The panorama of the rising and setting of the sun and constellations took place because of the daily orbit of the Earth. The sun and planets also moved around the central fire, but they moved more slowly because their orbits were larger than the orbit of the Earth. There was a very slow rotation of the celestial sphere itself. As it turned it generated the music of the spheres which could not be heard by mortals (except, it was rumored, by Pythagoras himself).

The Pythagoreans were ridiculed and persecuted because they believed in the movement of the Earth. It was regarded as an insult to the gods to suppose the base Earth to be in motion like other heavenly bodies. "Also," said the enemies of Pythagoras, "people in India, on the other side of the Earth, should be able to see the eternal fire." To save the theory, the Pythagoreans proposed a counter-Earth, moving around the central fire once every twenty-four hours so as to shade the people in India from its glare. "Why do we not see the counter-Earth?" "Why does it not obscure the stars?" The answers to these awkward questions concerning the theory were known only to the inner members of the secret cult.

There was a natural revulsion at such empty speculation about the universe, and men turned to the more practical field of humanities, engrossing themselves with the problems of ethics and government. Socrates, for example, found no satisfaction in the study of the universe, since no two astronomers who lived before him had agreed. Their systems had been based upon personal feelings and prejudices without any attempt to find out who was right. Socrates despaired of making any progress in natural philosophy; the truth would always be hidden unless it was revealed to someone by the gods. He did, however, formulate a system of logic in which it was possible to suggest a hypothesis and draw a conclusion from it. With logic he could make some progress, but, because the original hypothesis was always in doubt, he could never be sure of his conclusion. We are in the same dilemma today. The postulates of science can always be challenged, and if the challenge is successful a new theory supersedes the old. We recognize in this process the growth of knowledge, for changes of viewpoint are inevitable as we advance. But Socrates was not so optimistic; he feared that argumentation would carry us round in circles and we would never break the loop.

Plato was even more pessimistic than Socrates, claiming that we could never hope to learn by looking at nature. A pure essence of something might exist, but it would never materialize on Earth. There was no such thing as a real straight line, only the essence of one; no trees, only images of them; and there were no honest men, everyone on Earth was imperfect. This philosophy challenged the intellect; it threatened to turn man into a morbid introvert who distrusted the real world and his fellow men. Fortunately we were saved by Aristotle, a pupil of Plato, who saw a way to break the vicious circle of argument. Natural objects were consistent, the same cause produced the same effect and we could use the hard facts of physics as a hypothesis. We could then be sure of the hypothesis, for it would not change unless the world itself changed. He developed a system of logic to a very high degree, and wrote a series of books discussing everyday experiences in physics, biology, and astronomy.

As an example of his logic, let us see how Aristotle proved the suggestion that the Earth was a sphere. The moon is opposite the sun at a total eclipse; therefore, the darkening is due to the shadow of the Earth. The edge of the shadow always has a circular outline whatever the position of the full moon; therefore, the Earth is the rotational figure of the circle—a sphere. In a further proof, he came very close to the concept of the center of gravity. Objects always fall toward a common point, the center of the Earth, therefore they will pack themselves near to this center forming a sphere, where the objects are as close to the center as possible. The second argument is weaker than the first, because he could not be sure that objects did move toward the center of the Earth. His argument was weak because the initial premise was no more than a speculation. It required the gravitational theory and mathematics of Isaac Newton to substantiate it.

This weakness of the initial premise runs throughout Aristotle's work. It was the primary cause of the collapse of Greek science. Aristotle's system of logic was respected by all philosophers, but very few people challenged his initial postulates. Aristotle did not examine them carefully enough himself, he relied too heavily on the ancient notions of Plato and the people before him. For example he persisted in the notion that things moved only because a force was exerted on them by a type of soul within, or attached to, the body. He said base objects, such as earth and water, are always striving to reach the center of the universe, while fire and the soul of man tend to move upward to the skies. The Milky Way is caused by earthly vapors igniting as they rub against the celestial sphere. The supreme element which forms the substance of the stars has a separate motion of its own, which moves in a perfect circle around the center of the universe. The Earth is not rotating on an axis because, if it were, the objects on the surface would be carried around in circles which is impossible since they are impure materials. There is no force acting on the Earth to make it turn, and if it had been made to spin in the past, it would have slowed down and come to a halt. Why does the celestial sphere rotate in a clockwise direction? Because to move to the right is a pure motion, whereas to move to the left is a sinister motion. The planets are godlike objects carried around the sky on revolving spheres; if they were earthly objects moving through space we would surely hear them make a noise. The stars are isolated from the Earth, therefore no changes can take place in the sky. Furthermore, Aristotle erroneously concluded that the stars, sun, and the Earth do not spin on an axis, because the moon always holds the same face toward us.

Aristotle took one step forward and two steps back, but the back-

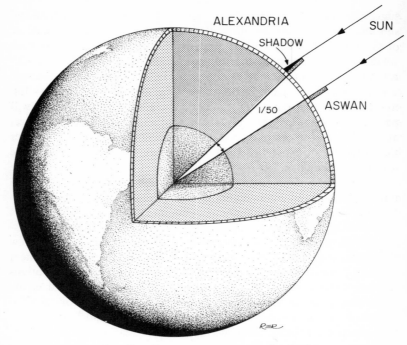

Fig. 11.   Eratosthenes measures the Earth

ward steps were not his fault. From the very make-up of his philosophy
we know that he was ready to be challenged for the progress of science,
yet no one was great enough to pit his wit against Aristotle's. After
the clouds of time and ignorance had closed around him, his writings
survived as a gospel of science—an unchallengeable set of truths concerning the nature of the universe. Before the darkness came, however,
three lesser men tried to carry on in the tradition of Aristotle. They
were Eratosthenes, Hipparchus, and Ptolemy.

Eratosthenes was the head librarian at Alexandria. From the established fact of the spherical Earth he proceeded to measure its size. On
a midsummer day there were no shadows at noon at Aswan in southern
Egypt, and the reflection of the sun could be seen in the water of a
deep well. Thus the sun was in the zenith, exactly overhead. At noon on
the same day at Alexandria, the sun was to the south of the zenith.
Vertical buildings cast a small shadow the length of which showed that
the sun was displaced from the zenith by one-fiftieth of the circumference of the heavens. Men were paid to pace out the distance between

Alexandria and Aswan and found it was 489 miles. Therefore Eratosthenes estimated the circumference of the Earth to be 50 times as great, or 24,450, and the diameter of the Earth to be 7,800 miles.

Hipparchus, on the island of Rhodes, decided that we should not talk about the motion of the planets and the stars until we knew exactly what this motion was. With this decision he became the first observational astronomer. He carefully prepared charts of the sky, showing the position and brightness of each star. By night he followed the motion of the moon and planets among the stars of the zodiac; by day he measured the altitude of the sun from the length of the shadow of an obelisk. From his work he discovered the drift of the equinoxes. The point where the ecliptic crosses the celestial equator is called the vernal equinox, and the sun is in this position on the first day of spring. According to his measurements, the vernal equinox, instead of being in the center of the constellation Aries, had moved eight degrees westward to the eastern edge of the constellation. The displacement was due to the slow precession of the Earth's axis, like the wobble of a spinning top, but Hipparchus did not know this. Since the time of Hipparchus, the vernal equinox has continued its movement and is now in the middle of the constellation Pisces. Hipparchus also found that the sun did not move at a uniform rate around the zodiac. This is because the Earth's orbit is not a true circle, but is an ellipse. Hipparchus, however, erroneously attributed the effect to a displacement of the orbit of the sun away from the center of the Earth.

Books by Hipparchus are rare, and we base our knowledge of him on the writings of Ptolemy, who lived some three hundred years later. Although Ptolemy made some observations of his own, he was primarily a theoretical astronomer. He used the principles of geometry, established by Euclid, to predict the motion of the sun, moon, and the planets. His system of planetary motion was put forward as a hypothesis, and was justified in his mind because, although cumbersome, it was a practical success. The Ptolemaic system was not an original idea; it was based partly on the epicycle of Apollonius and the displaced circle of Hipparchus.

In the Ptolemaic system all objects move except the Earth. A planet, like Mars, moves around a small circle, the epicycle. The center of the epicycle moves in a circular track, or deferent, around the Earth. Mars takes one year to move around the epicycle, and it takes 687 days for the epicycle to move around the deferent. The combined motion produces a looped path which nicely accounts for the retrograde motion of Mars when it is at opposition. Mercury and Venus, the planets be-

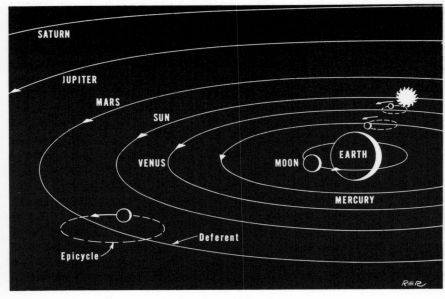

Fig. 12.    Ptolemaic system

tween the Earth and the sun, move differently. The center of the epicycle is set on an arm drawn from the Earth to the sun, and each planet
moves once around the epicycle in less than a year. The combined motion again produces a looped path, and the planets move in a retrograde
direction when they are closest to the Earth. The moon and the sun also
move around small epicycles, but in the opposite direction to the
planets. This accounts for the nonuniform motion of the moon and
sun, without requiring a retrograde motion.

With this system Ptolemy was able to foretell the position of the
planets and other heavenly bodies with great accuracy. He added one
final touch to bring the system to perfection. The centers of the defer-
ents were displaced slightly away from the Earth and this removed
the final disagreement between the observed motion and his predictions.
The world was presented with a triumphant theory, and no further in-
quiries seemed necessary. We were so close to explaining the workings
of the solar system, and yet so far from the truth. Our understanding of
the universe was little better than *the shepherds' view*.

PART II
# DEBUTANTE SCIENCE

An armchair astronomer at the
coudé telescope of the Paris Observatory. From an old French print.
(General Astronomy, C. A. Young,
Ginn and Company)

# CHAPTER 5

# THE GIANTS

I HAVE OFTEN WONDERED WHY THE DARK AGES WERE SO DARK FOR science, why the human mind hibernated, at least in western Europe, for a thousand years, and why the fruits of Greek thought were left to wither on the plant. For thirty generations masses of people existed with a life no better than the beasts of the forest, and yet did nothing to change their lot. Assassination and murder, licentiousness and greed, disease and starvation, were ever-present. Man had taken a blind, backward step and almost lost his footing on the Earth.

Some historians blame the system of government. Europe was divided up into small states, and most people were serfs or slaves. They worked hard on the land, growing crops with primitive tools. All their efforts went into a desperate fight for survival as they fed themselves and kept the lord of the manor supplied. Some historians blame Christianity. After the acceptance of Christ as the savior of mankind, Christians eagerly waited the Day of Judgment, when Christ would return. The bitter life on Earth was made endurable by the promise of heaven, and changes were looked for, not in this world but in the next. Some historians blame the Church, claiming that the monasteries with their tithes oppressed the people more severely than did the feudal system. Other historians point to the neglect of education, poor communications, and the absence of printed books. Perhaps the last suggestion is closest to the truth, for in the mind of man there is always the potential for progress if only he will use it.

By 1600 the forward movement was again well under way. The first stirrings occurred some four hundred years previous to this, but the movement was indistinct and difficult to recognize. The upper classes, supported by the toil of peasants, grew tired of spending their leisure in vice and lassitude. At first they turned to art for their enter-

tainment, copying and developing the old techniques of painting. Old
sculptures were discovered and copies were made to bring beauty into
the home. From these skills, developed by the stonemason, Renaissance
architecture originated. Then the man of leisure, both Christian and
Moslem, turned to the manuscripts of ancient Greece. At first the
manuscripts were read for amusement, and it became the fashionable
thing to do. Later there was a genuine desire to continue and extend
Greek science, and the rebirth of learning had begun. We are still
moving forward in this Renaissance even today, and all the products
of our modern civilization are the results of the faint stirrings within
the human mind at the end of the Middle Ages. We shall never know
exactly what caused the forward movement. These great minds could
easily have been wasted, like the talents of the many sages who must
surely have been born in medieval times. The Dark Ages could easily
have continued for another thousand years and be with us today.

The rebirth of astronomy can be followed more closely than other
phases of the Renaissance. Astronomy grew from the work of three men
Copernicus, Brahe, and Kepler, under a remarkable set of circumstances. Some people regard the happy juxtaposition of these three men
as pure chance; others regard it as Divine Providence. In 1450 the
churchmen of Rome felt secure, and thought that it was only a matter
of time before every country would pay homage to the Pope. They
enjoyed the beauty of Renaissance Italy, and tolerated the study of
Greek philosophy. In fact the churchmen themselves read the ancient
manuscripts, regarding them with almost the same reverence as they
regarded the Scriptures. Thus the works of Aristotle and Ptolemy became scientific gospels. A true churchman was expected to believe
without argument that the Earth was at the center of the universe, that
the heavenly bodies moved in orbits which were perfect circles, and
other Aristotelian pronouncements. But the early 1500's brought
many threats to papal supremacy. The printing press had been invented, and new ideas could be set forth in pamphlets for rapid distribution. Protestants were gaining a foothold, and the heads of European
states were breaking away from Rome. As a reaction, the various popes
tried to stop the forward advance and return to the ideas of 1450. It
became heresy to challenge the work of Ptolemy and Aristotle.

Both Catholics and Protestants realize today, of course, that it is
impossible to treat the words of a scientist as dogmatically true. The
ideas of the ancient Greeks have been replaced by wonderful discoveries that show the immense splendor and majesty of the universe. The
discoveries of science have given substance and depth to religion, but

in the 1500's these advances were stubbornly resisted. To make the first step from the old to the new needed a man who was courageous, yet careful; free-thinking yet tactful; subservient to the pope, yet respected by the intellectual Protestants. Such a man was Nicholas Copernicus.

Copernicus was a Polish priest, and carried out his research in the shelter of Frauenburg Cathedral. For thirty years he occupied one of the towers of the dormitory, and as a canon of the Church was provided with food, clothing, and materials for his work. He was strong-willed and persevering, trusting his own mind before the opinions of others. From his classic education he was familiar with the Ptolemaic system of planetary motion, and he also learned of the shortcomings of the theory. He debated the problem in his mind and decided that the motion of the planets could be described more easily if we regarded the sun as fixed, even though this view did not conform with the accepted beliefs. He argued that the sun was our source of heat and light, and was larger than the Earth. It would be more appropriate for the small Earth to travel around the sun than vice versa. If the Earth makes a circular path around the sun why should not the other planets do the same? The system of circular orbit was much less complicated than the one Ptolemy proposed. In particular the retrograde motion of Mars was simply a result of the Earth's overtaking Mars at opposition, and as the Earth passed by, Mars appeared to lag behind. Thus the primary epicycle would be needed no more, since it was invented purely to explain the retrograde motion.

Copernicus knew that the sphere of the stars was at a great distance, because it was large enough to contain the Earth, the sun, and the other planets. With the Earth in orbit around the sun it was quite simple to imagine a second motion, a spin on an axis. Then the rising and setting of the stars, and the rotation of the celestial sphere, would be an illusion. Copernicus could more easily imagine the Earth spinning on its axis than the enormous celestial sphere turning completely around once every twenty-four hours. He argued that the rotation could not be felt by people on the surface, because the motion was steady and the air was carried around with the Earth. To check his ideas, Copernicus made several observations of his own, and carried out calculations with the aid of trigonometry, which had been brought to a state of near perfection by Hindu and Arab mathematicians during the so-called Dark Ages of Western Europe.

Although Copernicus had made the first step in the rebirth of astronomy, his work was almost lost. He realized that his ideas might provoke controversy and be destroyed as a heresy. Pope Clement VII had certainly shown an interest in the work, but some of the Pope's advisers might be less approving. For thirty years he weighed his words carefully as he put his arguments into a book. He pointed out that Ptolemy's theory of planetary motion was not the only one to be proposed by Greek philosophers, and that one more theory, from a canon of the church, might not be improper. To avoid personal antagonisms he pointed out that the heliocentric theory was not entirely his idea; in fact it had already been suggested by the Greek philosopher Aristarchus. Also, all churchmen had been requested to help straighten out the errors in the calendar, and Copernicus suggested that his book had a practical value, because it would help the reform of the calendar. Finally he dedicated the whole work to the Pope in a beautifully written preface.

Copernicus had been diplomatic and he could do no more. To avoid rancor and any personal inconvenience, he planned to leave the book as a legacy, to be published after his death. One of his former students, however, George Rheticus snatched the manuscript, figuratively speaking, from the feeble hands, and had the book published at Nuremberg. Nuremberg was by this time a Protestant stronghold, and a Lutheran minister, Andrew Osiander, acted as editorial consultant. He coined the title for the book *Revolution of Celestial Bodies,* and to give the pill a coating of sugar, he inserted a second preface insisting that the work was only a suggestion, a hypothesis for simplifying the calculation of planetary motions. This second preface was nothing more than an apology, and was out of character with the rest of the book. Osiander did not sign the second preface and for many years we were in doubt as to the true intentions of Copernicus. We know now that Copernicus did not agree with the apology, but intended his book to start a revolution in thinking. However, Osiander probably helped rather than hindered the new astronomy, for the two prefaces made it difficult to denounce the book as heresy. At the time it looked as though Copernicus had recanted after all, just before he died.

The new book spread rapidly from Nuremberg among Catholics and Protestants alike. A copy was rushed to Copernicus, who by now was on his deathbed. He was too feeble to recognize his book, and in a few hours he had gone where no mortal criticism could follow. Some people scoffed at the book and the author, "How could the slothful Earth be moving?" Some people denounced it as a heresy, "There is nothing in the Scriptures to indicate a movement of the Earth!" Ironically enough, it was Martin Luther, the leader of the Protestants who was the most emphatic on this point. The Protestants were hypersensitive. Their only hope for salvation was to interpret the Bible for themselves, and adhere to every word in it. If Copernicus was right, Luther expected to find confirmation in the Bible. Some people, mainly the German and English astronomers, tried to follow through the arguments of Copernicus, and they calculated the positions of the planets according to his theory. From the practical standpoint they found that the Copernican system was no easier to use than the Ptolemaic one, nor did it give more accurate predictions. In retrospect we know the Copernican theory could never be completely successful because the planets move in orbits that are not exactly circular and at speeds that are not constant. Copernicus attempted to account for the discrepancies by introducing small epicycles, similar to those of Ptolemy. This, of course, was a backward step, and without the further work of Kepler and Newton the Copernican system would have remained as artificial as that of Ptolemy. But the seed had been carefully sown, Copernicus' sun-centered viewpoint was correct, and he has gained immortality by his efforts.

A theory, even if it is correct, must be proved by observations. When Copernicus died in 1543, he left only twenty-seven observations instead of the thousands that were needed.

Tycho Brahe was born in 1546 with a character well suited to the task before him—that of organizing observational astronomy. He was the son of a Danish nobleman, and received a fine education. He had boundless energy and was able to work both night and day on his labors. He forced his assistants along with him at the same pace until they fell exhausted. He was sensitive to the beauties of all art forms, particularly the works of his Creator as he saw them in the sky. Tycho had bad traits, but even they were used to advantage. He was bombastic and quarrelsome. At the university he argued with a fellow student as to which one knew more about mathematics. They fought a duel, Tycho's nose was sliced off, and he had to wear a false one of gold and silver for the rest of his life. But his arrogance impressed the kings and princes with whom he had to deal. He was conceited, claiming to be the world's greatest astronomer. Several plaques and inscriptions were put up in his house to this effect, but this conceit encouraged his pupils to become greater. Today we would label Tycho as an organizer, or perhaps as an operator.

A strange series of events brought Tycho into astronomy. When he was thirteen years old he saw a partial eclipse of the sun, and was impressed by the event. On November 11, 1572, he was startled to find a new star in the northern sky. Today we know that the star was a supernova, the explosion of a distant star. Only six supernova have been seen in our galaxy, and the event is very rare. Other people, of course, saw Tycho's star, and speculated on its nature. Both scholars and laymen were sure that the star was close to the Earth, perhaps closer than the moon, because it was so bright. Tycho, however, decided to measure the distance for himself. If it were closer than the moon the star should show a displacement when viewed from different cities on the Earth. Also it should be displaced from hour to hour as the celestial sphere rotated, because Tycho was on the Earth's surface and not at the center of the sphere. After several nights of work, Tycho obtained an accurate position for the new star by comparing it with other fixed stars nearby. To his surprise he found no parallax, and was forced to conclude that the new star was very distant, probably on the celestial sphere itself. The celestial sphere, which Aristotle had pronounced to be changeless, had changed.

Tycho wrote an account of his work in a booklet that was rapidly circulated and well received. He was invited by the King of Denmark to give a series of lectures about his new star. Tycho complied, and included in his talk some very forceful remarks about the need of systematic observations, and how it was the duty of a civilized nation to support astronomical research.

After the lectures, Tycho returned to Germany where he had spent his student days, but his words were still ringing in Danish ears. Tycho encouraged a rumor about his intentions for German citizenship and about the encouragement he was getting from German astronomers. King Frederick summoned Tycho to return, and asked him what he would need to begin astronomy in Denmark. Tycho recognized the opportunity for research, and at the same time could see a way to achieve his other ambitions. When the negotiations were completed he was given the island of Hven, a few miles off the shore near Elsinore Castle, and sufficient money to build and operate a fine observatory. He employed the best instrument makers to engrave quadrants and circles for the measurement program. Observations were made from balconies and turrets on the roof, and also from basement rooms with the instruments poking through windows at ground levels. Living quarters were provided for himself, his family, and his retinue of servants. There were many students and research assistants under his direction who were each provided with living quarters and laboratory space. The observatory was set in a landscaped park, with four avenues of entrance from the north, south, east, and west. It was a palace, it had all the splendor that money could buy, and Tycho named it Uraniborg, meaning "Castle of the Sky."

For more than twenty years Tycho and his assistants measured the position of stars and planets in the heavens, collecting the data needed for the next advance in science. As the angles were read off from the quadrants and entered in the ledger book, corrections were applied for atmospheric refraction, errors in the graduating quadrants, and other effects. The observations were undoubtedly more accurate than any that had been made before. Also there was an uninterrupted series of measurements over a period of twenty years, a continuity which is so important for theoretical work. Tycho's forceful character had made all this possible, but it was also the cause of the downfall of Uraniborg. His arrogance and overbearing attitude at last exasperated the Danish court and, on the excuse that Tycho had ill-treated one of the tenants on the island, his pension was withdrawn. Tycho, in a rage, packed up his book of observations and took his retinue with him into Germany. Uraniborg was plundered, and rapidly fell into decay. Today there is nothing left of this Castle of the Sky.

As he wandered around Europe, Tycho carried in his heart a disturbing fact, a secret hidden from everyone. He was not a mathematician, and was incapable of analyzing the data. He knew of the Ptolemaic and Copernican systems, of course, and of the argument about the movement of the Earth. During the course of his work he had proposed a third system, the Tychonic system, suggesting that the planets go round the sun and the whole assemblage then revolves around the Earth. This was a compromise between the other systems, for although the planets went around the sun as Copernicus suggested, the Earth was fixed and immovable according to the Aristotelian doctrine. Without mathematics his theory was an idle speculation. Tycho needed a mathematician to help him, otherwise his observations, his twenty years of labor, would be wasted. The only person who could help him was Johannes Kepler, a promising young mathematics teacher of eastern Germany, who had already shown unusual skill in dealing with the motion of planets. But old age was overtaking Tycho and he was destitute. Kepler was underpaid and had no money to travel. How could the two men meet?

Johannes Kepler was born a Protestant, and his religion was the force within him. He was sensitive and emotional, a mystic and a sage. As a Protestant, his salvation lay in the study of the Bible, rather than in the dogma of the Pope. The heavens were also a book written by God, to be studied as reverently as the Bible. He would work for years on a problem waiting for the day when divine inspiration would give him the answer. At the moment of discovery, when the solution lay open before him, he would feel elated and overjoyed. Sometimes the emotion brought tears to his eyes. His religion gave him the patience to struggle through the tedious analysis of Tycho's observations, and his religion brought him in touch with the book of data.

The imperial Emperor of Germany Rudolph II invited Tycho to his court in Prague. This brought Tycho within two hundred miles of Kepler, who was at Graz. The Emperor offered Tycho the position of imperial mathematician, and, although Tycho was by this time a little subdued by his travels, he was still able to negotiate for himself a large salary. He moved into Benatky Castle, set in the beautiful countryside near Prague, and immediately began to convert it into another Uraniborg. Meanwhile, in Graz, a new religious policy was inducted. Kepler was given the choice of becoming a Catholic or leaving Graz forever. He packed his household goods in two wagons and set off with wife and family for Prague. There was no time to exchange letters; Kepler relied on Brahe in his new-found glory to provide him with food and shelter. Tycho was overjoyed and gave Kepler and his family a warmhearted welcome. The meeting was charged with expectancy; one man had a scientific treasure chest, the other had the key.

Kepler became one of Tycho's assistants and was given a suite of rooms in the castle, but life as a pawn of Tycho was not pleasant. There was continual uproar in the castle, with carpenters, metal workers, and stonemasons rushing to the orders of their master. All Tycho's servants and assistants ate together at a large table with Tycho at the head. This system was used partly to make the assistants feel inferior as Tycho poked fun at them, and partly to impress upon them the prestige and grandeur of their master. Observational work and discussions with Tycho went on long into the night, but the data book was jealously guarded. On rare occasions the book was opened to a certain page for Kepler to see, but if he tried to turn the page and read more than his allowance, Tycho scowled. Before revealing the entire book, Tycho wanted some assurance that Kepler would prove the Tychonic system correct and the Copernican system wrong, but, of course, this was impossible; the truth could not be distorted. The verdict was predetermined by the observations and was beyond the whims of men. Kepler waited patiently. He felt that destiny had brought him to the book and that destiny would open it for him. Tycho died, Kepler took his place as imperial mathematician and began to study the observations.

After five years of concentrated effort, Kepler discovered the first two laws of planetary motion.

Law I states: *The orbit of a planet is an ellipse with the sun at one focus.*

Law II states: *A line drawn from a planet to the sun sweeps out equal areas in equal times.*

Tycho's accurate data had led him far from ancient beliefs. The truth was strange indeed. Instead of perfect motion taking the form of a circle it was an ellipse, a shape closely related to a circle. In fact a circle is a form of ellipse. We call the flattening of an ellipse "eccentricity." An ellipse becomes more flat or more elongated, as the eccentricity increases. Maximum elongation is reached when the eccentricity is equal to one. When the eccentricity is zero, the ellipse is not distorted and we have a circle.

In both the Ptolemaic and Copernican systems the true importance of the sun was not brought out. Ptolemy, of course, imagined the sun to be moving around the Earth. Copernicus still did not place the sun exactly at the center of the Earth's orbit. He adopted the view of Aristotle, supposing the Earth to move around a perfect circle. Since this

TABLE 2. THE PLANETS IN RELATION TO THE SUN

| Name | Distance from sun (million miles) | Sidereal Period P (years) | Semi-major axis a. (astronomical units) |
|---|---|---|---|
| Mercury | 36 | 0.241 | 0.387 |
| Venus | 67 | 0.615 | 0.723 |
| Earth | 93 | 1.000 | 1.000 |
| Mars | 142 | 1.881 | 1.524 |
| Jupiter | 483 | 11.86 | 5.203 |
| Saturn | 886 | 29.46 | 9.539 |
| Uranus | 1,783 | 84.02 | 19.18 |
| Neptune | 2,794 | 164.8 | 30.06 |
| Pluto | 3,670 | 247.7 | 39.52 |

did not agree exactly with his observations he was forced to assume that the Earth's orbit was displaced, and that the sun was not exactly at the center. Copernicus, therefore, did not regard the sun as steadfastly fixed, but imagined it to make a small movement of its own around the center of the Earth's orbit. But Kepler found the sun to be at the focus of the ellipse, a critical point in the geometry. This established more emphatically than Copernicus had done the true importance of the sun.

To draw an ellipse you can place a loop of thread around two pins stuck into a sheet of paper. If you place a pencil in the loop, draw the thread tight, and move the pencil around the pins, then you will trace out the figure of an ellipse. Each pin is at the focus of the ellipse. If the ellipse were a reflecting mirror, then light sent out from one focus would be reflected and form an image at the other focus. We know from the work of Newton that if the sun were at the center of the ellipse and not at the focus, then a planet would quickly change its course.

The second law was also a break with past philosophy. For centuries people expected to find uniform motion for celestial bodies, but now Kepler revealed a peculiar behavior—a planet moved faster when it was near the sun. Instead of a planet moving equal distances in equal time, the radius swept out equal areas. The truth, found by Kepler, is almost as simple as the dogma of Aristotle. But Kepler's law opens up new avenues for research. Why should a planet move faster when it is near the sun? Kepler took it as evidence for a controlling influence from the sun, some force producing the motion. He was very close to the theory of gravitation.

One more law lay hidden in the figures of Tycho, and Kepler worked hard for fourteen years to uncover it.

Law III states: *The square of a planet's period is proportional to the cube of the semi-major axis.*

Kepler's ambition, ever since his student days, had been to discover a relationship between the distances of the planets, for the harmony of God would then be clear to him. For this reason the law is sometimes called the "harmonic law." The law does indeed show an underlying influence between the planets and the sun. The harmonic law led Newton to his theory of gravitation. The period of the planet is the time taken for it to make one journey around the sun, starting and finishing at a line drawn from the sun to a distant star. It is called the sidereal period, and is shown as "P" in Table 2. The major axis of an ellipse is the longest line that can be drawn across the orbit. The semi-major axis is half this distance, and is called "a" in the table. For a circular orbit, the semi-major axis is equal to the radius. It is not too difficult to check Kepler's harmonic law by multiplying P x P, and seeing that it comes out equal to a x a x a. With the discovery of the harmonic law, Kepler felt that his destiny had been fulfilled.

Because of the rapid changes in religious beliefs, Kepler was refused Holy Communion by both the Protestants and the Catholic Church at the time of his death. In the eyes of the Church he was therefore damned, but he hoped to obtain salvation as a reward for his devotion to the study of the works of God. He thought of himself as a "priest of nature." He was buried in a modest grave in a churchyard in Regensburg. Two or three years later there was no sign of his grave, for Swedish, German, and Bavarian troops had turned the graveyard into a battleground. Yet the monument of his scientific work survived. For nearly two hundred years his laws were plagiarized, and the figure of Kepler was overshadowed by the great scientists who followed him. When in 1773 the original manuscripts, letters, and diary of Kepler were discovered they were purchased by Catherine the Great of Russia for the Pulkova Observatory. From the study of these documents we recognize the brilliance of Kepler, and see in him a streak of genius beyond the diplomacy of Copernicus, or the labors of Tycho Brahe.

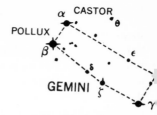

C H A P T E R **6**

# THE VIEW FROM
# THE TOP

Dᴜʀɪɴɢ ᴛʜᴇ sᴇᴠᴇɴᴛᴇᴇɴᴛʜ ᴄᴇɴᴛᴜʀʏ, ᴛʜᴇ ᴘʀᴇsᴛɪɢᴇ ᴏғ Iᴛᴀʟʏ ᴡᴀs high. The country had led the Renaissance movement in art and philosophy, and was the fountain of world religion, both for the Protestants and the Catholics. As the excitement of the new astronomy spread through Europe, people naturally turned toward Italy, expecting to see a scientific giant in that country too. Italian gentlemen, however, still looked upon education as a pastime for the leisure hours. It had become fashionable to study logic and Greek philosophy, but it was not fashionable to think for oneself. Any argument concerning science had to be based upon the "truths" of Aristotle.

Italy did not produce a brilliant scientist during the Renaissance, but it did produce one man, Galileo, who was essential for the advance of the debutante science. Galileo was more aware of nature than his fellow students, preferring to trust his own judgment rather than the words in the dusty books. As a student he refused to believe the statements of Aristotle, because they disagreed with his own experience. He argued with his fellow students until they were exhausted. He argued with his professors until his scholarship was cancelled and he was pushed out of the university without a degree. But Galileo was not disliked. He was always inventing things, and had shown a mastery of Euclidian geometry. His argumentation developed into an eloquence, and his facility with words made him a fine teacher. Whenever he gave a public lecture, people flocked to listen. Whether he talked about the stars, or a comet, or whether he lectured on the motion of cannon balls, he was always forceful and dramatic. On several occasions he dropped weights from the leaning tower of Pisa, to show the crowd below that Aristotle was wrong when he said, "A heavy object falls more rapidly than a light one." Galileo therefore had a ready audience, both inside and outside Italy, when he first pointed his telescope to the sky, and wrote of his discoveries in the *Sidereal Messenger*.

Europeans were fascinated to hear about the mountains on the moon. Most Greek scholars had said the moon was smooth. They were amazed to hear that the planet Venus showed phases like the moon. Venus evidently shone by reflected sunlight, whereas Aristotle had said the planets were self-luminous. The sun showed dark spots on its surface, and from the movement of the spots Galileo concluded that the sun rotated. If the sun were spinning surely the Earth could spin as well. Galileo's telescope showed four moons encircling the planet Jupiter. Here was a miniature solar system like the one Copernicus had in mind, and Galileo was quick to stress this point. He also used the observation to dispose of the argument which said that the Earth must be fixed, otherwise the moon as it went round the Earth would very soon be left behind. The four moons of Jupiter followed the moving planet, and Galileo argued our moon could do the same. Galileo and his little telescope encouraged such a healthy discussion in the Copernican system that in 1616 *The Revolution of Celestial Bodies* was placed on the index of forbidden books by the Vatican censors. Galileo was requested to return to mathematics, and keep his astronomical speculations to himself.

For sixteen years Galileo remained quiet, but then a friend of his was elected to become Pope Urban VIII. From previous discussions, Galileo knew that the Pope appreciated scientific work, and was rather favorable to the Copernican theory. So Galileo uncovered his carefully written manuscript entitled *A Dialogue on the Two World Systems*, and had it approved for publication by the Vatican censor. The censor read the pages with suspicion but did not see the trick. The dialogue was a play, a discussion between two professors and a man in the street called Simpleton. The eloquence of Galileo was apparent in every speech in the book, and at the end Simpleton was persuaded that Copernicus was right. Once more a breath of fresh air flowed through Europe, and many people regarded the book as a sign that the Vatican was modifying its stand. Unfortunately Pope Urban identified himself with Simpleton and was enraged. Further publication of the dialogue was stopped, existing copies were confiscated, and Galileo, although by now seventy years old, was summoned to Rome and forced to recant under threats of torture. But his book lived on and his beautifully worded arguments were all that were needed to tip the balance in favor of the Copernican theory.

Galileo has an important place in the history of science, but we do not regard him as anything more than an intelligent, hard-working mathematics professor. To be sure, he had an aptitude for invention, but he was surpassed by Leonardo da Vinci in this respect. He made telescopes and microscopes, but only after he heard about the invention from the Dutch. His astronomical discoveries amazed the public but they were not remarkable. Give any bright boy a dollar telescope, and he will point it at Jupiter, the moon, and Venus to discover for himself the wonders of Galileo. Nor did he recognize the great work that others were doing. He knew of Kepler's three laws of planetary motion, how the orbit was an ellipse and not a circle, how the sun was at the focus and not at the center, and how the planets did not move at a constant speed. But he did not emphasize this in his lectures, since he regarded Kepler as a mystic on the verge of insanity. He put the weight of his argument behind the Copernican system, which is not exactly true, instead of the system of Kepler which is correct. His most important contributions were in the field of mechanics, where he introduced the concept of acceleration, force components, and viscosity. In this he was a forerunner of Isaac Newton. Galileo died under house-arrest in 1642, broken in mind and body, blind, unable to sleep, and ridden with dropsy and ague.

Isaac Newton was born on December 25, 1642, the year Galileo died. Within two weeks of his birth there was a partial eclipse of the sun and a total eclipse of the moon. Twenty miles away, King Charles I was raising his standard in Nottingham, and civil war broke out in England. Apart from these happenings, the birth and childhood of Isaac Newton were uneventful. He was very good at making kites, sundials, and model windmills, and like the other boys he carved his initials in the woodwork of the school. Usually he finished near the bottom of the class when the grades came out. On one or two occasions, however, he worked a little harder than usual, and rose to the top. When he reached his teens, his widowed mother needed help to run her farm, so Isaac left school to do his share of plowing and marketing. By the time he reached sixteen, Mrs. Newton despaired of making her boy a farmer, for he had developed the habit of reading mathematical books behind the hedge, and engaged in weird experiments. On the day that Oliver Cromwell, the Great Protector, died, the country was hit by a severe storm with winds of hurricane force. Instead of leading the cattle to shelter, and securing the gates and barn doors, Isaac was seen jumping into the wind, and away from the wind, to measure its force. There was only one thing to do with him, send him to college.

At Cambridge University, Newton was for the first time in an atmosphere of learning. At the start, other students in the class were ahead of Newton, because they had paid more attention to their earlier studies. Newton rapidly caught up. He would read through a textbook before a lecture course commenced, and was then able to help the professor in the course, since he had a better grasp of the material. After graduation, Newton continued his studies at Cambridge for a master's degree, though he had to return to the farm once or twice because of the serious plague in the city. The three years after graduation, between the ages of twenty-three and twenty-six, were the most productive years in Newton's life. During this period he found the force of attraction between all the bodies in the solar system, the force of gravity. He showed that Kepler's three laws were a direct result of the law of gravitation, and the movement of all the planets was controlled by this simple law.

The derivation of Kepler's laws requires the use of calculus which was not available in Newton's day. Normally it takes a student one or two years to master calculus. Newton had to invent it before he could proceed with his research. He studied optics, discovering that white light can split up into its constituent colors by means of a prism. Before his time people did not realize that white light is a blend of all the colors of the rainbow mixed together. They thought that white was a pure color, and that if white light were distorted or made impure then a different color would result. Newton explained the cause of the tides in the ocean, the reason for the bulge at the Earth's equator, and the reason for the precession of the equinoxes. But beyond all this, Newton established for us the principles of the physics of motion.

In our everyday experience we come across many forces. As a car turns a corner we are thrown to one side. As the driver accelerates we are pressed back into the seat. If we inadvertently walk into a lamp-post, the lamp-post seems to return the blow. These experiences and other more complicated interactions are governed by Newton's three laws of motion.

The first law states: *A body will continue in a state of rest or uniform motion unless acted upon by a force.*

Here we recognize a break with Greek philosophy. An object moving along in a straight line at constant speed is in a state of rest. It will continue to move along forever; there is no need for us to intervene. For Aristotle all movement required a force, and an arrow flying through the air was carried along, according to him, by spirits or angels. Newton's viewpoint is entirely the reverse. The force is only required if we wish to stop the object or change its speed.

When first reading this law, some people doubt its truth. They argue that an automobile traveling along a flat, straight road requires a continual force, the engine must be kept running or else it will come to a standstill. If the engine is turned off, the automobile will certainly coast to a standstill, but this is because other forces are acting. Wind resistance, the friction of the tires and bearings all act on the automobile in the reverse direction. The car is acted upon by a resultant force, and cannot continue in a state of uniform motion. It is brought to a standstill, and then the frictional forces disappear. While we sit in the seat of the car, in the shelter of the interior, there is no wind acting on us, and there are no frictional forces. We can travel along a straight road at a uniform speed without the need for a continual force. It is just as though we were resting on a seat back at home. If, however, the car changes its direction or speed then according to Newton's first law, a force must be applied to our body. As the car swerves around the corner this force comes from the side of the seat, and if the door were not there to supply the force, we would be thrown through the opening to continue for a while along the same straight line we had before the car turned.

Newton's second law states: *To every force there is an equal and opposite reaction.*

This law underlies all our ideas on equilibrium. If an object is to remain at rest, then all the forces must cancel, otherwise it would begin to move. If objects are to remain at rest, as stated in Law I, then nature must supply the necessary forces. Consider a person sitting in a chair. His or her body is being pulled toward the center of the Earth by the force of gravity. It would leave its condition of rest, and begin to move toward the center of the Earth unless it were stopped by an equalizing force. The chair must supply an upward reaction to hold the person in position. Law II requires us to think very clearly about the behavior of objects, for when two objects come together each is exerting a force on the other, even if this force is not immediately obvious. Some people doubt that a chair can provide an upward force, a reaction, to keep them in position, but it supplies the force from the strength of its material. If this were not so, if the chair broke, for example, then they would begin to move under the action of gravity, and would not stop until they reached the floor, or some surface which was able to provide the required upward reaction to hold them in position.

Newton's third law describes the effects of an unbalanced force. When acted upon by a force a body will not move at a constant speed. So long as the force is present, the body will move faster and faster.

We say it accelerates. When the force is removed or neutralized by a reaction, acceleration ceases, and the body thereafter moves along at a uniform speed. The third law states: *Acceleration is equal to force divided by mass.*

In the automobile we feel a push from the back of the seat as the car accelerates. If our bodies are to accelerate with the car we must be acted upon by a force, and this force is applied by the back of the seat. If the seat is not strong enough to supply this force, then we are left behind, we fall backwards. If the driver presses on the brake pedal, a force acts on the car, and it slows down, it decelerates. If we also wish to decelerate, we must push the dashboard, so that we can feel the force supplied as a reaction by the dashboard.

These three laws show the clear thinking of Newton's mind. Without them the science of mechanics and physics could not begin. His recognition of gravitation as a universal force was equally important. The law of gravity states: *Between any two objects, there is a force of attraction which is proportional to the product of the masses. If the distance increases, the force decreases as the distance squared.*

Newton recognized this force to exist between all objects in the universe. Just as the Earth pulls a falling stone to the surface, so it pulls the moon. He showed that the moon was indeed continually falling toward the Earth. From the first law of motion we would expect the moon to move in a straight line unless a force were acting upon it. Gravitation causes the moon to deviate from a straight-line course, and Newton recognized that the moon in its circular orbit was continually falling away from the straight line. Motion in a perfect circle was a continual acceleration, unlike the state of rest supposed by Aristotle.

If we let a small object drop out of our hand, it will experience a resultant force, since the air is unable to provide a reaction. This unbalanced force is called the "weight" of the object. From the third law of motion, the force produces an acceleration of gravity, and this acceleration will continue until the object hits the ground. It is not obvious that the "mass" in the law of gravity is the same as the mass in the third law of motion. However, Newton made the assumption that this was so, for without this step further progress was impossible. With this assumption the acceleration of falling bodies will be the same, even though their masses are different. Galileo had shown this at Pisa. He was correct, of course, and the assumption linked the force of gravity with motion, but even today the philosophers of science argue about the implication of this step.

Newton's greatest difficulty was to calculate the force of gravity at the surface of the Earth. As we stand on the Earth, we are pulled by everything else in existence. Two people standing at arm's length experience an attraction of one-millionth of an ounce, while with larger objects the force is greater. A distant mountain range, the rocks beneath the surface, and the earth's core are all exerting a force. These forces have to be added together to obtain the resultant effect, the pull called your "weight." The calculation involves integral calculus. Newton had already developed this branch of mathematics during his three postgraduate years, calling it "inverse fluxions," but found it difficult to apply to the spherical shape of the Earth. Finally he solved the problem, finding the answer to be quite simple. He proved that the spherical Earth acted just as though all the mass were concentrated at one small point at the center, called the center of gravity. Having solved this integration he was then able to link the forces of gravity at the surface of the Earth with the forces existing between the Earth, moon, and other celestial bodies.

In 1687, Isaac Newton published his work in a book called *Principia,* or *The Mathematical Principles of Natural Philosophy*. It took the efforts of Sir Edmund Halley, Sir Christopher Wren, and other members of the Royal Society to persuade him to publish his work. Otherwise, it might never have reached us. Even in 1687 some of his work sheets had been lost during the twenty years that had gone by, and Newton had to start the calculations afresh. Nobody knows for sure why Newton did not publish sooner. One gets the impression from his letters that he did not regard his work as unusual, and felt that anybody else could do what he had done by sitting down for a while and thinking. He did not regard himself as brilliant; his fellow scientists were just rather stupid. He was also annoyed by criticism, and although he took great pains to answer a critic, he regarded such efforts as a waste of time. To avoid unpleasantness he would rather not tell other people of his work. We do not know how far Newton would have gone if he had worked throughout his life with the energy of his postgraduate years. In those three years he solved most of the scientific problems that interested him, and laid his pen aside for other matters. He was elected a member of Parliament, and for twenty-eight years was Master of the Mint. British coins made between 1699 and 1727 were pressed under his general supervision. His thoughts turned mainly to theology, though occasionally he would turn back to science, solving in a day a problem which had occupied his colleagues for several months.

The *Principia* was a masterpiece, solving the major scientific problems of the seventeenth century and giving in one volume more than could be gleaned from the combined works of all previous men. Alexander Pope summarizes the reverence and esteem in which Sir Isaac Newton was held at the time of his death by the lines:

> Nature, and Nature's Law, lay hid in night,
> God said "Let Newton be" and all was light.

But Newton himself would have disagreed with this epithet. What he had done was not unusual, other men could have done the same. Nature was there for anyone to see and there was a vast heritage of previous thinking to draw upon. In Newton's own words, "If I have seen further than any other man, it is because I stood on the shoulders of giants."

CHAPTER 7

# REVOLUTION

IN THE LAST TWO HUNDRED YEARS MANY CHANGES HAVE TAKEN PLACE. Galileo and Tycho would be amazed at the new instruments available to astronomers. Isaac Newton would perhaps be a little bewildered at the hundreds of different sciences developing today. Kepler would be thrilled to see data flowing from an observatory into a computing machine where laborious calculations are performed in a matter of seconds. The Renaissance started a revolution in our thinking and each new advance accelerates the process. Each generation students learn more about science as new discoveries are made by the student and professor working together in research. We are riding on the crest of a wave which is growing larger year by year. Whenever we look back we see a deep trough behind us, which makes us wonder what the giants of the past would have done if our modern instruments had been available to them.

The largest refracting telescope in the world is at the Yerkes Observatory, eighty miles northwest of Chicago. By means of this telescope, astronomers have learned important facts about the planets, the moon, and double stars. Most of the photographs of the moon that you see in textbooks were obtained with this instrument. The lens at the end of the tube is forty inches in diameter, weighs five hundred pounds, and was ground and polished to an almost perfect shape by the firm of Alvan Clark and Sons of Cambridge, Massachusetts. The steel tube of the telescope is sixty-two feet long, and, although it weighs twenty tons, it can be turned with fingertip pressure.

The funds for the telescope and observatory, constructed at a cost of $349,000, were provided by Mr. C. T. Yerkes, Chicago businessman. Mr. Yerkes was encouraged to be so generous by a remarkable person, George Ellery Hale. Although Hale at the time was only an assistant professor at Chicago University, he carried his plans of a giant telescope directly to the president of the university, and to anyone else who would listen to him.

A refracting telescope produces an image of stars by means of the large objective lens. The light is bent, or refracted, by the glass of the lens and so telescopes of this type are sometimes called refractors. If a plate of ground glass were placed at the focus, you would see the image of the star-field. The distance between the lens and the image is called the focal length. The size of the image depends directly upon the focal length, and if the focal length were doubled, then the stars would appear twice as far apart on the ground glass. The image can also be made to appear larger by viewing it through a magnifying glass. This lens is called the eyepiece. A short-focus eyepiece enables you to place your eye very close to the image, and hence obtain a larger picture. The magnifying power of the telescope is equal to the focal length of the objective divided by the focal length of the eyepiece.

The objective lens and the eyepiece contain more than one element. It is impossible to use a single lens successfully, because the refraction of the light produces a separation of colors, and the image develops colored fringes. The objective lens consists of two elements, a convex lens of a special glass called crown glass and a concave lens made of flint glass. The pair of lenses are cemented together in most refractors, but in the forty-inch Yerkes telescope the elements are separated by about eight inches. The eyepiece lens is also a combination of lenses of different types of glass which are carefully designed to prevent the separation of colors.

The objective lens is of large diameter for two reasons; it gives a large light grasp and a high resolving power. A human eye has a pupil no more than one-quarter of an inch in diameter, and does not collect much light. The light grasp depends on the area of the lens. Thus a lens forty inches across collects more than twenty-five thousand times as much light as the human eye, and if this light is carefully brought to a focus a person can see much fainter objects. With the eye you can see a fifth-magnitude star, and through a perfect forty-inch telescope you can see a star eleven magnitudes fainter—magnitude sixteen.

The resolving power tells us how much detail we will see through a telescope. The moon is about one-half a degree across as we see it in the sky, and with unaided vision we can see craters one minute of arc across, or one-thirtieth of the moon's diameter. With a telescope we can see more detail, and one minute of arc can be divided into sixty parts called a second. A telescope of one-inch aperture will resolve, in theory, two stars which are only 4.6 seconds of arc apart. The limit of resolution is inversely proportional to the aperture of the telescope. Thus a two-inch aperture will resolve to a limit of 2.3 seconds and, in theory, the Yerkes telescope will separate stars about 0.1 second of arc apart. Correspondingly this resolution would show craters as small as six hundred feet on the moon. High resolution is not always obtained, however, because the atmosphere causes dancing and blurring of the image. Under normal conditions we cannot use a resolving power higher than that of a ten or twenty-inch telescope, but on rare occasions when we have a perfect night we can use the full resolving power of the forty-inch Yerkes telescope. An astronomer taking a photograph is more troubled by the atmosphere than an astronomer looking through the telescope. An exposure usually requires several hours, and during this period the dancing of the image smears the light over the film. A visual observer can still see detail even though the image is dancing.

The largest optical reflector is on Mt. Palomar, fifty miles north of San Diego. The telescope weighs five hundred tons and, like the Yerkes refractor, resulted from the enthusiasm of Dr. Hale. He raised about ten million dollars for its construction, and he guided the team of designers. He lived to see the large glass disk carried from New York State to California by special train, but died ten years before the completion of the telescope. It is named the George Ellery Hale telescope in his memory.

A reflector functions like a refractor, except that starlight is focused to form the image by reflection from a large curved mirror. As in a refractor, the magnification depends upon the focal length of the mirror; the light grasp depends upon its area, and the resolving power depends upon its diameter. Since the mirror of the Palomar telescope is two hundred inches across, the light grasp is twenty-five times greater than the Yerkes refractor. You can see stars as faint as the nineteenth magnitude when you look through the eyepiece, and with a long-exposure film you can photograph stars at magnitude twenty-three. The theoretical resolving power is two-hundredths of a second of arc, corresponding to an object one hundred feet across on the moon, but this resolution is never realized because of the turbulence of our atmosphere.

Professional astronomers turned from refractors to reflectors because of necessity. It is impossible to build refractors much larger than the Yerkes telescope, because the crown and flint glass blanks cannot be cast greater than this size. Also a large lens would sag under its own weight, and lose its shape. The glass blank for a mirror, on the other hand, does not have to be perfect. Small bubbles and inclusions are not detrimental because the light does not have to pass through the glass. Imperfections become serious only when they interfere with the smoothness of the surface during the polishing of the mirror. The weight of the mirror can be supported more easily than a lens. The two hundred-inch mirror has thirty-six cells cast in the back in which supporting jacks can be placed, so the weight of the mirror is evenly supported as the telescope is pointed to various parts of the sky. The mirror is coated on its front surface with a film of aluminum, and can be recoated when the surface becomes tarnished after a year or two. Although the casting of the Palomar disk was difficult (sixty-five tons of molten pyrex were used), and the preparation of the mirror was a severe test for opticians (more than a year was required to grind and polish off five tons of glass from the blank), the Hale telescope does not represent the limit of our technology. Astronomers still require a telescope with a larger light grasp for penetrating further into space, and a person with the enthusiasm of Dr. Hale may soon begin canvassing for a four hundred-inch mirror. Meanwhile the two hundred-inch enables the astronomer to probe beyond the planets and stars to the galaxies at a distance of ten thousand billion billion miles.

For the amateur astronomer, the choice between a reflector and a refractor is based on different considerations from those of the professional. Both types give excellent views of stars, planets, nebulae, and the moon, but the view through a refractor is a little brighter than the view through a reflector of equal aperture. The tube of a refractor is closed at both ends, which minimizes the flow of air currents within the tube. A refractor is more robust, and does not fall out of adjustment so easily. It is also more easy to aim. On the other hand a reflector is less expensive than a refractor, and the amateur telescope maker usually prefers to make a mirror instead of an achromatic objective lens.

A professional astronomer seldom looks through a telescope. He removes the eyepiece and places a film at the focus. With a long exposure he can photograph objects one hundred times fainter than he can see, and he has a permanent record for later measurement. Whereas a hundred years ago people were eager to hear an astronomer describe the view through the telescope, now everybody can see for himself in the halftone plates of a book.

Some telescopes, like the Schmidt, have been designed entirely for photographic work, and it would be more appropriate to call them cameras instead of telescopes. The normal reflector has a mirror in the shape of a parabola, which gives a perfect image for a single star, but over a wide field the images deteriorate. The German optician, Bernhard Schmidt, reverted to a spherical mirror, and placed a thin glass correcting plate in front of the mirror to make it appear like a parabola. In this way tolerable images are produced over a wide field, and many stars can be photographed at the same time. In 1956, a survey of the northern sky was completed with the 48-inch Schmidt on Mt. Palomar. The position and brightness of millions of stars were recorded in an atlas, which would have taken a century to make by the older method of visual observation. Even with the modern instrument, the survey took several years, for more than a thousand photographs were necessary.

We discover the wonders of space by reading the message of light, yet an astronomer would find it difficult to tell you exactly what light is. Even the physicist has difficulty. Light behaves like a wave, an electric and magnetic field vibrating in unison and moving with a velocity of 186,000 miles per second. But light also behaves like a particle, called a photon. It is impossible to subdivide the photon because the waves seem to hold together in packets of fixed size.

Photons can be detected individually by a photo-multiplier, a photo-electric device. The photon hits a surface and ejects an electron. This small charge of electricity is then amplified until the signal is large enough to record. Photo-multipliers are very useful for the detection of faint stars. They also give a very accurate measure of brightness, because the electric current depends directly upon the number of photons coming in. The photographic plate and the human eye do not behave in this way. If the brightness increases a hundredfold, the eye and the camera only record a fivefold increase in their response.

The electromagnetic waves which form a beam of light have definite wave lengths. Each color corresponds to a separate wave length, and all wave lengths together form a spectrum. A color can be slightly changed by the movement of the source. This change is called the Doppler effect after Christian J. Doppler, an Austrian physicist, who was one of the first to discover it. The Doppler effect is very important to the astronomer, because the slight change in color is proportional to the speed of an object. If a certain line in the spectrum is displaced toward the red, then the astronomer knows that the object is receding from him. A shift toward the blue indicates approach. We can measure the motion of stars and galaxies with precision provided we can collect sufficient light.

The Doppler effect exists in all types of wave motion, and forms part of our everyday experience. For example, sound is a wave motion through the air, and hardly a day goes by without an illustration of the effect. The sound of an object that is approaching us has a shorter wave length and we hear a high-pitched note. A receding object has a longer wave length and a lower pitched note. There is a sudden decrease in the pitch of the whistle of a locomotive as it passes by, and an automobile horn shows the same effect. Even the hum from the tire or the roar of an engine shows a change in tone as it passes by. The radar sets used to measure automobile speeds also work by this principle. If your car were not moving, then the reflected signal would not increase in frequency. There would be no Doppler shift, and no speeding fine.

A spectroscope enables an astronomer to make a very thorough analysis of the color of starlight. Although the spectroscope is based upon the simple prism experiment of Newton, it represents the ultimate in refinement. Instead of Newton's hole in the blind, the light is let through a narrow slit, no more than one-thousandth of an inch wide. From the slit the light is led in a parallel beam through a series of four or more prisms. After refraction the light is focused again to form an image of the slit, and a separate image appears for each color in the original light. With a good instrument, as many as ten thousand different colors can be resolved in a spectrum.

Sometimes the prism is replaced by a grating, a thin glass plate on which thousands of fine lines are ruled. As the light passes through the grating, interference occurs and the colored beams are sent out at different angles. When extra resolution is required the spectroscope is set up in a long air-conditioned tunnel, and light enters the tunnel through a shaft about one hundred feet long. Spectroscopes have also been designed to work with invisible light beyond the ordinary spectrum. Some instruments have special diffraction gratings which work in the infrared region where the heat rays are found. Others use special quartz prisms for probing the ultraviolet spectrum. At the very long wave lengths electromagnetic vibrations becomes known as radio waves, and a study of the universe in this region of the spectrum has developed into the new science of radio astronomy.

Today a further revolution has taken place, for we are able to take our instruments above the troublesome atmosphere. Balloons are able to carry telescopes to a height of seventeen miles where they are above 98 per cent of the air and water vapor. Astronomers from the ground use remote control to point and focus the telescope. One successful flight can yield thousands of detailed pictures. Already Dr. Martin Schwarzschild of Princeton has changed our ideas about the surface of the sun by his pictures of the granulation. Soon the technique will be yielding information about the surface of the planets. Satellites and space probes can carry instruments completely out of the atmosphere to bring further discoveries about our environment. We can even recover the instruments and records after a successful flight. Ultimately the instruments will be established on the surface of the moon and planets to give direct measurements of conditions and to relay television pictures of the terrain.

CHAPTER 8

# DISCOVERY

WITH THE INVENTION OF NEW INSTRUMENTS CAME NEW DISCOVERIES. The Earth was recognized as an ordinary planet attending the sun; comets were seen to be clouds of glowing gas; meteors were found to be small fragments burning in the atmosphere, and it was discovered that the sun is a typical star. Telescopes, penetrating the cloud of stars surrounding the sun, revealed the huge system of the galaxy. Stars were found to be related to each other in a simple sequence, and their internal structure was explored by the astrophysicists. Beyond the Milky Way other galaxies were seen, extending our exploration of the universe almost to infinity. During the course of the development of our understanding, several important facts had to be ascertained before progress could continue. One of the foremost questions was "What is the size and shape of the Earth?"

The size of the Earth was found from the work of hundreds of surveyors with measuring rods using the method of the Greek scholar Eratosthenes; the shape of the Earth was discovered accidentally. The surveyors measured the distance in miles between two locations and also the difference in latitude. In 1500, a Frenchman, Jean Fernel, measured off the distance of one degree of latitude by counting the number of revolutions of the wheel of a carriage. In 1637 an Englishman, Richard Norwood, measured the 150 miles between London and York partly with a chain, and partly by pacing it out. Louis XV sponsored a survey in 1735 to obtain an accurate value of the Earth's diameter. Three scientists and two Spanish army officers measured the length of a three-degree arc in rough territory in Peru. Five other scientists measured the length of one degree in the frozen tundra of Lapland. Year by year the measurements continued, culminating in the formation of the International Association of Geodesy with its world-wide cooperation. The diameter of the Earth from pole to pole is 7,899.98 miles, and the diameter at the equator is 7,926.68 miles.

From the figures you can see that the Earth is slightly flattened at the poles, or is oblate. This oblateness is due to the spin of the Earth on its axis as the centrifugal force causes the equator to bulge. Its existence can be predicted theoretically, but it was discovered experimentally by the Frenchman, Jean Richer. He was sent by the French Academy to make astronomical observations in South America where he found that his clock, which had kept good time at Paris, lost more than two minutes a day at the new location. At first his discovery was disbelieved. Then other astronomers went to the equator and confirmed the result. They found that the beat of the pendulum was slow because the clock was thirteen miles further away from the center of the Earth.

The next problem was to determine the mass of the Earth. How much would the Earth weigh if, piece by piece, the rocks were dug out and placed in a balance? One of the first methods of measurement compared the attraction of a mountain with the attraction of the whole Earth. A weight on a thread was suspended near the mountain. It was pulled sideways by the attraction of the mountain, and downward by the attraction of the Earth. The forces are given by Newton's law of gravitation, and knowing the distance to the center of the mountain and to the center of the Earth, the scientist could work out the ratio of the mass of the mountain to that of the Earth. The mass of the mountain could be estimated by weighing a few samples of rock, and then measuring the size of the mountain. Thus from the slight deflection of the plumb line, the actual mass of the Earth could be found.

Several mountains were chosen, each with a regular shape which enabled the surveyor to estimate its total size. Pierre Bouguer went to Mt. Chimborazo in Ecuador, Francesco Carlini to Mt. Blanc, and the American T. C. Mendenhall went to the sacred volcano of Fujiyama in Japan. The British Astronomer Royal, Nevil Maskelyne, chose the beautiful hill of Schiehallion in the lowlands of Scotland, because it had been smoothed to an almost perfect shape by glaciers.

Sir George Airy used a different method to determine the mass of the Earth. He measured the period of oscillation of a pendulum at the top and at the bottom of a mine shaft. For his first experiments he chose the deep tin mines of Cornwall, but later in his career he showed a preference for coal pits. His most successful measurements were made in a disused colliery near South Shields. The work was quite dangerous. On one occasion Sir George almost suffocated in some foul air; on another occasion a superstitious miner set fire to the swinging pendulum during the course of the experiment.

The most accurate determination of the mass of the Earth has been made in the laboratory. A large sphere of lead was used to replace the mountain and the small gravitational force that it exerted was measured by a swinging balance. The most recent measurements give a mass of 6.6 thousand billion billion tons.

During the routine measurements of mass, surveyors have been surprised by the Earth's heaviness. If the Earth were made of granite and other ordinary rocks it would weigh only half as much. Even the early experiments with mountains and mine shafts showed the discrepancy, and there was much discussion as to the cause. In their routine measurements the scientists had discovered the heavy core which exists at the center of the Earth. The consequences of this discovery are described in a later chapter.

The distance to the moon was measured by the method of parallax. If you look at the moon you see it projected again a background of stars, and if you could move rapidly to a new position on the Earth the moon would appear in a different place. The apparent displacement is called the angle of parallax, and it is the angle in a triangle with its peak at the center of the moon. We have all used the method of parallax unknowingly since we were about three months old. The two eyes in our head are set about three inches apart for the purpose. They are at each end of a base line, and if we look at a nearby object we are forced to squint. The slight rotation of each eye measures the angle of parallax. This measurement is relayed to our brain where the trigonometrical calculation is performed and we immediately know the distance to the object. Our automatic range-finder fails if we shade one eye, or if the distance is greater than about a hundred feet, for then the three-inch base line is too small. To measure the distance of the moon, astronomers use base lines several thousand miles long. They cooperate, making simultaneous observations, and from the parallax angle they compute the distance. The moon is a little over two hundred thousand miles away, but the distance varies slightly because the orbit of the moon is not exactly circular. Radar astronomers have found a different way to measure the distance. Radio signals are sent off from the Earth, traveling with a speed of light, and from the time taken for the round trip they can find the one-way distance.

The distance to the sun is also measured by parallax, but since the sun is so bright it is difficult to measure its displacement against a

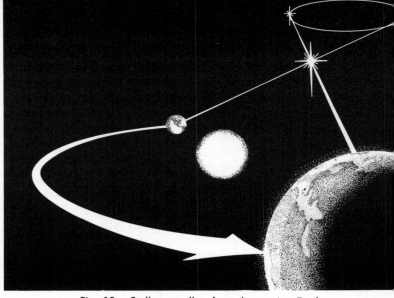

Fig. 13.  Stellar parallax from the moving Earth

background of stars. Astronomers solved the problem by using the
planet Venus instead. When Venus passes in front of the sun we can
see it projected as a black disk. As it moves, Venus is said to make a
"transit" across the sun. Astronomers in different parts of the world
see Venus in different positions on the disk, the displacement being
due to the effects of parallax. From the parallax angle it is a simple
matter to calculate the distance between the Earth and Venus. But
the ratio of the distance of Venus and the distance of the Earth from
the sun is known from Kepler's harmonic law. We can therefore calculate the distance to the sun as well as the distance to Venus. The distance to Venus is 26 million miles, and the distance to the sun is 93
million miles.

One of the most aggravating things to discover was the parallax of
a star. The stars are too far away to show a parallax with a base line
on the surface of the Earth. But the parallax appears when we use the
Earth's orbit as a base. Aristotle had commented that he expected the
stars to make a small movement in the sky if the Earth revolved about
the sun. Since the shift was not seen he used it as a proof of the im-
movability of the Earth. Copernicus was aware of the problem when
he put forward his theory. His observations showed no seasonal parallax which he explained as being due to the immense distances of the
stars. Tycho Brahe supported Aristotle, refuting the Copernican theory
because no parallax could be detected. By the eighteenth century the
absence of stellar parallax was becoming a source of embarrassment.

1. Uraniborg, the observatory of Tycho Brahe in Denmark

2. Eclipse observers wait for the weather to lift in New England

3. The 200-inch telescope of Mt. Palomar

4. Evolution of the solar system

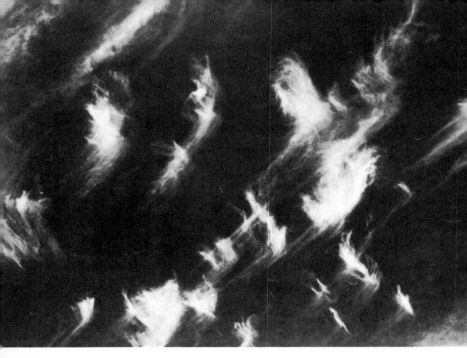

5. Cirrus clouds, forerunners of a storm

6. Cumulonimbus, a dramatic thunderhead

7. The inferno of Venus

8. The plains of Mars

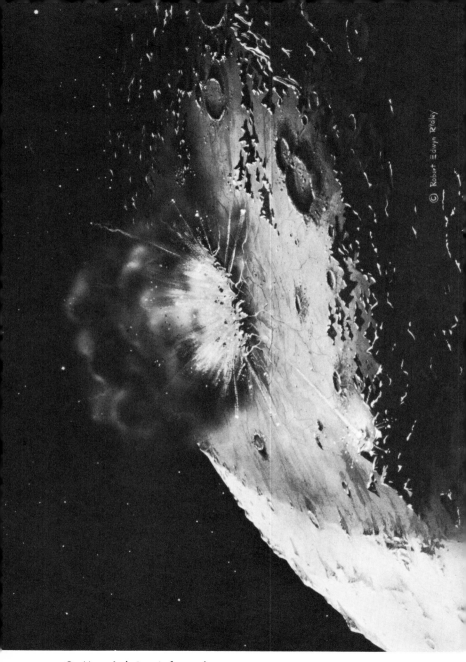

9.  Mare Imbrium is formed

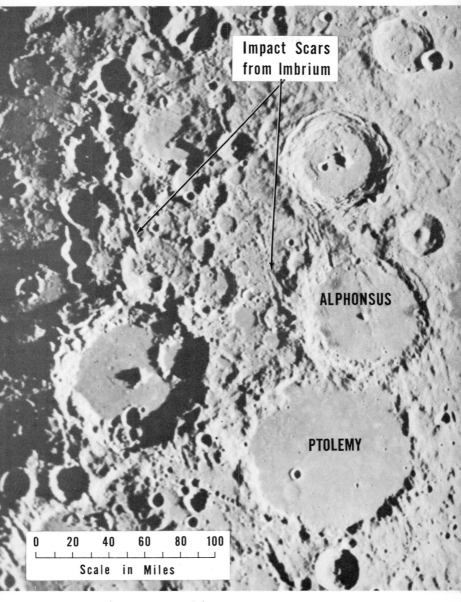

Impact Scars
from Imbrium

ALPHONSUS

PTOLEMY

0   20   40   60   80   100
Scale  in  Miles

10.  A region on the moon near Alphonsus

11. The moon near last quarter

12. The moon near last quarter

13. The moon almost full

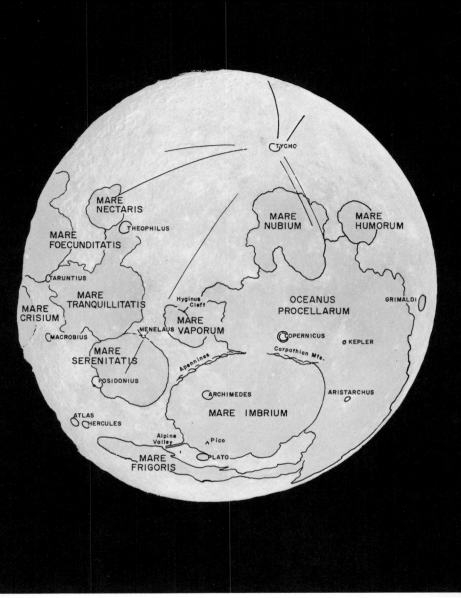

14. The moon almost full

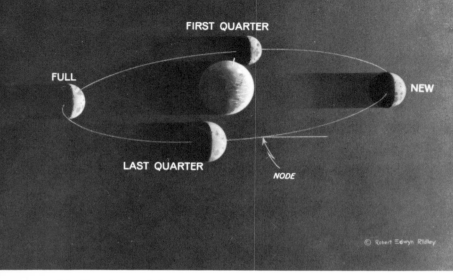

15. The phases of the moon

16. Voyager explores Mars

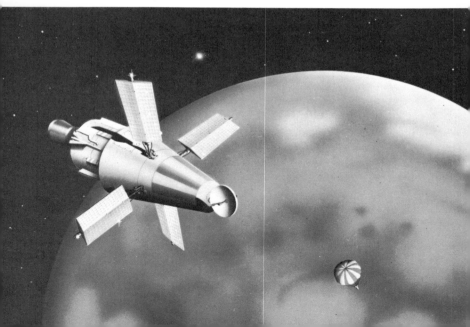

Astronomers were convinced of the truth of the heliocentric system with the Earth moving around the sun. The stars must show a seasonal displacement, however small it was, otherwise there was something wrong with the foundations of astronomy. The pressure was on. Who would be first to discover stellar parallax?

In 1704 Olaus Römer announced the discovery of a displacement of the bright stars Sirius and Vega. Unfortunately the result was wrong because of an error in his instruments. He had measured the right ascension of the stars by means of a clock, but the clock was sensitive to temperature changes, running slower in the daytime than it did at night. Some thirty years earlier, Robert Hooke had tried to be first in the discovery by fixing a long-focus telescope in his lodgings. He cut a hole in the roof and set the objective lens in a special box with a lid to keep out the rain. The starlight was brought down through a hole in the bedroom floor into his study. By lying on the floor and looking up, he hoped to detect slight displacements of the star gamma Draconis from the vertical. He was thwarted in the attempt because the lens fell down one night and was smashed. Samuel Molyneux and James Bradley repeated the work on gamma Draconis and found a displacement to and fro of forty-one seconds of arc. At first they thought it was parallax but after a while they realized the effect was due to the aberration of light. As the observer was carried along by the Earth, the beam of light from the star was apparently displaced. This displacement is seen quite often in a rainstorm. As you stand still the rain appears to come down vertically, but if you move along in a car the direction of the raindrops shows an apparent displacement which makes them splatter on the windshield. Although Bradley had not discovered stellar parallax, his result was of great interest, for aberration showed conclusively that the Earth was moving around the sun. It gave a further impetus for the actual detection of stellar parallax.

After several false alarms, caused by poor instruments and over-enthusiastic observers, the parallax of a star was successfully measured in 1838, by the German, Friedrich Bessel. His success was due partly to his choice of star, and partly to his skill as an observer. There are two thousand stars visible to the naked eye and Bessel had to guess which one was nearest to the Earth before he started his long series of measurements. Römer took the brightest stars, Sirius and Vega, but these stars are bright not because of their nearness but because they are giant stars. Vega in particular was not a very fortunate choice, for among the stars visible to the naked eye there are hundreds which are closer than Vega. The parallax of Sirius is greater but through a telescope it is a brilliant object and difficult to measure. Bessel chose the fifth magnitude star 61 Cygni, a double star with a wide separation of the two components. It also has a large proper motion, changing its position in the constellation by ten minutes of arc every century. Bessel's choice was fortunate, there is no other naked-eye star closer than 61 Cygni among the thousands in the Northern Hemisphere. The parallax was one-third of a second of arc, about the width of a human hair at a distance of 16 feet. Yet Bessel's accurate work revealed this small displacement to the satisfaction of the astronomical world. He had set the scale of stellar distances. The stars were indeed at tremendous distances from us; 61 Cygni was 67 million million miles away. As Sir John Herschel presented Bessel with the gold medal of the Royal Astronomical Society he said "It is the greatest and most glorious triumph which practical astronomy has ever witnessed."

Not all astronomical discoveries are received so well. Sir William Herschel, the father of Sir John, has been immortalized for his discovery of the planet Uranus. Keats wrote in a sonnet

> Then felt I like some watcher of the skies
> When a new planet swims into his ken. . . .

but at the time of the discovery Sir William was made to feel very uncomfortable. He was an amateur, and observed with a homemade six-inch reflector set up in the street outside his house. It was March 1781, and he was carrying out an ambitious project, a systematic inspection of every star and nebula in the sky. On the thirteenth of the month he was examining a region in the constellation of Taurus when he came upon the planet Uranus. He knew it was not a star because it showed as a disk instead of a point of light, and it moved from night to night against the background of stars. Since the beginning of history there had been seven wanderers, the sun, moon, and five planets, and Herschel did not wish to interfere with the magic number. He conservatively called Uranus a "comet" and wrote a letter to the Royal Society about his discovery.

Herschel had used an unusual method for fixing the position. He had measured the distance between Uranus and the background stars to within two seconds of arc (using a micrometer of his own making). Professional astronomers using a system of graduated circles determined the position of stars individually without reference to the background. They had difficulty in reaching the accuracy that Herschel had obtained with his comparison method. They were skeptical of his results. Furthermore, Herschel had used faint stars of twelfth magnitude, which were not on the star charts, and the professionals at first could not find the object he was talking about. Even the famous comet hunter of France, Charles Messier, wrote to Herschel suggesting that he had not observed for a sufficient number of nights. In his report Herschel said the magnifying power of his telescope was two thousand. This again threw doubt on his work, because the focal length of the eyepiece would have to be one-thirtieth of an inch and the members of the Royal Society were sure that nobody could make such a lens. But Herschel was speaking the truth. He was an exceptional craftsman. A hundred years later some of his eyepieces were measured, and his statements were confirmed. Some of his lenses were no bigger than a fly's eye, and had been ground and polished by Herschel by some process that he did not disclose.

The value of Herschel's discovery was realized in the end. He was elected a member of the Royal Society, was made president of the Royal Astronomical Society, and was knighted. He was appointed Royal Astronomer to King George III, (there already was, of course, an Astronomer Royal) becoming a professional at a salary of £200 per year.

There was also unpleasantness in the discovery of Neptune, which was found in two ways, mathematically and with the telescope. Uranus did not move smoothly between 1800 and 1820, but appeared to lag behind. Wild explanations were put forward; perhaps the law of gravity did not apply exactly to the new planet, or maybe Herschel's original observations were wrong. Actually Uranus was lagging because it was being pulled by the planet Neptune, invisible in the depths of the solar system. Three mathematicians decided to find out where Neptune was by using the gravitational theory. These men were Bessel, John C. Adams, and Urbain J. J. Leverrier, and they worked independently. Bessel unfortunately died early in his career and did not complete the task. John Adams was a student at Cambridge University when he resolved to tackle the problem, and he began work as soon as he graduated. Within two years he had found the orbit of the unseen planet, and he went to London to give the Astronomer Royal, Sir George Airy, its predicted position in the sky. Sir George had had a busy summer visiting the Cornish tin mines, railroads, lighthouses, and breakwaters in France, and was unable to see him. Adams returned to Cambridge in disappointment. Nevertheless he continued his calculations and sent Airy a revised set of figures the following year. We now know that Adams' position was correct to within one degree, and the astronomers only had to point their telescope and they would have seen the planet Neptune.

Airy was still apathetic when the new calculations arrived. Although he was a mathematician himself, he somehow had the idea that it was impossible to predict the position of an unknown planet. Then he received a communication from Leverrier and his apathy changed to a mild form of panic. Leverrier, working quite independently, was predicting the same position for Neptune as was Adams. The calculations were obviously correct and it was clearly the duty of the Astronomer Royal to point the telescope. As usual Airy was very busy, and detailed Professor Challis of Cambridge Observatory to make the search. Professor Challis also had no faith. He measured more than three thousand star positions in the search, but did not have the incentive to plot them on a chart. If he had done so he would have discovered Neptune, because he observed it on August 4 and August 12, 1846. Meanwhile astronomers at the Berlin Observatory were also searching, and there Professor J. Galle found Neptune on September 23.

For several years afterwards there was a rancor in Europe. Airy had not publicized the work of Adams, and when the English claim was put forward Adams was regarded as an impostor. The argument was carried on rather fiercely between the top men in the academies of France and England, but the two mathematicians kept in the background. Adams himself was very shy, and made no public statements about the episode. In the end Airy and Challis were blamed for their handling of the matter, and Adams and Leverrier were given joint credit for a unique and remarkable piece of work.

The discovery of Pluto produced an enigma. Uranus overtook Pluto in the constellation of Capricornus in 1834 and afterwards began to lag behind once again. Percival Lowell repeated the calculations of Adams and Leverrier, and predicted the existence of a trans-Neptunian planet in the constellation Taurus. He carried out an energetic search for four years, photographing the sky every available night. He actually photographed Pluto on several occasions, but the image was faint and he overlooked it. Lowell's search was ended by his death in 1916.

Three years later the calculations were repeated by W. H. Pickering of Harvard Observatory, this time using the lag in the planet Neptune. The calculations showed that Pluto had now moved into the constellation Gemini, and Dr. Milton Humason, of Mt. Wilson Observatory, undertook a search. He photographed Pluto twice in 1919. The first time Pluto's image was masked by a flaw in the film, the second time it was exactly in front of a star. Pluto had still escaped detection.

Ten years later another search was begun at Lowell Observatory. Photographic plates were exposed by night and examined by day in a herculean effort. In ten thousand hours of work about ninety million star images were examined, and Pluto was found by Clyde W. Tombaugh not more than five degrees away from the predicted position. The Lowell observers proceeded with caution, checking the movement of Pluto for almost two months before announcing the discovery. It was an all-American achievement from the initial prediction to the final detection.

There was something odd about Pluto, however. It was fainter than predicted and did not show as a disk in the telescope. Lowell's calculations put the mass of Pluto at seven Earth masses, Pickering's put it at two. If Pluto had this mass, the astronomers argued, it must be a compressed object with a density five times as great as lead. If Pluto does not have this mass, then the calculations are invalid. This would mean that Pluto was not pointed out by the mathematicians, but by the finger of fate.

The riddle is not yet solved. Dr. Dirk Brouwer, of Yale, has re-examined the motion of Uranus and Neptune. He concludes that Lowell and Pickering overestimated the mass, and the true figure is close to 0.8 of the Earth's. Dr. Gerard Kuiper and Dr. M. Humason measured the diameter using the 200-inch Hale telescope. They found it was 3,700 miles across, less than the planet Mars. The revised density is still much greater than the Earth, some thirty times as heavy as water. Many suggestions have been put forward. Perhaps there is another planet out there beyond Pluto, disturbing the motion of Uranus and Neptune. Perhaps Pluto is a frozen ball of ice, and as it glistens in the sunlight, we measure the glint from the surface and not the true diameter. In size it would then resemble the Earth more than Mars and the density would be normal. But this question is beyond our reach at the moment. The answer, like so many others, lies in the discoveries of the future.

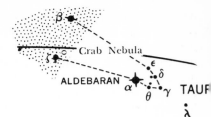

CHAPTER 9

# WHITE ELEPHANTS

MOST OBSERVATORIES HAVE A BASEMENT OR AN ATTIC WHERE instruments are laid aside ignominiously. Obsolescence is of course unavoidable; sooner or later instruments are replaced by better models, and by comparison the older models look hopelessly inept and useless. If an instrument has served us well there are no regrets when it is laid aside. It may even take on new value as a museum piece. Sundials, for example, were essential before the pendulum clock was invented, and portable sundials were needed until we had pocket watches. To examine a collection of pocket sundials, some made of ivory, some made of brass, each one an individual sample of craftsmanship, is a fascinating step into the past. The owner of such a sundial opened up the case, faced due south with the aid of a magnetic compass needle, and read the time from the shadow cast by the sun. Primitive alarm clocks were also available. A lens focused the sun's rays to a burning point which moved steadily as the sun traveled across the sky. A toy cannon could be set to fire at a prearranged time when the sun's image reached the fuse. Although today we prefer to use more conventional timepieces, sundials were essential to our forefathers and deserve an honorable place in history.

Observatories themselves have become outdated as city lights have encroached around them, but usually astronomers adapt their work to the changing conditions to keep the observatory alive. In 1847 Harvard College Observatory mounted a fifteen-inch refractor which, together with a similar one in Russia, was then the largest telescope in the world. The telescope and its luxurious red velvet seat were in service for fifty years or more, but the lights of Boston eventually made observing difficult. Nowadays Harvard astronomers do theoretical work in the confines of an office and travel to New Mexico or South

Africa to make their observations. When the Royal Observatory of Belgium was troubled by lights from the city of Brussels, the instruments were moved to the small town of Uccle. Similarly, when the Royal Greenwich Observatory was smoked out of London, it was moved to Herstmonceaux Castle in the clear air of Sussex. By adapting to the changing conditions, these observatories have continued to be important in research.

Some instruments ordered by observatories were never used. Hundreds of the circles engraved by Edward Troughton unjustifiably became basement relics. To place an order with Troughton a person walked through to a back parlor on Fleet Street, in London, and spoke into an ear trumpet. Troughton's soiled wig and snuff-stained clothes gave little indication of his ability, but his craftsmanship was superb. Astronomers of the time, however, failed to use Troughton's genius to the full. Some instruments, on the other hand, by the nature of their design and construction, could never be successful, and were destined to cause embarrassment and chagrin to the owners. One of these instruments was the long-focus telescope.

A refracting telescope has two main defects called spherical and chromatic aberration, which spoil the view through the telescope. Spherical aberration occurs when the surface of the objective lens is part of a sphere. The image is blurred because the rays of light are not brought to a focus exactly at one point. Chromatic aberration is produced when light is split into different colors by refraction at the objective lens, which causes the image to have colored fringes. One way to avoid spherical aberration is to grind nonspherical surfaces, but this trick was not known in 1650. Chromatic aberration was not overcome until special crown and flint glasses were made a hundred years later. Seventeenth century astronomers tried to avoid the problems of aberration by building longer and longer telescopes, but in doing this they met troubles much worse than aberration.

Johannes Hevelius was very successful in mapping the features of the moon and he used a homemade telescope that was twelve feet long. Two brothers in Holland, Christian and Constantine Huygens, read of his success and decided to build their own telescope. They ground lens after lens and made telescopes that were 12 feet long, 23 feet, and finally one 123 feet long. Several years of work went into the making of the telescopes and many troubles occurred in melting the glass, grinding the lens, and making the telescope tube.

By the time they reached the 123-foot telescope, the brothers had given up the idea of a tube altogether. It was impossible to obtain single sections of wood long enough to make the tube, and joints would weaken the structure. A post 100 feet high was set up in a field, and the object glass was mounted on a ball-and-socket joint. The joint was fastened to a table which could be raised or lowered by hauling on a rope. To look through the telescope the observer stood on the ground and pointed the eyepiece toward the top of the mast. To make sure that the eyepiece was 123 feet from the objective, a piece of string, exactly the right length, was stretched between the two.

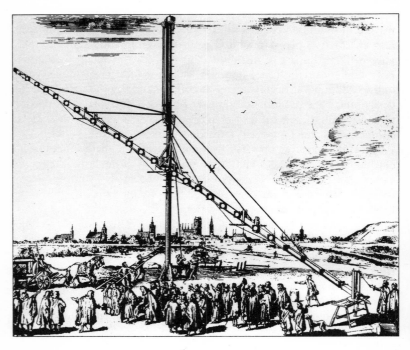

Fig. 14.   Hevelius erects the 150-foot telescope on the shores of the Baltic near Danzig

Christian Huygens had great difficulty in using the telescope. In the first place it was difficult to see the top of the mast on a dark night and he had to search for the objective by shining a beam from a flickering lantern. Then he had great difficulty in pointing the telescope. The object glass was turned by pulling the string, but the ball-and-socket joint would twist in the breeze, and the platform would slip down the mast. When he was looking at a bright object, Huygens could find the image by bringing it to a focus on a piece of oiled parchment, but even when the telescope was correctly sighted there was no convenient way to allow for the steady westward drift as the celestial sphere rotated.

Constantine Huygens continued to extend the focal length, and made object glasses for telescopes 170 and 210 feet long. The Dutch brothers found these lenses impossible to use, and presented them to their rivals in England. Isaac Newton received the 170-foot lens and in turn presented it to the Royal Society of London. The Reverend G. Burnet received the 210-foot instrument and, finding it an embarrassment, followed Newton's example. The Royal Society received the lens of the 123-foot telescope directly from the hands of Christian Huygens in 1692, but the Dutchman did not include the 100-foot pole in the gift.

The fellows of the Royal Society were delighted with Huygens' generosity, and at once looked around for a high building on which to place the lens. Unfortunately the London of Queen Anne's day could not provide a building of the requisite height or stability. St. Paul's Cathedral was under construction, and Sir Edmund Halley was ordered to try out the scaffolding, but apparently he did not think it suitable. In 1710 the instrument was finally erected eight miles north of London on the top of a maypole taken from the Strand. Either the Londoners wanted their maypole back, or the countryfolk disapproved, for satirical verses were often found nailed to the instrument when the astronomers arrived for work in the evening. Very little was accomplished however, because of a poor image due to the motion of the air and the shaking of the pole. After a while the lens was taken down and handed over to William Derham, vicar of Upminster. The vicar found Huygens' lens was a great burden on his stipend, especially since long poles cost nearly $300. For several years he tried to use the instrument but saw nothing worthwhile through his makeshift mounting. The lens was finally returned to the rooms of the Royal Society, where it remains to this day.

When Hevelius in Danzig heard of the long telescopes in Holland, he decided to build longer telescopes for himself. He owned a brewery, and therefore had sufficient funds to employ local glassworkers, carpenters, and steeple jacks. Progressing from 60-foot and 70-foot telescopes he finally built one longer than the one in Holland. The Danzig telescope was 150 feet long, and was erected on the seashore by the Baltic. It was necessary to make the telescope in four sections, because the longest planks available were only 40 feet. Instead of

Fig. 15. Christian Huygens attempts to use the 123-foot aerial telescope

making a solid tube Hevelius reduced the weight of the telescope by making an L-shaped housing with just a bottom and one side. The telescope was stiffened along its length by wire stays and was suspended at six different points to prevent its bending under its own weight. As it was close to the Baltic, the telescope could not be left permanently in position, but was brought out and erected during the evening when Hevelius desired to observe. This process was usually watched with interest by a group of burghers from the town. Several assistants would haul on ropes to set the telescope high on the mast. Others would place in position the observing table and Hevelius would then point the telescope, making the final adjustments on the winches at the eyepiece end.

In his books Hevelius tells us how easy it was to mount and use the giant telescope, but other writers tell a different story. It took several hours to move out from Danzig and place the telescope in position. The telescope was really too delicate to be handled by horse-power and rough hands. Sometimes the wooden planks warped or dew settled on the ropes, twisting the telescope out of line. The slightest breeze caused it to swing and the entire framework to quiver like a reed. No doubt the telescope was looked at more than it was looked through, for despite Hevelius' optimistic account, no important discoveries were made with the instrument.

Long-focus telescopes are monuments to futility. Admittedly Huygens discovered Saturn's largest moon, Titan, and the true nature of Saturn's rings; Cassini in Paris saw a marking in the rings and four new moons, but these discoveries were not a direct result of the monstrous telescopes. Spherical aberration was minimized to some extent by the long focus, but chromatic aberration was not, and telescopes of twelve- or fifteen-foot focus would have served the astronomers just as well. Perseverance and observational skill were the two qualities that enabled Huygens and Cassini to make discoveries despite the limitations of their instruments.

The last long-focus telescope was constructed in 1900. It was built in a tunnel more than 200 feet long, and light was reflected into the lens by means of a mirror. Chromatic aberration was partially overcome by a special combination of different glasses in the 49-inch diameter lens, and it was placed on view in the Universal Exhibition at Paris. Millions of people paid an admission fee to look through the monster, but at midnight they were turned away as French astronomers took over for a night's work. Very little was accomplished, however. To see any chosen star, the mirror at the end of the tunnel had to be swung to the correct position. This was done by command, the orders being carried along the tunnel by a telephone to the assistant at the end. To focus the giant, the eyepiece assembly was moved backwards and forwards on a railroad track.

It was a financial disappointment as well as a scientific one. The admission fees didn't cover the cost, nor would the French government buy the telescope when the exhibition closed. It was taken apart and the lens was stored in the basement of the Observatory of Paris.

Chromatic aberration was finally overcome by Sir Isaac Newton when he designed and constructed the first reflecting telescope. The metal mirror reflected light rays of all colors to a common focus, producing a clear image without spurious colored fringes. Successive improvements were made in the reflecting telescope during the eighteenth century, Sir William Herschel of England being the world's authority.

Herschel neglected his music career to grind hundreds of mirrors. His telescopes were unsurpassed for clarity of detail, and were a convenient length to handle, some ten or twenty feet. As he mastered the polishing technique his mirrors became larger, and his ultimate goal was to cast and polish a mirror forty-eight inches across. A large mirror, he argued, would show more details of the planets, moon, and star clusters, than a small one. Unfortunately this is not true, because the atmosphere of the Earth breaks up a wave front into sections about three inches across, and these sections interfere with each other in a telescope. As a result the view becomes blurred. The best view is obtained with mirrors between six and ten inches in diameter; further enlargement of the mirror only makes the image grow worse. Large mirrors show faint objects, but the definition of planetary detail and close double stars is limited by the atmosphere.

By the time Herschel was Royal Astronomer to George III, the desire to build a forty-eight inch telescope was irrepressible. A sum of £4,000 was set aside by the King for the construction of the telescope, but casting a forty-eight inch mirror was a difficult problem. Herschel could remember his unfortunate experiences of 1781, when he tried to cast a twenty-four inch mirror in the basement. The molten bronze, two-thirds copper and one-third tin, burst through his mold and flowed over the flagstones on the floor. Some of the stones began to crack and some exploded. Workmen ran for their lives leaving Herschel to collapse exhausted on a heap of bricks. The forty-eight inch mirror was therefore cast under contract by a firm in London.

Month after month the mirror was ground and polished. A team of twelve men was needed to move the polishing tool over the mirror,

Fig. 16. Sir William Herschel peers into the 48-inch telescope at Slough

each man grasping a handle provided at the edge. Meanwhile passengers in a stagecoach between London and Bath saw a wooden pyramid growing behind the house of Herschel. The latticework of poles and ladders was needed to support the telescope and the observing galleries. The whole structure rotated on rollers around a brickwork track, moved by a man at a windlass. Thirty-five workmen swarmed around laying bricks and hoisting spars. One was a smith who set up a forge to rivet together the sheet-iron tube. The tube, which had been put together in a large barn a quarter of a mile from the house, was forty feet long and five feet in diameter. Before the tube was placed in position visitors could not resist the temptation of walking through it. Dukes, princesses, the King and Queen made the trip. George III walked through the tube several times, becoming accustomed to the darkness. On one occasion he led the faltering Archbishop of Canterbury by the hand saying "Come my Lord Bishop, I will show you the way to heaven."

The telescope itself was a failure, though Herschel himself would never admit it. The climate of England allowed no more than a hun-

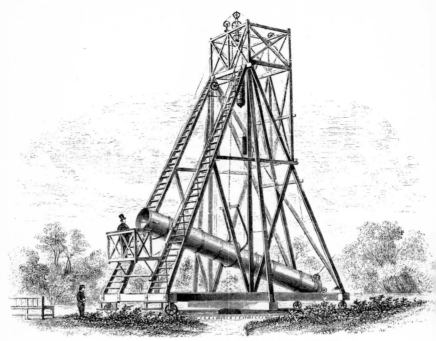

Fig. 17.   Lord Rosse with his 36-inch reflector

dred hours of observation time each year. Much time was lost in organizing and instructing the team of men who turned the winches and hauled at the ropes. The mirror tarnished and had to be taken out and polished by the team of twelve men every six months to maintain the performance. Even under the best conditions Herschel could not see the detail he had hoped for because of the turbulent distortion within the atmosphere of the Earth. He was disappointed with his forty-eight inch, and did not write many accounts of its performance, nor did he give any details of the method of construction.

The telescope fell into disuse and disrepair until it became a public danger. It was dismantled by Herschel's son, Sir John, who with his family sang carols in the giant tube before it was laid aside in the garden at Slough. Later, during a storm, an old tree was blown over, destroying most of the tube. Only a small portion of the blacksmith's work now remains among the moss and ivy.

As the Herschel telescope was being dismantled another giant reflector was under construction in Ireland. William Parsons wanted to build the largest telescope in the world, and he had sufficient capability and money to do it. When his father died, William became the third Earl of Rosse inheriting a fortune, a seat in the House of Lords, and the ancestral estate of Birr Castle. If Herschel had obtained one hundred hours of good sky each year in England, Lord Rosse could not hope for more than ten or twenty in Ireland, because his ancestral home was in a maritime climate and close to the Bog of Allen. Nevertheless Rosse taught himself the art of polishing a metal mirror. By 1840, Rosse had completed a thirty-six inch telescope and managed to test it for a few hours through some breaks in the overcast sky. From the contemporary drawing we can see that Rosse's telescope was almost a copy of the Herschel forty-eight inch. Rosse can be seen standing at the observing gallery. Apparently he insisted on wearing his top hat when the drawing was made, but no doubt he removed it when observing.

His ambition next turned to a seventy-two inch mirror, a telescope with an aperture of six feet. Lord Rosse was not deterred by the absence of skilled labor in Ireland. He had an unofficial feudal control over the nearby village of Parsonstown, and recruited his workmen from there. The village smith and several other villagers were trained by Parsons over the years, becoming very efficient at melting, grinding, and polishing mirrors. Many hands were available as the time for pouring the seventy-two inch disk drew near. Three large furnaces, fired by Irish peat, were burning all day to melt the copper and tin. Four tons of metal were melted, and two thousand cubic feet of peat were burned. The stokers continued to work as the sun set, and at nine o'clock in the evening Lord Rosse was ready to pour. He formed the mirror in the open, lifting out the glowing crucibles with three cranes and tipping the contents into a circular ring of sand. Lord Rosse could see the faces of his laborers illuminated by the orange glow, and beyond them the walls of the castle. Overhead the clouds parted to reveal a brilliant moon in a star-studded sky. Ironically enough, such fine observing conditions could seldom be repeated in the years that were to follow. Lord Rosse was satisfied with the casting and it was trundled along a railroad into an annealing oven where it was left to cool for sixteen weeks.

Five castings were made altogether before a perfect mirror was obtained. One was accidentally broken, another cracked in the annealing oven, and two had imperfections on the surface. Human muscles were spared during the years of grinding and polishing, for Lord Rosse

Fig. 18. The 72-inch giant at Birr Castle

designed a special machine driven by a steam engine. Meanwhile masons, carpenters, and the smith were at work on the supports for the telescope and the tube. The tube was made of sheet iron, riveted together, and was slung between two walls like a gigantic gun barrel. You can see from the illustration how the walls had been tastefully designed by the architect to blend with the castle, and how the observer mounted the battlements to look through the telescope.

We know that atmospheric turbulence was bound to interfere with the performance of the telescope even if the mirror were perfect. In fact the definition of the six-foot reflector would be no better than the performance of a present-day six-inch. Also Rosse had made a bad mistake in the mounting. Slung between the two walls, the telescope could point only in a southerly direction, and as a star or planet rose in the east and traveled across the sky it could be seen in the telescope for only a short time at transit. If the weather were cloudy at transit the observer would have to wait twenty-four hours before the object was visible again. The telescope took four men to operate it, and one to look through it. One man, usually the strongest, raised the giant tube by turning a winch, the process taking about five minutes. Another pulled the tube slightly from side to side, while a third pulled the observing gallery up and down to keep the observer near the eyepiece. The fourth workman relighted the lamps when they blew out.

It has been said of Lord Rosse that his interest ceased once the last nail had been driven home, and the largest telescope in the world adorned the grounds of his ancestral estate. Yet he did manage to make a few observations; in particular he noticed the spiral structure of the nebula in Ursa Major. Also many important scientists came over from

England and Europe to use the instrument—weather permitting. One astronomer stayed at Birr Castle hoping to see the Orion nebula. He stayed four weeks but it was continually cloudy. Sir George Airy, the Astronomer Royal, ventured across the Irish Sea in 1848, but saw nothing of interest, because of the ever-present mist and fog. Although he was an English gentleman, in letters to his wife Sir George described the weather with adjectives such as "entirely clouded," "vexatious," "hopeless," and "absolutely repulsive." In 1908 the telescope became unsafe and was taken apart by the son of William Parsons, the fourth Earl of Rosse.

Lord Rosse spent a great deal of money on his telescope. Perhaps he was driven by an intense interest in research, or perhaps he enjoyed the visits of important scientists to his home. It is interesting to speculate on his reaction if he were asked today to finance the construction of a six-hundred inch reflector. Although such an instrument would cost a fortune, with modern photography its light grasp would enable us to penetrate to distant galaxies on the edge of the universe.

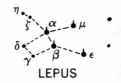

LEPUS

# VOYAGES OF
# ASTRONOMERS

WHEN CAPTAIN JAMES COOK SAILED FROM PLYMOUTH ON THE twenty-sixth of August 1768 he carried with him orders from the Admiralty to be somewhere in the South Pacific by June of the following year. On board the converted coal bark *Endeavour* he had two reflecting telescopes, a pendulum clock, a quadrant, and an astronomer. Charles Green, formerly an assistant at the Royal Greenwich Observatory, had been detailed to make observations on the forthcoming transit of Venus when the planet would momentarily be silhouetted against the bright disk of the sun. Such an event was very rare, taking place not more than twice a century, and gave astronomers their only chance of determining the distance between the Earth and the sun. If astronomers at different latitudes observed the transits simultaneously, then they would each see Venus in a different position on the sun. The apparent displacement gave, by simple trigonometry, the distance to Venus and also the distance to the sun. Such a measurement was of fundamental importance to eighteenth century astronomers, who hoped to fix for all time the exact size of the solar system (which was then regarded as the entire universe). As John Winthrop had said during a spirited appeal in the Harvard University Chapel for support of a transit expedition—how else, if we do not know the size of the universe, "can we hope to attain a just idea of the grandeur of the works of God?"

The Royal Society of London had worked hard to finance Cook's expedition and had finally appealed in a written prayer to George III for royal support to honor England and benefit science in general. The King generously provided £4,000 from the treasury, hoping no

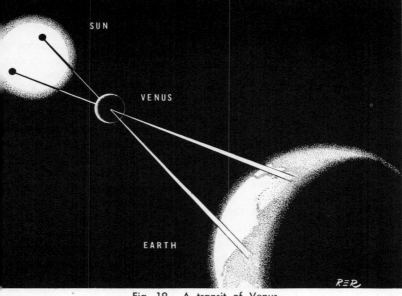

Fig. 19. A transit of Venus

doubt to quickly replenish it from the newly imposed Stamp Tax in the colonies. In addition to the astronomer, the ship's complement was joined by a wealthy businessman, Mr. Joseph Banks, later to be knighted for his work on this expedition. Sir Joseph had loaded the ship with a fine library of books on natural history and had employed two artists and four scientists at his own expense. Sir Joseph never stated the exact amount of money that he invested in this expedition but it is estimated that he must have spent at least £10,000, a sizable fortune in those days.

James Cook had already proved his scientific bent in his observations of an eclipse of the sun. He was also known as an efficient and humane ship's master. Eighty seamen voluntarily transferred from H. M. S. *Dolphin* to the *Endeavour* which was construed as a compliment to Cook, although it may have been due in large measure to a rumor that the expedition would stay a while at a certain South Sea paradise that had been found by the *Dolphin* on its previous voyage.

With high spirits the crew of the *Endeavour* sped directly to Tahiti, reaching the island on April 13, 1769. They immediately renewed the close friendships that had been made with the womenfolk of the island on their previous voyage. In spite of such distractions, they had the telescopes and clock set up by June 3. Both Charles Green and Cook observed from morning to late afternoon the passage of Venus across the sun, and the weather was perfect. When compared with the results of astronomers in other parts of the globe, science at last had a reliable measure of the distance to the sun. Furthermore, Joseph Banks and his assistants made a thorough study of the plants, animals, and people on the island, and Cook named the group of islands surrounding Tahiti the Society Islands in honor of the Royal Society of London whose prayer to the King had made the expedition possible.

On the way home to England the *Endeavour* made the first coastal survey of the North and South Island of New Zealand and raised the Union Jack in southeast Australia, claiming the territory for King George. Cook's skill as a navigator carried the *Endeavour* safely through the perils of the Great Barrier Reef, but he was powerless to control the fatal scurvy that began to spread from member to member of the crew. A native of Tahiti who had joined the crew followed his instincts, going ashore to eat wild berries and fruit. Noticing that the scurvy left him, Cook encouraged the rest of the crew to drink fruit juice. They too quickly showed signs of improvement. After that incident British vessels carried limes which is how the Britishers acquired the nickname "Limeys." One member, however, had a different viewpoint. Charles Green insisted that it was undignified for an Englishman to copy the habits of a native and he refused to eat anything that had not been loaded on the *Endeavour* back home in Plymouth. He died of scurvy and the sea was enriched with the body of one astronomer. Although saddened at the demise, the members of the Royal Society were relieved to learn that the observational results had been saved.

Other astronomers observed the transit from different latitudes. A Frenchman with a long name, Jean-Baptiste Chappe d'Auteroche, made a correspondingly long ocean and cross-country journey to Cape Lucas in lower California. His party was made up of an artist, a clockmaker, and an engineer named Pauly. They were all transported free of charge by the Spanish government. The clockmaker, of course, was needed to repair the inevitable damage to the delicate mechanism of the grandfather clock they took along caused by its buffeting in the Atlantic and its manhandling across Mexico. The engineer went along to make a geographical survey and possibly to take note of Spanish fortifications on the way. Two astronomers of the Spanish navy also were in the group and undoubtedly stayed close to the French engineer.

After repairing the clock and telescopes Chappe successfully determined the exact longitude of Cape Lucas from observations of the moons of Jupiter and then made every preparation for the transit of

Venus. During the preparations, a plague, which was spreading through the local population, claimed the lives of several of the assistants. Even as Chappe made the exacting observations of the transit, the disease was swirling around him also and finally dragged him to his death. Only Pauly survived, to bring back Chappe's papers, the instruments, and the knowledge of the misfortune.

Scientists on other expeditions took similar risks. John Dymond and William Wales were chosen by the Royal Society to go to the Hudson's Bay Station, but owing to the hazards of the journey it was not thought prudent to pay them their £200 stipend until they returned. The surveyor, Charles Mason, went to Ireland and his partner, Jeremiah Dixon, sailed to Hammerfest in Norway, way above the Arctic Circle, both under orders from the Royal Society of London. Russian astronomers ordered twenty-one new telescopes from London, a sizable order for the eighteenth century, and transported them to many stations scattered from eastern Siberia to the southern Ural Mountains.

Not everybody traveled though. George III stayed at home and saw the transit from Kew. There was also much activity in France, Italy, and the New England colonies. Interest spread through New Jersey, Delaware, Pennsylvania, and Maryland and the observations were made with such precision as to evoke a commendation from the British Astronomer Royal, the Reverend Nevil Maskelyne. In Providence, Rhode Island, a wealthy merchant, Joseph Brown, had become fascinated by the astronomical rarity, (a transit occurring not more than twice every hundred years) and at his own expense had imported some fine instruments, setting them up in an observatory close to the present-day Transit Street. To encourage popular interest he paid for a cannon to be fired exactly at noon the day before the transit so that the public who were within earshot could mark the shadow from the sun and determine exactly a true north-south line. Cannons were also fired by the astronomer Maximilian Hell in the ruined fortress of Wardhus, Norway, to celebrate the successful completion of the observations.

In part, the interest in 1769 was caused by a transit of Venus that had occurred eight years before. This earlier transit was the first one to be studied systematically by astronomers for the purpose of determining the distance to the sun, but the results from the various expeditions were not as accurate as the scientists had hoped. After laborious calculations and bitter debates the distance of the sun had been found to be somewhere between 75 million and 100 million miles. This uncertainty was far too great for the meticulous astronomers, and the errors in the observations threw considerable discredit on the profession. The astronomers had many good excuses, however. One cannot hope to obtain a precise measurement from a phenomena like the transit of Venus when there is no previous experience on which to draw. Also, the year 1761 fell in the middle of the Seven Years War and there were many military, transportation, and political difficulties that troubled the expeditions.

Mason and Dixon, who were later to survey the famous demarcation line between Maryland and Pennsylvania, were making preparation in Portsmouth, England, during the foggy days of November and December 1760. They were lodged comfortably in the White Hart Tavern, together with their telescopes and an accurate pendulum clock that had just been made by Mr. John Ellicott. The Royal Society of London approved of their choice of accommodation and, in fact, allocated each man a generous liquor allowance to buoy him up through the troubles ahead. In the early New Year the expedition boarded the *Seahorse* and was warped out into the waters of the English Channel which, like the other oceans of the world at that time, was under the control of the British navy.

It was therefore somewhat of a shock for them to sight the thirty-four gun frigate *Le Grand* of the French navy. It was even more disturbing for Mason and Dixon to have to participate in a violent engagement with the enemy so close to the British shore, before they had time to overcome the convulsions of a serious bout of sea-sickness. The *Seahorse,* badly damaged, managed to get disengaged from the French frigate and groped back toward Portsmouth, carrying eleven dead and thirty-seven wounded. Mason and Dixon flatly refused to go out again on the expedition. They pointed out to the Royal Society that it was not safe, that probably Bencoolen, their destination port, was already in French hands, and that their astronomical instruments had been damaged. But these arguments made very little impression in London. The expedition had been prepared at considerable expense, many important national figures had been involved in the money raising, from the Duke of Newcastle to George III himself, and furthermore the international reputation of England was at stake.

With veiled threats the astronomers, together with their repaired instruments, were placed aboard another ship with orders to fight their way through to the East Indies whether these islands were in the hands of the French or not. By the time they had crossed the Bay of Biscay and the South Atlantic, Mason and Dixon felt far enough away from London to make their own decisions. To avoid the dangers of the Indian Ocean an observatory was set up on the Cape of Good Hope where much wine was drunk and successful measurements of the transit of Venus were made.

It was more dangerous for a Frenchman to be sailing the ocean in the Seven Years War than it was for an Englishman, and with this thought in mind the French Academy of Sciences wrote to the British Admiralty to request a safe passage for the astronomer Pingré in his voyage to the Indian Ocean. The request was politely received and Pingré was given a written passport containing general orders to all British commanders not to molest his person or effects upon any account, but to suffer him to proceed without delay or interruption. Pingré therefore felt safe, at least from enemy action, when he sailed in the *Compte d'Argenson* one night in January 1761. He trusted nature and the elements less than he trusted the British, and at a farewell dinner in Paris he told his friends that it might be the last time he would eat in Paris, for he might never return again.

Captain Marion of the *Compte d'Argenson* had other views as to the relative dangers of the voyage, and when five British warships were sighted one day out from France he mounted the cannon and cleared the deck for action. Since the gun deck had been partitioned off to provide private cabins for the astronomers, it was a considerable inconvenience to be called to action, for the cabin partitions had to be torn down. Pingré in his diary complained bitterly of this disturbance, especially as, like Mason and Dixon, he was not taking easily to the motion of the boat. Fortunately Captain Marion managed to outsail the British ships, and by following similar evasive action whenever he sighted a sail on the horizon he was able to take his passengers and cargo without mishap down to the Cape of Good Hope.

Some time was lost off the coast of Africa because Captain Marion had to go to the assistance of a French supply ship, the sole survivor of a six-ship fleet that had unfortunately encountered the British navy. Although the supply ship was able to revictual the *Compte d'Argenson* with quantities of fine white wine, Pingré deplored the delay and began to think that he would never reach his destination, the island of Rodrigue, in time for a glimpse of the transit. He therefore transferred to a boat that was going to the Isle of Rodrigue to pick up a load of turtles and he landed on the shore with only nine days to spare.

Pingré was too busy during this period to write much of the physical hardships that he endured, but we know that the shore of the island is particularly treacherous and the climate not ideal for Europeans. He mentions the construction of a very crude observatory building to protect the instruments from wind and dust and deplores the rusty state of the pendulum clock. The instruments were reconditioned and the clock was persuaded to go by the application of oil extracted from turtles on the island. June 6 was a fine day, yielding very successful observations of Venus.

After the transit the island of Rodrigue was visited by Captain Robert Fletcher, supposedly of the British navy, who was interested to find the French astronomers in such an isolated spot. Pingré produced his passport, taking care to draw attention to the signature of Admiral Anson on the safe passage and the unchallengeable protection that this piece of paper gave to the French expedition. In spite of the passport, Captain Fletcher unceremoniously opened fire, burned their boat, and took away their supply of food and wine. Gradually the French were reduced to starvation and despair; Pingré noted with disgust in his diary that this was the first time in his life that he had been reduced to drinking water. Nevertheless, the party continued scientific activities making a very thorough study of the flora and fauna of the island, and collecting specimens of seaweed, animals, and plants. They were rescued by the next turtle boat and transferred over to the very first vessel they met that was bound for France.

Although the usual evasive action was taken, it was impossible to escape from further naval engagements. The protective passport was again shown whenever the occasion arose, but it was never honored. Whether it had been countermanded by order from the British Admiralty or whether the news of the attack on Mason and Dixon had spread through the fleet we shall never know, but Pingré's collection of live monkeys, plants, and other specimens was gradually pilfered and destroyed. Pingré was indeed lucky to reach Paris again in possession of his life.

The most unfortunate astronomer to chase the path of Venus was surely Guillaume le Gentil, who devoted his astronomical career to the problem but was destined never to make an observation. His troubles commenced on the twenty-sixth of March 1760 when he left Brest on board a fifty gun bark, thus allowing himself adequate time to be ready for the transit in the following year. His destination had been selected by the French Academy; he was to proceed to the French possession of Pondicherry on the east coast of India. One of his fellow passengers had committed suicide, but the voyage was otherwise without incident. Although pursued by a British fleet, le Gentil arrived safely at the Isle de France. By this time Pondicherry was effectively besieged and blockaded by the British and did not offer much prospect as an observatory site. However, a powerful rescue fleet was assembling for the relief of Pondicherry and le Gentil elected to go along with them.

As the fleet was preparing to sail, it was struck by a severe hurricane that caused great damage to the gunboats and many men were drowned. Fortunately le Gentil was saved and wrote to the French Academy for permission to go to Batavia instead of Pondicherry. He caught a severe attack of dysentery and decided that maybe the easier route would be once again to attempt to reach Pondicherry; this time he boarded a troop ship.

Approaching Pondicherry on *La Sylphide,* le Gentil learned that all French resistance at Pondicherry had been overcome making it useless to proceed further. Having wasted so much time, le Gentil was grieved to find that June 6, the day of the transit, would place him on the high seas somewhere in the Indian Ocean. June 6 was a clear day with a wonderful view of the sky in which the small silhouette of Venus could clearly be seen making its passage across the sun. For an astronomer it would have been easier to bear if the sky had been clouded over, for no worthwhile observations could be made from the bridge of the tossing *Sylphide,* nor could the longitude of the observing point be accurately determined.

While waiting in the Isle de France for a ship to return him home, le Gentil made detailed studies of the geography, geology, and astronomical folklore of the area. In fact, he stayed so long that he decided his best plan would be to remain in the vicinity of India so that he could better prepare himself for the second transit of Venus that was to occur in 1769.

From his calculations he established that it would perhaps be wise to watch the transit from Manila, some four thousand miles further eastward. He therefore wrote to the French Academy for permission to change his observing program. Before receiving a reply he shipped for Manila, setting up an observatory and commencing a very active astronomical program. The final decision of the Academy was that Manila would not be a suitable site—in fact, Pondicherry was still to be preferred. The actual choice, however, was left to le Gentil who was then torn between his own conviction and his respect for the authority of the Academy. He decided to act on the advice of the

Academy and return to Pondicherry, but he left a telescope with a missionary in Manila and gave him a set of detailed instructions as to what to do when the long-awaited transit occurred.

Pondicherry was still under British domination, but the occupation force was extremely friendly and cooperative. In fact le Gentil could have had no better treatment even from the French. An observatory was constructed for him on the ruins of the old French fort; he was provisioned and given every assistance he asked for. Le Gentil made observations for several months under perfect sky conditions to establish the exact longitude of Pondicherry and prepare himself for the transit.

On the eve of the transit he was so excited that he could not sleep and stayed at his telescope all night, preparing himself for 7.00 A.M. when Venus was to pass from the edge of the sun. The sun rose on a clear horizon and the conditions could not have been better. Unfortunately a small cloud floated by at 6.50 A.M. and did not leave the sun until 7.20 A.M. Once again le Gentil had been thwarted and the only outlet he had for his grief was the voluminous entry made in his diary for that day. (Ironically enough, at Manila it was clear.)

Such is the fate which often awaits astronomers. I have wandered almost ten thousand leagues over great stretches of sea, exiling myself from my home country, only to watch a fatal cloud which came to disport itself in front of the sun at the exact moment of my observations, robbing me of the fruit of my troubles and labors.

After further hardships he landed at Lisbon, made a rough overland journey to Paris, and reached home after an absence of eleven and a half years. During his absence he had been legally declared dead. His estate was in the process of liquidation when he arrived, so that he had tremendous difficulty in recovering even his own possessions.

Although he was a frustrated astronomer, his life ended on a happy note. He exchanged the elusive Venus of the sky for one more mortal; he married, had a charming daughter and all his previous tribulations were assuaged.

A total eclipse of the sun is another phenomenon that sends astronomers scurrying over the surface of the Earth. The full glory of an eclipse can be seen only within a small black area some 100 miles in diameter where the shadow of the moon falls, and it is the ambition of every astronomer to place himself in this small black spot. The spot travels at 2,000 miles per hour along the eclipse track which can be accurately calculated beforehand. Careful preparations are made for each eclipse of the sun, with many rehearsals of the detailed observational program that must take place during the few seconds that the moon's shadow spends over the chosen site. If an astronomer could travel to every eclipse track he would still not have more than a few minutes' working time available each year because total eclipses are rare, occurring not more than two or three times a year. If it is cloudy, or if equipment fails on the day of the eclipse, then he must wait many months before it is possible to observe again. Even then the next eclipse track may cross inaccessible parts of the world where his courage and travel allowance cannot take him.

Eclipse expeditions have given us a fundamental knowledge of the sun. The faint outer atmosphere of the sun, the corona, was first described by the amateur astronomer Francis Baily when he traveled to Pavia, Italy, to observe the eclipse of 1842. Baily had previously excelled himself during an eclipse that had occurred near his home in England in 1836. He was impressed by the changes that occurred in the thin crescent of the sun as it was gradually obliterated by the edge of the moon. The sunlight shone through the valleys along the rim of the moon, and each valley appeared as a brilliant spot of light. The phenomenon was promptly called "Baily's Beads" and has held this name to his honor ever since.

The red-colored chromosphere could be seen by nineteenth century astronomers only during the brief phase of totality, so a considerable number of expeditions had to be made before it was recognized to be the lower layers of the glowing atmosphere of the sun. In 1870 Professor Charles A. Young of Princeton solved the mystery of the chromosphere by looking at it through a prism. The prism separated the light of the chromosphere into its constituent colors, and as the moon covered the sun not one crescent but many were seen through the prism, each representing an individual wave length that was emitted by the atmosphere of the sun. It is more difficult to make this observation than to describe it, since the crescents can be seen for only a fraction of a second just before, and just after, the total phase. Because of its short duration it has become known as the "flash spectrum," and nowadays elaborate photographic equipment records the details of the flash spectrum during each eclipse.

A total eclipse of the sun is a thing of beauty as well as a rare scientific event. Most people are taken by surprise when the bright disk of the sun disappears and the full glory of the corona becomes visible. The daylight sky turns to night, producing varicolored hues through which the stars and planets shine. The wispy, pearl-colored corona stretches out away from the sun for several diameters and at the base of the corona crimson prominences are seen twisting from behind the dark outline of the moon. In 1842 when Sir George Airy was observing in Turin he found that the large crowd which gathered to watch the eclipse were awed at the spectacle. As the moon encroached on the sun the low buzz of thousands of Italian voices gradually subsided until there was a hushed and reverent silence when the full corona appeared. But in Milan, during the same eclipse, the public was exuberant; Baily's Beads were greeted with bravos, the corona was cheered, and finally every throat burst out with a chant "Long live the astronomers."

The year 1869 was a gala one for eclipse observers in the United States. Not only did the eclipse track stretch across the continent from Alaska to North Carolina, but the federal government was very generous in providing equipment to make sure that important astronomers were able to observe. Astronomers of lesser importance were accommodated by the network of railroads that was then stretching across the new territories. Free passage was given to all bone fide observers and their instruments and personal effects were also transported free of charge. Some railroads even set up special observation cars for the eclipse, being confident, no doubt, that the stockholder would readily approve of such charitable support for the progress of science. Thus the thin black line across the states was heavily packed with astronomers and interested citizens who, at almost every point, had a perfect view of the marvelous spectacle.

Another eclipse of importance to the United States fell on June 8, 1918. It was an all-American eclipse, occurring in the northwestern states and being unobserved by European astronomers because of their involvement with the final stages of World War I. The American eclipse was recorded at a temporary observatory set up in the fair ground at Baker, Oregon. The portrait painter, Mr. Howard Russell Butler, went along with this expedition, for he had been commissioned to paint the sun's corona. As he himself stated, it was a most disquieting undertaking, for usually he was able to persuade his subjects to sit placidly for several hours at least so that he could adequately represent them on canvas, yet the corona was only going to show itself for a brief 112 seconds. Nevertheless, perched advantageously on a high stepladder, and using a rapid shorthand technique, he was able to produce an accurate and valuable impression of the eclipse in colored oils. Such labors have now been replaced by colored photography.

Of course not all eclipse expeditions are successful for the scientist, and many times the layman also comes away disappointed. New Englanders will long have memories of the disappointment of October 2, 1959, when the sun was due to be eclipsed at the instant it rose above the eastern horizon. Many people looked toward Cape Ann in the swirling mist and drizzle when the shadow of the moon could be detected only by the unusual double dawn that it produced. The efforts of other expeditions have been wasted by a small cloud coming along at just the wrong moment, as with le Gentil at the transit of Venus. Large-scale preparations were made in the spring and summer of 1958 to go to a small island in the South Pacific that was important for one fact only, that it lay exactly on the thin black line. A great deal of equipment was carried over the reefs to be set up among the palm trees of Danger Island by scientists supported by the United States Navy and Air Force. A thunderstorm obliterated the eclipse and the equipment had to be dismantled and stored in readiness for the next opportunity. The next eclipse was on the other side of the Earth, visible from the Canary Islands if, of course, the weather were clear. Unfortunately the experiences of Danger Island were repeated in the Canaries, but the undaunted astronomers re-crated their equipment, once again bracing themselves for a continuation of the globe-trotting activities.

Sometimes, but not too often, the scientific results are lost through sheer incompetence. In an expedition to the West Indies in 1886 very few results were obtained even though the sky was perfectly clear. One person did not point the telescope in the right direction, another telescope was accidentally smashed a few days before totality, an assistant gaped at the corona in a mesmerized fashion forgetting to press the camera trigger, and two native policemen who were protecting the observatory stood around blocking the light from the measuring photometers. To make matters worse the few photographs that were obtained by this expedition were seized by customs officials, delaying the development of the plates and making the photographs worthless.

The voyaging French astronomer, Pierre César Janssen, was trapped in the siege of Paris when the eclipse of December 22, 1870, was about to take place. He had already been to Peru to make magnetic measurement, to Japan and Algeria to see the transits of Venus, and to many other solar eclipses, so the German army was not going to deter him from his appointment with the moon's shadow. He was also spurred on by international competition; the United States had appropriated $29,000 for the support of its astronomers, and England had supplied a ship to take Sir Norman Lockyer to a favorable spot in the Mediterranean. There was considerable rivalry between Janssen and Lockyer. They had both discovered an easy way of observing solar prominences, and the French government was planning to strike a medal in their honor with the name of Janssen on the front of the medal and Lockyer on the back. Pierre Janssen procured a balloon and made a spectacular flight through the bullets of the German army down toward the eclipse track in the Mediterranean. Racing against time by stagecoach and horseback he established himself on the predicted path of the moon's shadow. Unfortunately on the day of the eclipse it was cloudy. Janssen was probably consoled a little to hear that Sir Norman had been shipwrecked, and, although unhurt, was prevented from observing the eclipse because of clouds.

Each voyager, from le Gentil to Janssen, was helping in his own way the progress of the new science that had emerged from the Renaissance. He was conscious of the responsibility of his profession; he realized that as well as working for posterity he would also obtain recognition from his patrons and colleagues; and as he traveled, observed, and lectured he drew a feeling of satisfaction from his labors. The physical hardships of the past are seldom repeated today, but the spirit of the early scientists is still with us. If there is any phenomenon visible from which astronomical data can be extracted, an expedition will surely be organized by astronomers who are building on the heritage of the *debutante science*.

# PART III
# A SEARCH FOR KIN

The first drawing of the surface of Mars, November 28, 1659, at 7 P.M., and first drawing of Saturn's ring, 1657, both by Christian Huygens. (*Splendor of the Heavens*, T. E. R. Phillips and W. H. Steavenson, Robert M. McBride, and *Popular Astronomy*, Camille Flammarion, Appleton-Century-Crofts, Inc.)

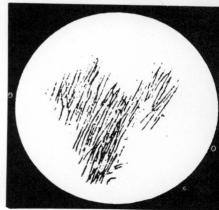

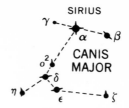

SIRIUS

CANIS MAJOR

C H A P T E R 11

# THE EARTH'S BEGINNING

IN THE BEGINNING . . . A MORTAL SCIENTIST CANNOT CONTINUE THIS sentence with absolute certainty, because he has to start with conditions as they are now, and work backwards in time through many areas in which his knowledge is incomplete. It would be like asking a child to give an account of his birth or a description of his conception. Religious scriptures explain the creation of the Earth in picturesque ways, but no two accounts agree exactly. Some of them however do come quite close to the scientists' idea of creation, or, at least, to the successive stages of development that must have taken place.

The scientist today knows many more facts than were known to people one or two thousand years ago. He had to explain much more than the ocean and the dry land, the sun by day and the moon by night, man and other living things. The Earth is a tiny globe of rock made up of the rarest elements in the universe. It is surrounded by a thin shell of atmosphere containing large amounts of oxygen, a remarkable element essential to animal and human life. The Earth is accompanied through space by eight other planets each quite different from the Earth in size and composition. All the planets move in orderly fashion, in almost circular orbits that are tilted very slightly from a flat plane called the plane of the ecliptic. Dominating and controlling the motion of the planets we find the massive sun, much larger than the planets and different from the Earth again. The sun is a star and not a planet, shining with its own light and continually sending out to the planets enormous amounts of energy. Whereas the planets have collected to themselves the rare elements of the universe, the sun and stars are of average composition, being composed almost entirely of hydrogen. In exploring the origin of the Earth we must at the same time try to explain the many wonders that exist in the universe besides the Earth.

The questions are too great to be solved by the mind of a single man and many scientists have contributed to the modern ideas on creation. Immanuel Kant, the famous German philosopher, suggested that in the beginning there was an immense, cold whirling cloud of dust and gas. This suggestion is accepted readily by astronomers today because their telescopes show dark clouds of dust existing between the stars which must be very similar to the cloud that Kant had in mind. We can see these dark clouds only when they are in front of a bright region of the sky. The photograph shows a few of them silhouetted by a bright cloud of gas in the constellation Serpens. (See Plate 29) Although on the photograph we see minute black specks, the distances involved are very great, and each speck is about ten billion miles across, as large as our present solar system.

The French mathematician Pierre Simon Laplace took Kant's idea a little further and suggested how he thought the planets and the sun were formed. The cloud was spinning and at the same time shrinking in size. Thin veils were shed at intervals to form the planets and the mass at the center collapsed to form the sun. Unfortunately Laplace's hypothesis breaks fundamental laws of physics and mathematics and must be wrong. Calculations show that the shrinking mass would tend to spin faster and would not produce the slowly rotating sun that we find today.

Laplace's failure was followed by two or three other suggestions which also led scientists along the wrong path. These suggestions had to be abandoned with the Laplace hypothesis. Perhaps the sun had already formed and another star passed close by, tearing out a long stream of material. The planets, it was suggested, might condense around the sun and the passing star would then go on its way. Unfortunately, calculations show that the hot material from the sun would disperse and not form planets. Even if by some unknown process planets did condense, the orbits would not be the almost perfect circles that we find today. Perhaps the sun had a twin companion, and a passing star collided with the twin. From the debris of the explosion we might be able to produce the planets. From the way the stars are scattered in space a collision of this type is unlikely, and if it did occur it seems impossible that planets would form from the hot material of the stars. Both the close encounter theory and the collision theory fail on a further count; they do not explain how most of the planets have obtained satellite companions, a set of moons forming a type of miniature solar system.

Our modern theory returns again to the suggestion of Kant, but avoids the pitfall of Laplace. To produce the theory we have needed the combined efforts of many astronomers, mathematicians, chemists, and geologists. The new theory, which we will call the "whirlpool theory," now explains so many of the details of our present existence that we feel sure it correctly accounts for the broad features of evolution and the developments of the past. Many astronomers have contributed to the theory, notably the German, C. F. von Weizsäcker, the Dutchman, D. ter Haar, and the Americans, Gerard Kuiper and Harold Urey.

The theory begins with a large cloud of gas in space and describes what happens from this stage onward. The actual creation of the cloud of gas, of course, is beyond the scope of the theory and no attempt has been made to explain the creation of the original material. The gas contained the "cosmic mix," the mixture that is found everywhere in the universe. In every 1,000 atoms, 900 were hydrogen, 97 helium, and the remaining three atoms were heavy elements such as carbon, oxygen, or iron. Agitations within the gas were gradually smoothed out and the cloud took on a slow rotation. The rotation did not go along smoothly; in fact from the density of similar clouds, as shown in Serpens, we know that turbulence must have developed. The swirling cloud must have looked something like a whirlpool, with small eddies forming and re-forming as the whole structure turned. A large eddy at the center of the cloud contracted more rapidly than the rest and formed a dark object that we call "proto-sun."

In the cold depths of the cloud surrounding the proto-sun, the gases combined together to form compounds, such as water and ammonia. Some solid dust crystals began to grow; metallic crystals such as iron and stony ones like silicates. It is impossible for a spinning cloud to remain spherical. The cloud is forced by gravity to flatten out into a disk. Very soon the whirlpool must have taken on a flattened appearance, like a phonograph record with the proto-sun blocking the hole at the center.

Eddies were still forming again in the whirling disk. Some of the swirls were torn apart as they collided; some were broken up by the gravitational pull of the proto-sun. The fight for survival was a simple one. To hold itself together against the forces of disruption, an eddy had to collect a certain critical amount of substance. In the battle within the wheeling system some eddies gained and some eddies lost material. Ultimately a series of nine large swirling disks developed around the sun, each one being at this stage a proto-planet. The proto-planets were sufficiently large to hold together by the force of their own gravitational field, and as they moved around the sun they acted as scavengers, sweeping up the material left over.

At this stage the proto-sun began to shine, fitfully at first and very dull red, but very soon turning into the golden yellow star that we see today. The proto-sun was about one hundred times larger in diameter than the proto-planets, and this difference in size caused it to become a star and not a planet. The size was sufficient to trap all the hydrogen which began to burn deep in the interior by a process of nuclear fusion. The development of the sun is a separate story to be described later. At the moment our interest is focused on the development of the proto-planets, particularly proto-Earth.

There was just enough material in the swirling proto-Earth to repeat the whirlpool process once more. A mass grew at the center, and a single eddy dominated the surrounding space, sweeping it clean of all material to form the proto-moon. The Earth and the moon weighed much more at this stage in their history than they do at present. The proto-Earth weighed at least 1,000 times as much as the present-day Earth and was about 80,000 miles is diameter. The Earth would have been unrecognizable, a whirling cloud of ice particles and solid fragments, a dusty snowstorm. The slimming process then followed. There were two reasons why the Earth lost such a lot of weight, and why the lighter atoms and compounds such as hydrogen and water, were evaporated away. One source of heat was the energy liberated by the collapsing mass. The collision among the particles as they smashed their way down toward the solid surface generated large amounts of heat. The heat was intense enough to vaporize the ices and even to melt the solid dust particles that were present. By this time the Earth might have been molten throughout, from the core at the center right through to the surface. As the proto-Earth continued to sweep through space, more and more debris crashed to the surface with a further generation of heat. The Earth was probably a seething mass of lava, carrying molten iron and other compounds in solution. At this time the heavy iron and nickel mixture sank to the center to form the molten core that the Earth has today.

The hydrogen and other gases escaped into the atmosphere above the molten rock, but the gases did not stay with the Earth for long—the second source of heat was in action. The rays of the sun were now pouring out in full intensity, breaking up the compounds in the atmosphere and blowing them by light pressure away from the proto-Earth to be lost again in space. Thus most of the hydrogen and the lighter elements were removed from the Earth, leaving a high concentration of the rare elements of the universe which are so essential for the formation of rocks, plants, and our own bodies.

The story of the Earth has almost reached the point where it can be taken up by a geologist. When the Earth stopped collecting material, and the bombardment from the sky ceased, the surface cooled a little and became solid. A crust formed and the dry land appeared. But the Earth was not ready to support life; the surface was too hot to walk on and the atmosphere contained poisonous methane and ammonia. There were large quantities of carbon dioxide in the atmosphere as well. Molten lava flowed from fissures in the newly formed crust, carrying to the surface small amounts of steam that had been trapped in the molten interior. Geologists think that the early volcanic activity brought to the surface most of the water that forms the present-day oceans. The oceans are, of course, immense, but they represent only a small fraction of the total material of the Earth.

After a million years or so the volcanic activity decreased, and sunlight broke up some of the water molecules into hydrogen and oxygen gas. The hydrogen escaped into space, and the oxygen then became an important chemical in the atmosphere. It oxidized the ammonia forming the nitrogen that we find in the atmosphere today, and it removed the methane, turning it into carbon dioxide. Year by year the Earth became cooler as heat was radiated away, and soon it was cool enough for the volcanic steam to condense into water. At first the raindrops spattering on the hot lava changed back into a hiss of steam, but eventually the Earth cooled down sufficiently to permit pools of water to collect on the surface. Then it rained. All the water in the seven seas fell in one continuous deluge. Gradually the shallow areas in the wrinkled crust filled, and the oceans appeared on the face of the Earth.

Scientists are sure that these events happened in the past, in the order described here, but no one is able to tell the duration of each phase. The dust and gas of the whirlpool probably began to collect some five billion years ago. We can divide the creation of our Earth into five periods, each lasting about one billion years. At the end of the first period the sun was shining as it is now, and the proto-planets were in an advanced stage of formation. After two billion years the Earth was a hot volcanic body with a heavy atmosphere, a poisonous one incapable of supporting life. This atmosphere is described as a "reducing" atmosphere because it contained large quantities of hydrogen liberated by the interaction of water vapor and metallic iron. The reducing atmosphere was a suffocating one; without oxygen nothing could burn, or oxidize, or breathe. During the third period, the solid crust formed and the oceans appeared. During the fourth period the generation of hydrogen ceased, and oxygen was released in the atmosphere by the breaking up of water molecules in the ultraviolet light from the sun. This brings us to the beginning of the fifth period, a date approximately one billion years ago. At this time the Earth had settled down to a form that we would recognize today. The age of the oldest rocks that can be measured by radioactive dating, the Pre-Cambrian, is between 700 million and 1,000 million years and the astronomer's time scale joins up approximately with the geological time scale.

When did life appear on the Earth? If we are asking about man, the two-legged creature who is able to speak and think constructively, then the answer is "quite recently." The sequence of evolution, outlined in *The Origin of Species* by Charles Darwin, began during the last billion years of history, and Homo sapiens finally evolved only one hundred thousand years ago. But if we take a more general definition of life, a collection of molecules capable of absorbing energy from their surroundings and reproducing molecules similar to themselves, then life began to stir in the ocean during the third and fourth periods, some three billion years ago.

The first oceans were warm and contained no salt. Salt in the sea is of very recent origin by the astronomical time scale, it has been washed out of the dry land during the last 200 million years. The primitive oceans formed under the reducing atmosphere and contained many complex compounds of carbon, hydrogen, and oxygen. Some of the compounds were amino acids, similar to those found in living substances today. Some at least of these compounds were alive, extracting energy from their surroundings and promulgating the strain. Even today we find red bacteria and some species of algae that thrive on hydrogen, and we think that they are the disappearing progeny of the living chemicals that first appeared on the Earth.

The first oxygen to appear in the air was greedily absorbed by the rocks, but after the initial oxidation of the crust was completed a little oxygen was left over for life. Organisms using oxygen developed rapidly, and out of the primeval ooze emerged the first strains of animal life. Animals obtain energy by burning carbon in their bodies, breathing out carbon dioxide. Plant life also developed, capable of breaking up carbon dioxide and liberating oxygen. A happy balance was achieved, with the plants absorbing the carbon dioxide exhaled by the animals, and the animals thriving on the oxygen liberated by the plants.

The other proto-planets followed a different course of evolution that was not so hospitable to life. Mercury was the nearest proto-planet to the sun, and under the intense heat was not able to retain the moisture. The gravitational pull of the sun interfered with Mercury and Venus, the two planets forming close to the sun, and both planets were prevented from spawning a moon. Venus is between the Earth and sun, with surface temperature of at least 500° F. Even today the surface of Venus is too hot for oceans to form. The steam issuing from its volcanic surface is broken into hydrogen and oxygen; the hydrogen escapes, the oxygen is lost in oxidation processes. Until water condenses on the surface, no life can form.

Beyond the Earth the planet Mars has been through the five stages of evolution of the Earth. The surface cooled, water condensed, and the erosion flattened the surface. Sunlight again broke up the water molecule into hydrogen and oxygen, the hydrogen escaped and the oxygen was absorbed by the surface. The waters may have been a sufficient breeding ground for life on Mars, but the generation of life was abortive because the water disappeared. Either the hydrogen escaped and the oxygen was absorbed, or the water lies frozen like a Siberian permafrost beneath the dusty surface.

The major planets, Jupiter, Saturn, Uranus, and Neptune, were too far from the sun for the water to remain a vapor. The water encases the planet in an icy mantle, and the atmosphere is composed of methane and ammonia. The major planets are therefore permanent records of the early stages of the Earth. If they could be brought closer to the warming influence of the sun, the water would evaporate and dissociate, oxidation would begin, and perhaps life would develop. Jupiter, the largest planet, formed from a very large proto-planet. It was so large, and so far from the sun, that most of the hydrogen was retained. Proto-Jupiter was not quite large enough to form a star, but numerous moons formed in the outer regions of the proto-planet and today can be seen circling Jupiter like a miniature solar system.

Today astronomers look upon the Earth as just an ordinary planet. Because of its initial size and distance from the sun, the Earth was able to develop on its surface a scum that we call life. Is this life a unique accident or are there other inhabitants elsewhere in the universe? While astronomers were following the old theory of a close encounter between the sun and another star, they were pessimistic. The chance of a close encounter was extremely remote and we felt we were the only inhabitants among the hundred billion stars of our own galaxy. But the whirlpool theory makes us optimistic once more. The formation of a star and planets follows quite naturally if we concede the existence in space of whirling globules of dust and gas. Sometimes the whirlpool breaks into two or three components and forms two or three close stars. Sometimes it breaks into a central star with an attendant family of cold solid planets. From a study of binary stars we think that the chances of a planetary system forming are about one in a thousand. This chance is quite high when you remember that there are many stars in the universe.

The original size and density distribution in the dust cloud is quite important. The density in the disk surrounding the proto-sun has to be very close to a critical limit, called the "Roche density," before the proto-planets will form. Once this process starts, then the chain of events moves relentlessly forward, and the proto-planet that forms in a radiation field of about two calories per square centimeter per minute will develop in the way that the Earth has done. Astronomers, chemists, and geologists are sure that oceans, air, and land will appear. Once these conditions for the existence of living organisms are met, biologists are certain that life will begin to stir in the primeval ooze.

# CHAPTER 12

# LAND, SEA, AND AIR

An astronomer gazes into the night sky to learn what he can about other worlds, but one world lies at his feet and requires no telescope to aid his vision. At one time it was possible for a man like Aristotle or Newton to embrace the whole field of scientific knowledge. Today this is impossible, not so much because our minds are limited but because the field of knowledge has extended and no single brain can cover the entire area. Astronomers reluctantly leave the most accessible planet, the Earth, for other scientists to study. Today we know far more about the Earth that did the Greek scholars or the natural philosophers of the Renaissance, and the knowledge is divided into dozens of sciences. Each science offers to the student a lifetime of study and research. How amusing it is to hear a young person announce "I am going to be a scientist!" Is he going to be a geologist, physicist, or biologist? Or is he going to study a crossbred science such as geophysics or biochemistry? By the time a student gets to college he finds there are many choices before him when he decides to become a scientist.

Geologists study the rocks at the Earth's surface. Where the surface is split open, such as the Grand Canyon, Arizona, the geologist thinks he is probing deeply but, taking a perspective view, he is limited to the surface crust and a few scratches in it. The seismologist probes more deeply; he can follow earthquake waves almost to the center of the Earth. The tides, the coasts, and the profile of the seabed are the life's work of the oceanographer, and the winds and clouds above the surface belong to the meteorologist. On the dry land the botanist works with plants, the zoologist works with animals, and the sociologist works with people. In the ocean the conchologist studies shells, the helminthologist watches worms, and the ichthyologist follows the life history of fish. The discoveries made by Earth sciences could not be described in a single volume; we would require a whole library, and the story of the Earth is still unfolding.

We are most familiar with terra firma, the solid ground on which we walk. The continents are made of granite, a light-colored rock in which glassy crystals of silica are embedded. The granite has broken through to the surface in many places—Canada, New England, and Pikes Peak, Colorado. Over the rest of the continent the granite is covered by a thin veneer of sediments, deposited by water. Wind, rain, and sun in turn beat upon the solid rock as it is exposed. Part of the rock is dissolved and is carried in solution to the sea. Part mixes with the soils to be used as food by vegetation. The remainder crumbles into small particles which are deposited as sand and clay. A sandy shore may one day become a hard rock once again, when rain falls and carries acid between the particles. After thousands of years the grains become cemented together as a sandstone, and when this, by some upheaval, is exposed, the process of weathering starts again. Clay can be converted into a hard rock called shale, and vegetation can be turned by heat and pressure into peat, coal, and oil. The sediments can be very thick in places, several miles deep at the Gulf of Mexico, but they are still thin when compared with the granite of the continent. The roots of the continent go down fifteen miles; like an iceberg there is more below the surface than above.

Man, so far, has not been able to dig down more than a few miles into the Earth, but the roots of the continents have been mapped by seismologists. Deep in the Earth a section of rock cracks under the extreme pressure, causing the surrounding rocks to vibrate. Immediately above the fracture the vibrations shake the surface, bringing buildings to the ground in a pile of rubble. The waves from the earthquake also spread downward into the Earth and carry news of the disaster to the other side of the globe. Seismographs record the shape of the waves as they pass through the Earth and the scientist obtains an X-ray picture of the interior. By studying the reflection of earthquake waves seismologists found that continents were islands of granite floating on a heavy crust of basalt. Basalt contain no silica crystals and is dark in color. In places the basalt has been forced up from the depths by volcanic action. It has extruded up to the surface in some romantic places of the world—Fingal's Cave in Scotland, the Giant's Causeway in Ireland, and Hawaii.

In 1909, a Croatian seismologist named Andrija Mohorovicic, noticed that waves were reflected from a depth of some twenty miles. He had found the bottom of the crust, the boundary between the basalt, and the inner mantle of the Earth. The boundary became known as the Mohorovicic discontinuity, or "Moho" for short. The Moho has now been traced under the five continents and the seven seas. Around the entire Earth the crust fits snugly over the mantle.

Scientists, of course, would like to check their X-ray picture. Reflections show that the mantle makes up most of the Earth, extending from the Moho down to a depth of 1,800 miles. Earth tremors move

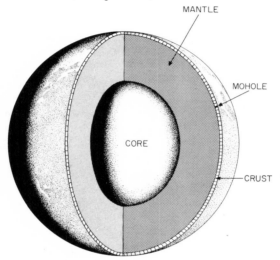

Fig. 20.   Crust, mantle, and core of the Earth

through the mantle with the same speed that they move through olivine. Olivine is a heavy green stone that is sometimes ejected from an active volcano. We presume that the inner mantle is made of olivine, but we would like a proof. If the dream of American geologists comes true we may have a proof, for they are planning to drill a shaft to the Moho. The task will be difficult, straining the resources of the mining engineer, but a sample of the mantle can be obtained in no other way.

Already test borings have been made off the Island of Guadalupe in the French West Indies. The American drilling barge, *Cuss I,* was maneuvered by radio control while a diamond-studded bit penetrated the ocean floor. The "Mohole" itself will be punctured in the ocean floor, probably off Guadalupe, for there the crust is not more than four miles thick.

As the drill punctures the crust, the temperature will rise 100° per mile, and at the Moho itself the temperature is expected to be about 500° F. The drill will force its way into history, from the recent sediments on the ocean floor to the first sediment that was ever laid on the basalt crust. From the fossils in the rock, paleontologists will read the story of life in the primitive oceans. Only the sea can tell us about the very beginnings of life, for the primitive fossil remains on the continents have been destroyed by volcanic upheavals. Radioactivity helps to keep the crust warm, and radioactive elements will be traced as the drill moves through to the Moho. Below the Moho we will find the composition of the mantle, and will know for sure the chemistry of the largest region within the Earth.

Below the mantle, some 1,800 miles down, we reach another boundary, the boundary between solid and liquid. Solid material can vibrate from side to side, like a plucked string, but liquids cannot. A liquid can only transmit compression waves. The transverse waves pass freely through the mantle, and we know that it is solid. The core of the Earth blocks transverse waves and only permits compression waves to pass. From the shadow cast by the core we know that the core is liquid and is 4,300 miles in diameter. Recent work shows that the liquid core may itself have a solid kernel some 2,000 miles across.

The core of the Earth is made of iron and nickel, or, at least, we are led to believe this by the following clues. When astronomers first measured the mass of the Earth they found it a little heavier than expected. The interior must be made of a substance more dense than the rocks at the surface. The calculated density of the center is what we would expect from iron and nickel under pressure. Early navigators soon discovered the Earth's magnetic field, generated in the interior. Physicists today think that a core of liquid iron would account for the magnetic field and also its variability. Meteorites, fragments of a broken planet, sometimes fall to the Earth, and many of these are made of iron. Perhaps the iron once formed part of an inner core similar to the Earth's. These are of course speculations. We can be certain only when a hole is punctured from the Moho down to the bottom of the mantle, but the shaft would be nearly two thousand miles deep and nobody knows how to make such a hole!

Every continent is an island, a granite bastion clothed in soil and surrounded on all sides by the ocean. The meeting place of land and water is the most fertile region on the globe. Life first developed in the shallow waters surrounding the ancient continents, where the warm rays of the sun flickered through to the trilobites crawling on the continental shelf. Plants were stranded by the tide, along the old shore line, and left to adapt themselves to a life on the barren land. Across the shore line the first air-breathers crawled to develop, breed, and evolve. Man still clings to the sea, building many fine cities at the water's edge.

The meeting place of land and water is not a quiet zone. Many times in the past the sea has rushed in, leaving large tracts of sand which later became sandstone. A thick layer of Potsdam sandstone can be traced across the United States from New York to Wisconsin. Other incursions by the sea have left layers of chalk and limestone, the accumulation of millions of tiny seashells. Many times the sea has retreated as the granite block was lifted by the crust and the water was shaken off. But there is always an edge to the sea, and along this edge erosion of the continent continues. Waves, helped by the wind, move across the ocean to crash against the shore, grinding the rocks to fragments and rolling the debris over the continental shelf like a sedimentary carpet.

One hundred miles or so from the shore the continental shelf ends, and we move into the deeps of the ocean where sunlight does not penetrate. In some places there are canyons in the ocean floor almost six miles deep. For many years marine biologists thought the canyons were devoid of life; nothing could live under the crushing pressure and there was no food supply. But recently a weird shark with puckered gills was caught at a depth of half a mile. Its nearest relative seems to be a shark that became extinct thirty million years ago, according to the fossil record. Then in 1952 a coelacanth emerged from the depths and was caught off Madagascar. A coelacanth is a fish with primitive legs, one of the first creatures to crawl on the land. Biologists were thrilled at the catch, for the coelacanth was also thought to be extinct, the last specimen being cemented in the rocks some sixty million years ago. Some of the fish that live in the darkness carry luminous feelers than can be switched on when they search for food. Others have adapted themselves by growing a luminous skin and large eyes. Life in the deep, however, is completely dependent upon the life at the surface. The fish are scavengers, and feed on decaying fragments that sink to the bottom. When the surface supply fails they turn carnivorous and feed on each other.

The moon heaps up the waters of the ocean by its gravitational pull. Physicists say that the water conforms to an "equipotential surface," and their calculations predict two bulges, one toward the moon and one on the opposite side of the Earth. Without mathematics we can imagine the bulge beneath the moon to be caused directly by the pull of the moon. The opposite bulge is a little more difficult to explain. The moon travels around the Earth once a month, and the Earth itself is moved slightly out of position by the moon. In fact the Earth and moon are both making a monthly journey around a point called the center of mass, which is on a line from the center of the Earth to the center of the moon. Although the Earth's orbit around the center of mass is quite small, the motion is sufficient to produce a centrifugal force. This acts on the ocean and forms the bulge on the opposite side to the moon. As the moon moves, the tidal surface follows. The two bulges always point toward and away from the moon.

We must not forget, however, that the Earth is also spinning on its axis. The oceans are carried round by the Earth and do not move relative to the land, but the surface of the water rises and falls to conform with the shape of the tidal surface. Thus, as the Earth spins, we have two high tides and two low tides a day. In the middle of the ocean the water is raised a few inches by the moon, but along the shore the water rushes up the continental shelf and the rise and fall can be many feet. The sun helps the moon in its tide making, but at a distance of ninety-three million miles the effect of the sun is only half that of the moon. Every two weeks the sun and moon pull together and we have exceptionally high tides, called spring tides. Between the spring tides, the sun and moon pull against each other and produce a smaller rise and fall, called neap tides.

The tidal wave is greatly hindered as it travels around the world each day by the five continents. Twice a day, the sea rushes into narrow constrictions like the Irish Sea and the Bay of Fundy. The waves smash against the rocks fixed to the shore and to the ocean bottom, dissipating two billion horsepower. If this energy could be harnessed it would supply heat and light for a thousand cities. At the moment it is wasted in the noise of the surf and the erosion of the coastline. Because of the tides the Earth is gradually slowing down, and the span of the day is growing longer. The increase is imperceptible during our lifetime, for no more than one-thousandth of a second is added to the day each century. Nevertheless, astronomers, with their precise measurement of time, can detect the change. So long as there are continents breaking through the surface of the oceans the Earth will continue to slow down. Ultimately the moon will stop

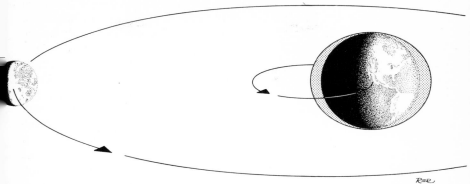

Fig. 21.   The tides raised by moon and sun

the Earth spinning and force us always to face the moon, just as the Earth in the past slowed down the rotation of the moon.

In addition to tides there are large-scale currents in the oceans, churning continually like a Gargantuan whirlpool. The waters of the North Atlantic turn around completely once every six months, so that a bottle thrown in from Cape Hatteras in January has a fair chance of returning in the summer, after a journey past the shores of Europe and through the Azores. Oceanographers trace the currents with marked buoys; some contain messages with a reward for the person who returns the bottle and some contain radio beacons that can be followed from a ship or airplane. In the olden days the currents were found by bitter experience. A captain would sail for days on end and yet make no headway. He gradually became aware that an ocean current was impeding him.

The Gulf Stream forms the northern edge of the Atlantic whirlpool, flowing from Florida along the North American coast toward Europe. The water passes through the heat of the tropics where the oxygen content is reduced. Sea creatures move away from the suffocating water which then takes on a blue coloration. The blue Gulf Stream shows up in contrast with the green and fertile waters of the North Atlantic. Ocean circulations are of great benefit to the continents, because they store up heat from the blazing sun of the tropics and carry it northward to the colder climates. The Gulf Stream is thus the central heating system for western Europe. At times, though, it is a little inadequate.

Our terrestrial water supply is limited. There is just enough to fill

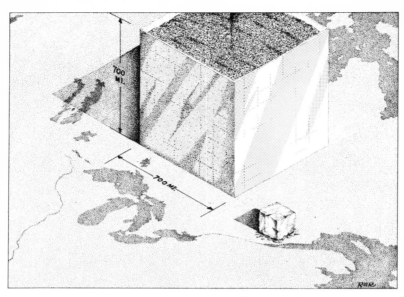

Fig. 22.    The Earth's supply of water and air

a tank seven hundred miles long, seven hundred miles wide, and seven hundred miles high. To fill the tank we would have to pour in all the oceans, drain all the rivers and lakes, and melt the ice from the polar regions. Even then it would not be quite full. We would need the moisture in the atmosphere and the liquid stored in plants, animals, and human bodies to bring the level to the brim. Without this water, life would cease. Moisture evaporates from the sea and is absorbed by insects and plants; rain water collects for the use of man, and insects thrive in the dampness of the soil. At the river mouths the water is returned to the sea, carrying with it minerals and a fresh food supply for the sea creatures waiting on the continental shelf. We have a single water supply that is shared by all forms of life. If the supply were cut by half, then half this life would disappear.

Just as our water supply is limited, so is our supply of air. If all the oxygen and nitrogen were frozen solid we would have an ice cube one hundred miles high, and one hundred miles long at each edge. With this amount of gas we can support all the life on the Earth. Mars has one-tenth, and the moon less than a millionth of this quantity. A touch of sunlight would vaporize the ice cube, and the gases would diffuse around the Earth to form a life-giving layer. The force of gravity holds the gas near the Earth's surface, and prevents its escaping into space. Because of the pull of gravity, the air pressure is greater near the surface of the Earth. The pressure decreases by a factor of ten for every ten miles of altitude. Thus if we could fly twice as high as Mt. Everest the pressure would be a little less than one-tenth of the sea level value, and breathing would be impossible without artificial aid. The temperature also decreases as we ascend, until at a height of eight miles it has dropped to $-67°$ F. The lower layers of the atmosphere are heated by contact with the warm earth and the heat gradually climbs upward from the surface.

If we go above the eight mile level, the temperature no longer falls, for we enter the quiet stratosphere. Convection from the ground cannot penetrate the stratosphere, and so no clouds form. Clouds, storms, and the circulation of the air is limited to the lower region, called the troposphere.

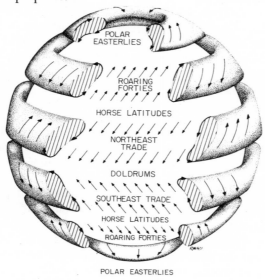

Fig. 23. Circulation in the troposphere

The troposphere provides us with all our weather, both good and bad. Wind and rain, hail and snow are all produced by the action of sunlight as it warms the lower layers of air. The hottest regions of the Earth are near the equator, and here warm air is continually rising. The air rises to the ceiling of the troposphere and then moves northward for about two thousand miles, where it cools and descends once again to the Earth's surface. To complete the circulation, the air flows back along the surface toward the equator, forming the steady "trade winds." Where the air is rising and where it is falling there can be light breezes, which, in the days of sailing vessels became notorious. The calms at the equator earned the name "doldrums," and the second region of fickle winds at latitude 25° became known as the "horse latitudes."

You may notice from the illustration that the trade winds are deflected to the west instead of blowing directly toward the equator. This deflection is due to the Earth's rotation. A wind at the equator travels 25,000 miles as it turns with the Earth, and therefore has a speed of about 1,000 miles per hour toward the east. A wind in the horse latitudes does not move so fast; it travels at 860 miles per hour. When a wind leaves the horse latitudes it always retains the easterly speed of those latitudes. In traveling south the air mass is left behind by the Earth's rotation and drags over toward the west. It is fortunate for us that the wind is deflected in this way. The northeast trade wind helped the flow of commerce from Europe to America during the days of sail. Without the trades Columbus would not have reached the West Indies in 1492.

The equatorial circulation stirs the air over the temperate latitudes and causes a second circulation in the opposite direction. Thus around latitude 40° the prevailing winds are from the southwest. These winds are not as gentle as the trade winds, nor are they so constant. In fact, especially in the southern hemisphere, these latitudes are called the "roaring forties."

We can now see the hand that stirs the water and produces the currents in the ocean. It is the wind pressing continually on the waves at the surface, transmitting its motion to the waters beneath. In the Atlantic for example, the Gulf Stream is helped along by the southwest wind and the return current down through the Azores is aided by wind of the northeast trade.

The southwesterly winds carry moist tropical air toward the north. The tropical air mass rubs shoulders with the cold air over the pole caps, and the meeting place of warm and cold air is called the "polar front." Most of the time warm and cold winds slip by each other, leaving the polar front undisturbed. But sometimes a kink develops, as a tongue of warm air curls into the polar front. The warm air is lifted, a circulation develops, and a storm is born. Along the advancing edge of the warm air, wispy cirrus clouds reach out to give warning of the approaching storm. Hour by hour clouds thicken as a drizzle turns into a steady rain. At the western edge of the tongue, the cold air is advancing on the warm air, and the meeting place is called a "cold front." Here the warm air is forced to tremendous heights, shedding its moisture in majestic cumulo-nimbus clouds. These cumulo-nimbus clouds can sometimes reach almost to the top of the troposphere, and the violent convection generates a thunderhead. If the cold front falls on top of the tongue, the air becomes very unstable and tornadoes develop.

Let us leave the troposphere and explore the region beyond. Sixty miles up we enter the ionosphere where atoms are broken up by the ultraviolet light from the sun. Each atom splits into a positive ion and an electron. A vast layer of electrons forms a mirror in the sky for radio waves, and a short-wave broadcast is bounced around the world when it hits this layer. There is a faint glow from the ionosphere as atoms release the energy previously absorbed from the sun. Normally the glow is so faint that it cannot be seen with the unaided eye, but at times it is augmented by the beautiful forms and colors of the Aurora Borealis.

From the United States and Europe the Aurora Borealis is seen in the northern sky and is known as the "northern lights." On the rare occasions when a great display is about to take place, a pale green arc appears over the northern horizon after sunset. Sometimes deep red clouds appear in the sky, and the arc takes on the form of a hanging curtain or drapery. At the climax, long shafts of light stand in the sky, extending upward until they meet in a crown. The forms move against the starry background; they sway and pulsate and sometimes appear like a flaming inferno. All of this excitement is caused by the sun as it disturbs the atmosphere of the Earth. Where there is no atmosphere, there can be no aurora. The sun extends a long corpuscular stream which is released from a flare at the surface of the sun, and reaches the Earth after a journey of ninety-three million miles. The protons and electrons of the stream penetrate our atmosphere, colliding with the atoms of oxygen and nitrogen to cause them to shine. During an aurora, a piece of the sun is presented with majestic pomp to the Earth.

No one can say exactly where the atmosphere ends. Above the ionosphere there is still a tenfold decrease in pressure for every ten miles of ascent, so that the pressure decreases a million-million-fold by the time we are 120 miles above the surface. The air becomes thinner and thinner as we go up, and there is no definite edge. At a

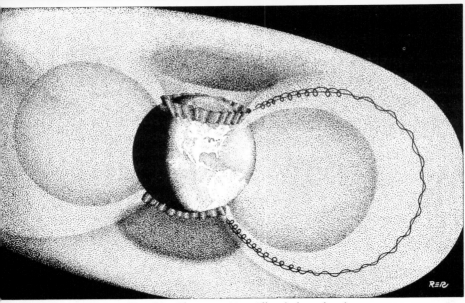

Fig. 24. The outer Van Allen belt and polar aurorae

height of 500 miles, however, the air has become extremely thin. Atoms in the rarefied air can move about freely without colliding with each other. The layer at an altitude of 500 miles is regarded by most scientists as the top of the atmosphere, for beyond it we move into a region where atoms no longer behave as a gas. Atoms are continually moving out into space on long, independent paths, finally to be turned by gravity and brought into the atmosphere once again. The region is filled with a continual spray of molecules, atoms, and electrons.

Beyond the atmosphere we are in outer space, the region into which we send our artificial satellites. Dr. James Van Allen, a physicist of the State University of Iowa, was very much surprised to find intense cosmic rays out there. Outer space is not empty, it is radioactive! Electrons and protons from the sun become trapped in the magnetic field of the Earth, and spring to and fro between the northern and the southern hemispheres. Their motion is controlled by the Earth's magnetic field, and they are forced to spin in a tight spiral around a line of force. At any instant, millions of particles are moving from pole to pole, and they form a doughnut-shaped ring around the Earth. It takes four seconds for an electron to spring from Alaska to the antarctic and back again, and it makes the trip a thousand times or more. Ultimately the particle approaches the surface of the Earth too closely at the northern or the southern end. It collides with an atom and joins the gas of our atmosphere. The supply of particles for the

Van Allen belt comes from the sun. When the sun is active, the Van Allen belt engorges the corpuscular stream and becomes filled to over-flowing. Particles then spill in a zone around the polar regions of the Earth, and people on the ground see the aurora.

What does the Earth look like from above? From the top of the atmosphere, at a height of five hundred miles, you can see a wide panorama, with a curved horizon sweeping between the misty atmosphere and the darkness of space. Mountain chains and lakes spread before you like a map, but highways and railroads are too small to be seen. By day the sunlight glistens from the mirror of the ocean, and at night the larger cities show as a hazy glow. From the moon you need a powerful telescope to see the lights of a city, and the signs of civilization are difficult to recognize. With unaided vision you can discern the broad features of America and other continents, set in the dark blue of the oceans. Storms viewed from above look pure white and change from hour to hour as they grow and drift across the globe. You can see the two storm belts of the roaring forties separated by the clear zone of the horse latitudes. Surrounding the equator is a band of small white spots, the tropical thunderstorms. Although you could recognize the broad features of our planet, you would not see details of civilization—the cities, roads, and cultivated farmlands, so familiar to us on the surface. This must be remembered when, back on the Earth, at the bottom of the hazy atmosphere, we point our telescopes toward the other planets in the solar system.

C H A P T E R  13

# VENUS AND MARS

APART FROM THE MOON, OUR NEAREST NEIGHBORS ARE VENUS AND Mars. When Venus passes between the Earth and the sun it is just twenty-six million miles away, and Mars, as it overtakes the Earth, comes as close as thirty-five million miles. Venus makes a close approach every nineteen months, and just before inferior conjunction it appears as a brilliant evening star. Favorable occasions for seeing Venus can be worked out from the sequence of evening star dates— January 1961, September 1962, April 1964. At maximum brilliancy, Venus outshines every other star and planet, and can even cast a faint shadow. Astronomers who try to cloister themselves in the depths of an observatory dread these dates, for multitudes of people phone, write, and call to report their "discovery" of a flying saucer or comet. Mars also makes its appearance rather infrequently. Favorable occasions occur some two years and one month apart, when Mars shines with a ruddy hue at midnight and rivals Venus in brilliance. Favorable dates can be worked out from the sequence of oppositions—February 1963, March 1965, April 1967. Mars and Venus present themselves for only a few months during the year, and on these occasions astronomers roll back the domes, point the telescopes, and scrutinize the surface of these planets.

Venus is rather frustrating. She hides herself in a thick white veil of cloud and no one has ever seen her surface. We are forced to engage in sleuthing to uncover the secrets of Venus.

Some light reflected from the clouds has been analyzed in the spectroscope. Some of the rainbow colors of sunlight are missing, for they have been absorbed by gases in the atmosphere of Venus existing above the clouds. One absorption band shows us very definitely that carbon dioxide is present in large quantities. Another absorption band shows us definitely that water vapor is present, although in the past scientists doubted whether water vapor really existed. To be sure, the water vapor absorption band appeared quite strongly in the spectrum, but, they argued, the absorption could easily be taking place in our own atmosphere and not the atmosphere of Venus. Commander Malcolm D. Ross and physicist Charles B. Moore took off one day in 1959 from South Dakota in the gondola of a stratosphere balloon. Charles Moore was a scientist and his task was to point an electronic spectroscope at Venus when the balloon reached sufficient altitude. At a height of 80,000 feet the balloon was above 98 per cent of the Earth's air, and the absorption bands that Mr. Moore found could not have been produced by earthly water vapor, but must have come from Venus. Although airborne for over a day, Moore was able to observe Venus for only a few minutes. The huge plastic balloon swayed and lurched and twisted. This encouraged air sickness in three different ways, and in the gondola a temperature of −40° F. gave cold comfort to the occupants. The descent was rather uncontrolled; batteries and other heavy objects were jettisoned to slow the fall and prevent the disruption of the fluttering balloon. The gondola landed on a slope and rolled. The parachute was caught by the wind and dragged a quarter of a mile so that the gondola and its occupants bounced along like a rolling stone. Fortunately Ross and Moore were unhurt, and the scientific records were taken immediately to be analyzed by Dr. John Strong at the Johns Hopkins University.

Radio astronomers have listened to the faint hiss coming from the surface of Venus. Radio waves occur in the spectrum beyond the infrared, and can be thought of as very long wave length heat rays. They pass unhindered through the clouds and bring information about the surface. The strength of the radio signals indicate a surface temperature of 500° F., 300° hotter than boiling water. We can well imagine what a visitor to Venus would see. As he dropped below the cloud bank he would see a landscape illuminated by a gray light similar to a dull day on Earth. Here and there would be the red glow of a molten lava bed welling up from the interior. Fierce winds would lash dust and sandy particles in a searing blast across the desert—hardly a place for life, at least for the next billion years or so.

Although Mars overtakes the Earth every two years, some oppositions are more favorable than others for the astronomers. The orbit of Mars is quite elliptical so that the planet is sometimes close and sometimes far away from the Earth. Every fifteen or seventeen years we have a favorable opposition when Mars is only thirty-five million miles away, such as September 1956 and August 1971. During unfavorable oppositions, such as March 1965, Mars can be up to sixty-two million miles away, almost twice its minimum distance. Most of the discoveries about Mars have been made at favorable oppositions, and astronomers are eagerly awaiting 1971.

Mars is a planet similar to the Earth in many respects. It is the only planet whose surface we can study, as the others are covered with cloud or are too far away. Through the telescope we see large expanses with an orange hue, and these areas are dry desert regions so often referred to as the "Red Sands of Mars." There are dark markings which can be seen each night on the planet as it rotates, and these are permanent features. The dark markings have been studied and mapped in great detail from 1800 to the present day, but we still do not know very much about them. Even the color of the markings is in dispute. Some observers say the color is olive green, some say gray or blue. There is good excuse for the disagreement. Through the telescope the image of Mars never remains steady, it is always rippling and becoming blurred due to the disturbances in our own atmosphere. It is almost like looking at something at the bottom of a swimming pool when the surface is disturbed. Telescopes, especially refractors, produce false color fringes, and then the red glare of the desert regions of Mars is always present to upset your estimate of color. At the North and South Pole of Mars we find the white polar regions, which are thought to be snowfields like the arctic and antarctic regions of the Earth. Occasionally a yellow cloud of dust is stirred from the desert to move over the surface at thirty miles per hour as a dust storm. At the last favorable opposition, astronomers were disappointed to find the entire planet engulfed in a storm which obscured the details of the surface.

Landing on Mars would be more pleasant than landing on Venus. The sun shines warmly from a deep blue sky, and the temperature never goes much higher than a pleasant 70° F. Pearly clouds make a delicate canopy overhead, and your feet would be comfortable in the soft sand. No one would need a raincoat, for it never rains on Mars.

There are some disadvantages however. The temperature of 70° occurs in the tropics at noon, elsewhere it is rather colder. At sunset the temperature drops to 0° F. in the tropics, and probably just before dawn it goes down to −30°. At the poles in the winter it is −150° F. The average temperature on Mars is, in fact, below freezing, close to 0° F. If you push your toes deeply into the soft sand you may come across a layer of ice. The dusty surface acts as a heat insulator and the heat from the sun does not penetrate very far. A few inches below the surface the temperature must be close to the mean temperature of 0° F. and the ground is permanently frozen. Beware of that smudge on the horizon; it is an advancing cloud bank of dust that will soon swirl around you to choke out the air and obscure the sun. Conditions on Mars would be a little worse than those obtained by placing the Gobi Desert on top of Mt. Everest. You would find half as much atmospheric pressure on Mars as you do on top of Everest, and pressurized space suits would certainly be required. We have detected carbon dioxide, but there is at the most only a trace of oxygen present. The oxygen has been locked into the surface materials and is not available for you to breathe.

Water vapor has been suspected on Mars but not definitely proved. A spectroscopic proof will not be available for some time, unless we can persuade Mr. Moore to enter the gondola once again. We have evidence to show that the white polar caps are made of frozen water in the form of light snow or hoar frost. In infrared light, Gerard P. Kuiper found the pole caps appeared almost black, just as ice and snow are dark when photographed with an infrared filter on the Earth. As the seasons change on Mars the pole caps respond as if they were a light dusting of hoar frost, about a quarter of an inch thick. During the winter months the pole cap spreads across three million square miles of the surface, and clouds and mist hang over them. With the first days of spring the clouds disperse a little, and the pole caps begin to shrink. Along their edge a dark fringe appears which is thought by many astronomers to be a soggy region of thaw. As summer comes the pole caps shrink further, the south cap disappearing completely. The snow lingers for a while at two small areas that must be elevated areas. Named the Mitchell Mountains, in honor of the discoverer, they are probably nothing more than low hills some five hundred feet high.

While the pole cap is melting a remarkable change takes place on the surface of the planet. At the beginning of summer a wave of moisture seems to spread across the planet down toward the equator, for the dark areas change their color. The darkening wave moves along at twenty miles per day breathing life into the planet. Astronomers believe that the wave is a moisture wave from the evaporating pole caps, but what sort of life is present to respond to the moist polar breeze?

Map after map of the dark areas has been made through years of careful study. Now we have a name for all the prominent features on the planet, each name reflecting the home country and character of the astronomer. We have narrow strips, Ambrosia and Nectar, reaching over to Solis Lacus, the lake of the sun. We have Arabia, Utopia and Hades, Sabaeus Sinus and Mare Erythraeum. Looking through even a small telescope it is easy to see Syrtis Major, a dark tongue shaped like the continent of India. It was the first feature to be seen from the Earth, being observed by the Dutch physicist, Christian Huygens, on November 28, 1659, at 7 P.M., just after dinner. The name for this imposing region is not well chosen, literally translated it means the Great Bog. We are sure that the dark regions are not lakes, seas, or bogs; they are something dark that rests on the surface. We are sure that the "something" is alive, for as the sand is blown over the area the dark marks quickly reappear. Something alive is forcing its way up through the choking sand. The American astronomer, William Sinton, studied the spectrum of the feeble reflected light and showed that carbon hydrogen bonds were present in the dark areas but not in the bright. The C-H bond is fundamental to all forms of life on the Earth, both plant and animal, and is unlikely to be produced by nonliving chemicals. But Kuiper found the dark areas did not reflect back infrared light like leaves and plants on the Earth. He found the coloration was similar to lichens, the odd union where fungi and algae join together to live on each other. Thus large expanses on Mars are probably covered with gray-green mold that we find on walls, rocks, and mountaintops here on Earth. A lichen can grow and thrive under very extreme conditions. It can even grow when the average temperature is below the freezing point of water, as it is on Mars, and it requires a very modest amount of atmosphere and moisture.

The dark areas spread and move from year to year on the surface of Mars. There is a dark area called "Thoth-Nepenthes," near Syrtis Major, that doubled in size between 1948 and 1954. If the lichens are spreading they must have moved six hundred miles in six years, one mile in three days. At that rate a small town would be overgrown in about a week—almost as virile as the spores described by H. G. Wells in *War of the Worlds!* Botanists are quite anxious to obtain specimens of the Martian vegetation to find out how it thrives under such bleak conditions. Let's hope the specimen bottle is kept tightly corked, and that Martian vegetation is not encouraged to spread on the Earth.

Strange things have happened during our study of Mars. Two moons were discovered at the favorable opposition of 1877 by the

American astronomer Asaph Hall. He named them Phobos and Deimos, "fear" and "panic," appropriate attendants for the God of War.
These two moons are astronomical impossibilities; they could not have
condensed from material in the original proto-planet like the other
moons in the solar system. Phobos goes around Mars in a period of
7 hours and 39 minutes, faster than any other natural satellite. Deimos
also has a short period, making a revolution in 30 hours. Both moons
are very close to Mars. The orbit of Phobos is only 3,700 miles above
the surface, a little higher than the American artificial satellite Vanguard I. As time goes on, Phobos may be drawn closer and closer by
atmospheric drag until it crashes into the surface of Mars. The
peculiar satellites of Mars were described quite accurately by Jonathan
Swift when he wrote the imaginary account of Gulliver's travels. Swift
had predicted these odd moons by clairvoyance, 157 years before
Hall saw them. The moons are quite small, only a few miles in diameter
at the most, and some Russian astronomers believe the moons to be
of low density, almost hollow shells. Perhaps they are artificial satellites, the last fling of a civilization before it perished.

Occasionally bright flashes occur on the planet. A bright speck
flares into view and remains visible for a few seconds. These flashes
are not seen very often, as there is no warning as to when and where
they will appear. Mars does not show any mountains or volcanic peaks
so it is unlikely that the flashes are the eruption of a volcano. Perhaps
a large meteor has crashed through the atmosphere to cause an explosion on impact with the surface. Perhaps the flash is a severe electrical discharge generated in the swirling dust.

The strangest happening in the study of Mars was the discovery
of canals. While Hall was tracking the moons in the favorable opposition of 1877, the Italian astronomer, Giovanni Schiaparelli, was carefully mapping deserts and dark regions. Suddenly, during a brief
instant when the atmosphere became still, he saw a series of faint lines
crossing the deserts. He hardly believed what he saw, but he caught
glimpses of the lines on several more occasions through the night.
Finally he announced his discovery, describing the lines by the Italian
word "canali." The word has two meanings, natural channel or man-
made canal. Schiaparelli meant the former, but, by a horrible mis-
translation, the latter meaning was used when his story was printed in
English. Thus the legend of the canals on Mars was born. Other
astronomers had great difficulty in seeing the canals and, when at the
opposition of 1879 Schiaparelli announced that some of the canals
had doubled, all sorts of doubts were raised.

The problem of the canals was dealt with energetically by the Bostonian, Percival Lowell. Dr. Lowell was not a professional astronomer, though he had obtained a thorough education in many subjects including mathematics and physics. He might be described as an intelligent intellectual with independent finances. In his own words, he was a man of many moods, and his interests ranged from flowers and trees to Esoteric Shintoism in Japan. Finally his imagination was caught by the planet Mars, and largely with his own money, he built an observatory at Flagstaff, Arizona, to study the surface details of the planet. The observatory was named after him and his body lies buried on the hillside near the dome.

If Dr. Lowell made any mistake, it was in the science of what we now call public relations. If you think you can see a network of lines on a planet, and that these lines are canals dug by intelligent people to conserve a dwindling water supply, then you should proceed in your research with caution, for such an astonishing conclusion is bound to produce violent reactions from both astronomers and the man in the street. Lowell, with his overflowing enthusiasm, encouraged widespread publicity of his work, making extensive lecture tours and writing books in which he categorically stated that he had proved intelligent life to exist on Mars. His ideas produced headlines for the front pages of newspapers and were excitedly discussed around the world. Even today when you give an "open night" lecture about the planets someone in the audience is sure to ask "Can astronomers still see the Martians and their canals?" It is a pity that he did not emphasize the split of opinion; on the one hand stood Percival Lowell, on the other hand stood the world of professional astronomers.

Even under the best conditions, astronomers like Barnard and Hale could not see the canals. Keen eyesight, a good instrument, and exceptionally clear weather were needed before the lines could be seen and even then only momentary glimpses were obtained. E. M. Antoniadi in Europe probably had eyesight as keen as Lowell's, but failed to see the canal network. Under high magnification he found many of Lowell's canals were better described as a disorderly array of small dark patches. A picture of Mars, without canals, was set up at a Greenwich school in London, and the boys drew what they saw through a telescope. Most of them were convinced that they saw canals, and this was taken to show that the canals were an illusion. Lowell was derogatory about the suggestion, calling it the "small boy theory." The French astronomer, Flammarion, repeated the experiment, and his boys did not draw a single line.

It was pointed out that the canals must be twenty or thirty miles wide to be seen from the Earth, and could hardly be excavations. Lowell explained that we were looking at a wide belt of vegetation irrigated by water from a narrow channel in the center. Why were some canals double? The second canal was used to return the water to the pole cap. How did the water manage to flow on the flat surface of the planet for distances of twenty-five hundred miles? Lowell claimed that there were pumping stations at regular intervals along the course. But the theory of intelligent beings finally met an argument impossible to answer. The water vapor in Mars' atmosphere is below the limit of detection, and absorption in the atmosphere shows the air pressure to be less than one-fifth of the pressure on the Earth. As the pressure is reduced, water boils at a lower temperature (mountaineering Englishmen find they cannot brew good tea above an altitude of two thousand feet.) Water could not exist for long as a liquid on Mars. It must either be in the air as water vapor, frozen at the poles as hoar frost, or frozen below the ground as ice. Thus it is quite impossible to have open seas or lakes on the surface, and long, open cuts with rushing water are out of the question.

Today we support Antoniadi's viewpoint. Irregular patches of vegetation are scattered in the Martian deserts, and from the Earth the patches can give the illusion of lines. No water is pumped down to the desert oases, but a moisture wave swells out during the summer months to darken the desert life. The pattern changes from year to year as the desert sand blows across the green, and as the vegetation struggles to gain a foothold in new territory. A definite answer will only come when we are able to visit Mars in person and tramp over the surface. It may take years; perhaps by that time our own water supply will have disappeared and two giant artificial satellites will be circling the dying Earth.

CHAPTER **14**

REGULUS

# JUPITER AND SATURN

BEYOND THE PLANET MARS WE ENTER A REGION OF FRAGMENTS called the "zone of the asteroids." Instead of a single large proto-planet, two or three smaller bodies formed. It is dangerous to have two objects in a similar orbit because the chance of collision is high. The Earth, Mars, and other planets travel in orbits of their own, but the less fortunate asteroids must have collided in the past to form the debris seen today. Some of the fragments are deflected by Mars and fall to the Earth as meteorites. Others can be seen as starlike points of light reflecting back the sunshine from the depths of space.

Ceres, the largest asteroid, is 480 miles across. Because it is spherical, and not irregular in shape as most other asteroids are, we infer that it has managed to avoid a collision so far, though one day it too may be shattered. G. Piazzi discovered Ceres from Sicily, and named her after the goddess of the island. The practice of using mythological names has been followed for most of the other 1,600 asteroids, but nowadays the weakness in classical education is appearing; one or two fragments are forced to scurry around with such names as Chicago, Rockefellia, or just a plain number. By observing the meteorites in our hand and the airless bodies in space, we are certain of one thing—the asteroids are not an abode of life.

Instead of a single planet forming between the orbit of Mars and Jupiter, several small planets formed, and from their collisions came the zone of fragments. Jupiter was the cause of the abortive planet. Circling around like a giant buzzard, Jupiter, with his gravitation, tore the proto-planet apart again every time it tried to form. Jupiter is the largest planet in the solar system, with one thousand times the volume of the Earth. Through the telescope Jupiter is a pretty sight, showing its colored cloud belts and its four famous moons. The spectroscope shows us that certain wave lengths of light are absorbed, and we know that ammonia and methane gas must be present in the atmosphere. By observing stars through the edge of the atmosphere, astronomers find that the average mass of a molecule is less than the mass of ammonia and methane. We conclude that the bulk of the atmosphere is made up of the lighter molecule of hydrogen. Thus Jupiter's atmosphere consists of hydrogen with traces of the poisonous gases, methane and ammonia. This is in agreement with our ideas concerning the creation of the planets. Proto-Jupiter was large enough and far enough away from the sun to retain most of its hydrogen. The temperature so far away from the sun is $-200°$ F., which means that water and carbon dioxide are completely frozen out. No oxygen can be liberated by photo-dissociation of water molecules, nor can oxygen be produced by plants from the carbon dioxide. The clouds in the atmosphere must be ammonia crystals, and perhaps below the clouds snowflakes of solid ammonia are incessantly falling.

Storms on Jupiter can be seen quite easily with even a small telescope. Most of what we know about Jupiter's weather has been revealed through the patient observation of the amateur. Circling the equator is a bright zone of clouds. Coloration changes from year to year, and sometimes from night to night, but the equatorial zone is usually white. Sometimes small dark storm clouds appear and are carried along by the wind. A fierce westerly wind is always blowing in the equatorial zone, carrying the clouds around the planet at two hundred miles per hour. Jupiter seems to have a jet stream just like the Earth, but the cause of the wind is not known. On either side of the jet stream we see north and south equatorial belts. Darker clouds form in these belts, usually of a brownish hue, and storm centers develop where the jet stream meets the belt.

Next to the dark equatorial belt we find the south tropical zone. Like the equatorial zone it is light in color, varying from yellow to pale gray. This zone is the most interesting one on Jupiter because of the remarkable things that have been seen in it. From time to time the "Great Red Spot" is uncovered, and can be seen with even small telescopes. The telescope had not been invented for very long when the versatile physicist, Robert Hooke, saw the spot in 1664, and the Italian, Giovanni Cassini, confirmed his observation in the following year. There is a picture of Jupiter in this book showing the cloud belts and the Red Spot. "Spot" is a depreciatory term since the area of coloration extends for 30,000 miles around the zone. There is room for three Earths to be placed in the spot and there would still be room left over. The spot may be even larger below the clouds; it seems to spread below the clouds, affecting their growth. You can see a large hollow that has been scooped out from the equatorial belt.

Since Hooke first noticed it, the Red Spot has played a remarkable game of hide and seek. For most of the eighteenth century, astronomers could see "Hooke's spot" on Jupiter, but not much interest was aroused. By 1880, however, the spot had enlarged and taken on a brick red coloration according to some observers. By 1890 the color had toned down to a pink, and later it faded to a dull gray. This color still changes from year to year, and the shades are so varied that it is sometimes difficult to describe them. Astronomers have used such terms as salmon pink, pinky red, carmine, and tawny, until we wonder in perplexity what this chameleon spot will do next.

At first one or two people thought that a volcano was erupting on the surface of Jupiter, causing a red glow in the clouds above, or perhaps coloring the clouds with a plume of dust. Careful observations over the years have given us a very firm denial of the volcanic hypothesis, for since at least 1831 the spot has been moving slowly backward and forward over the surface of the planet. The spot has pushed its way around the temperate zone three times while we have been watching. From 1830 to 1880 it moved steadily eastward at a walking pace of two or three miles per hour. It hesitated for a year or two in 1880, while it was very conspicuous, and then began to move westward again at three miles per hour. There were some minor hesitations in the first part of the present century but since 1936 the spot has resumed the westward drift at a slightly increased rate.

At the present time we think that the Red Spot is a solid object floating in the Jovian atmosphere. This idea explains the wandering of the spot and the behavior of clouds in the vicinity. As the huge red island, or continent, floats higher in the atmosphere, it breaks through the cloud tops and shows as a large colored oval. But from the laws of physics we know that angular momentum must be preserved. Just as a pirouetting ballerina will slow down when she extends her arms, so the red island will move more slowly as it floats high in the atmosphere and is moved away from the axis of Jupiter. We would expect the Red Spot to lag behind once it has broken through the cloud tops, and this does indeed seem to occur. The floating island broke the surface in 1880 and 1936 when the spot was conspicuous. Immediately afterwards the spot began to lag behind, and drift slowly westward. When the island submerges, the clouds close over the top and the Red Spot becomes inconspicuous. At these times it gains speed and moves toward the east. The explanation of the color changes is a problem for chemists. Some think that the floating island consists of ammonia crystals with an admixture of impurities such as sodium. When liquid ammonia containing about 4 per cent of sodium is frozen, remarkable color changes occur. These colors range from reddish bronze to blue and are similar to the colors, and color changes, seen on Jupiter.

We have seen another peculiar object in the tropical zone, a dusky rectangular marking with white clouds at either end. The marking is a little larger than the Red Spot, but it has not persisted over the centuries. The earliest sighting is dated 1900, which confines the event to the present century. Even today, after more than fifty years of observation, we have no idea of the nature of this object. Officially it is called the Disturbance.

The Disturbance at discovery was moving slowly, at two or three miles per hour, toward the east around the tropical zone. This was quite interesting, for the Red Spot at that time was moving westward around the zone, and a collision was inevitable. Interest increased as the collision date drew near, and during June 1902 many telescopes were pointed at the planet. Nobody was able to guess beforehand the course of events; the Red Spot did not break up, the Disturbance was not halted, nor did the Disturbance and the Red Spot join together and move forward as a single object. The Disturbance accelerated on approaching the Red Spot, faded, and then reappeared on the other side. The Disturbance seemed to go under, over, and around the floating island, for a dusky ring surrounded the spot and its brightness was reduced. From this we infer that the Disturbance itself was not solid, but was probably a persistent storm in the tropical zone. After the encounter, the Disturbance re-formed on the other side of the Red Spot and continued the eastward motion, while the Red Spot was not deviated and continued its westward drift. Although the Disturbance is probably atmospheric, how could it form again after dissolution, and why was the Red Spot unaffected by the storm?

This collision occurred on ten occasions altogether, and nine times the Disturbance emerged successfully and continued to drift around the tropical zone. The tenth encounter was in 1939 when the Disturbance did not reappear as in the past. The last sighting was made in December 1939 by Reverend T. E. R. Phillips, past director of the Jupiter section of the British Astronomical Association. All that could be seen was a faint shading in the tropical zone, the Disturbance apparently being stretched and dissipated over a distance of more than fifty thousand miles. Perhaps the Disturbance is quiescent and will reappear, or perhaps it is completely destroyed. Only by continuing observations through the years ahead will we know the answer.

We do not know for sure what conditions prevail below the clouds, but by using a pencil and paper and the laws of physics we can make an intelligent guess. By comparing the speed of our own moon with the moons of Jupiter, we find from Kepler's third law that Jupiter is 318 times more massive than the Earth. From the theory of Isaac Newton we deduce that the gravitational pull is two and a half times greater than on the Earth. If you weigh 150 pounds on Earth you would weigh 375 pounds on Jupiter. Gases also weigh more on Jupiter, and the atmosphere below the clouds must be under great pressure. These immense pressures will cause the ammonia and other gases to condense into liquid droplets, and when the pressure reaches a critical value the liquid has the same density as the gas.

Let us imagine a visit to Jupiter. As you approach the planet for a landing, you dip through the cool ammonia crystals in the cloud tops and begin your descent. As you go lower the sunlight is obscured by the clouds and the pressure and temperature of the atmosphere increases. The ammonia crystals turn to liquid droplets, at first bronze-colored, and then blue, as the ammonia solution and its impurities change phase. At the level of critical pressure, huge blobs of liquid would appear, slinking like submarines through the deep. Somewhere at the bottom of the murky sludge, perhaps some hundred miles below the top of the clouds, you would touch the solid surface of Jupiter, a frozen waste of ice.

Calculations enable us to explore further and go below the solid surface. The average density of Jupiter is one and a third times the density of water, and the cloud must be composed of light material, such as ice and frozen gases. The behavior of ices can be predicted, because this behavior depends to a large extent on pressure and temperature. The equatorial bulge of Jupiter gives us another clue about the interior. The degree of oblateness shows that the planet has a dense central core. So if we were to burrow down into Jupiter we would pass through concentric shells of ice. Perhaps the frozen hydrogen, which would be found in great quantities, would revert to a metallic phase under great pressure. About fifteen thousand miles from the center we would strike a heavy core which by now may have cooled sufficiently to be solid. This core contains iron, nickel, and the other heavier elements that we find so abundantly on the Earth.

Jupiter has four large satellites and eight smaller ones, making twelve altogether. Two of the large moons are as big as the planet Mercury, and two are similar in size to our own moon. Thus the giant planet has giant moons. Galileo was the first person to see the moons and he named them the "stars of Medici," in honor of his patron, the Grand Duke of Tuscany, numbering them in order of their distance from the planet, I, II, III and IV. It was January 7, 1610, when Galileo first saw the moons. The next evening a Dutchman, Simon Marius, also made the discovery, quite independently, and named the moons from mythology after sons and daughters of the gods, Io, Europa, Ganymede, Callisto. When Simon at last spoke up, his claim was swamped by the prestige of the savant. Branded as an impostor, he was ostracized, and his romantic and appropriate names were rejected.

The Galilean satellites are a pretty sight, set like pearls on a thread and moving to and fro as they circle the planet. Hour by hour the panorama changes, following a predicted sequence with the regularity of clockwork. Sometimes a moon passes through the shadow of Jupiter, and then it is totally eclipsed, remaining invisible for an hour or so. Sometimes the moon passes behind Jupiter and seems to be swallowed up in the cloud belts as it disappears. On the near side of the orbit a moon passes in front of Jupiter, and then it is seen as a bright disk against the background of the clouds. The moon is followed by its small round shadow which is producing an eclipse of the sun within the small black spot.

Although the moons move with the regularity of clockwork, they seem to fall behind schedule when Jupiter is far from us. This is caused by the finite speed of light—it takes light several minutes longer to reach us when Jupiter is further away. A Danish astronomer, Ole Römer, was the first to explain the irregularity and announced his discovery of the speed of light in 1675. Like most important advances of knowledge, it was not immediately accepted. In fact more than fifty years elapsed before scientists agreed that Römer was right, and during this time his discovery was ridiculed and his name scorned. Did not every sane man know that light traveled from place to place instantaneously?

The other eight satellites are small, not more than a hundred miles or so in diameter, and revolve at great distances from the planet. To conform with Galileo, and, perhaps, to insure the rejection of Marius, each moon upon discovery was given a number. Because of the earthly feud, the eight moons of Jupiter have become the only natural moons in the solar system without a proper name. Satellite V is very close to Jupiter, and completes a revolution in just under twelve hours. Satellites VI, VII, and X takes 260 days and the remaining moons take nearly two years to go once around the planet. The outer moons, with a two-year period, are loosely held in the Jupiter system, the gravitational disturbance of the sun distorts their orbits and causes them to wander in irregular ellipses. Jupiter may one day lose these moons, because his control is so weak. Indeed we think that the outer moons may not be original members of the Jupiter system, but have been captured from the asteroid zone. They certainly do not behave like normal moons; they have high eccentricities and are moving around Jupiter in retrograde orbits, that is to say when viewed from above the North Pole they revolve in a clockwise direction.

The god Jupiter was omnipotent for the Romans, controlling the heavens and unleashing storms, thunderbolts, and pestilence on the Earth. More and more we find the planet has been appropriately named. Jupiter's great mass influences the motion of all other planets in the solar system and even produces a measurable displacement of the sun. Now we find that Jupiter sends out strong radio signals. When played through a high-fidelity system you hear terrifying noises, rumbles and cracks, grindings and groans. A Jupiter sound track would have made appropriate background music for the ancient Roman temples.

The honor of discovering Jupiter's noise goes to Dr. Bernard Burke and Dr. Kenneth Franklin of the Carnegie Institute of Washington, who, working inside their radio laboratory, noticed that signals were displayed on the radio recorders when Jupiter was in the antenna beam. As radio scientists, they were unacquainted with the beauty of the night sky, and Jupiter to them was just a number in the ephemeris tables. When one of them noticed a bright white star sometime after the discovery he asked its name. He learned with embarrassment that it was Jupiter.

Jupiter transmits at irregular intervals with wave lengths between 10 and 20 meters in the amateur and commercial short-wave bands. No doubt the signals have caused annoyance to radio operators for a long time, but have been classed with the general term "interference." Surveys have enabled us to locate the source of noise. The transmissions come from one or two white storm regions a little to the south of the great Red Spot, and the noise seems to be more intense when the storms are passing close by the Red Spot. We do not imagine, of course, that the signals are produced by intelligent life. Some violent electrical disturbances must be taking place in the cold darkness below the clouds. People have suggested Jovian thunderstorms, turbulent upheavals with a rain of liquid ammonia, or earthquakes within the ice at the surface which send out shock waves through the ionosphere. Perhaps charged particles are pouring into Jupiter from the sun. We must listen and track for several more years before we can answer this riddle.

If Galileo was delighted when he first turned his telescope toward Jupiter, he was perplexed when he looked at Saturn. Instead of one planet he saw three set out in a row, and the large companions failed to move around Saturn like normal moons. Month by month the companions grew smaller until finally they vanished from view. Galileo could not believe his eyes. Italian philosophers of other schools began to doubt his other observations and his telescope. Professor Libri of Pisa denied the Jovian moons and would not consent to put his eye to the telescope. When Libri died soon after, Galileo politely hoped that he "perceived them on his journey to heaven." Galileo himself died before the problem was solved. The honor of solving the problem of Saturn's companions goes to Christian Huygens of Holland, who in 1656 was the first person to recognize the rings. He concealed his discovery by writing in code "aaaaaaa, ccccc, d, eeeee, g, h, iiiiiii, llll, mm, nnnnnnnnn, oooo, pp, q, rr, s, ttttt, uuuuu." A coded announcement was not unusual in the seventeenth century. It allowed the astronomer time to verify a startling result, and protected him from ridicule and persecution. Three years later, Huygens was satisfied and published the translation of the anagram. The letters, when rearranged, formed a Latin sentence that said "Saturn is surrounded by a flat ring inclined to the ecliptic and nowhere touching the planet."

The ring system is amazing. It is 170,000 miles across and less than 10 miles thick. We see the rings from the side, and as Saturn moves around the sun every twenty-nine years the rings appear to open and close. These variations perplexed Galileo and the early observers. When the Earth was exactly edgewise to the rings, Galileo could see nothing. When the rings were open, his imperfect telescope showed them as two side companions to the planet. Giovanni Cassini first noticed the dark line which separates the rings into two portions. It is called Cassini's Division in his honor. Inside Cassini's Division is a bright ring, Ring B, and outside is a fainter ring, Ring A. A third and very faint ring can just be seen with a powerful telescope. It is called the Crepe ring because of its diaphanous nature.

If the rings were solid, the outer edge would spin around faster than the center, like a wheel or phonograph record. A Doppler shift of spectral lines shows that Ring A on the outside moves more slowly than Ring B, so the rings cannot be solid. They must consist of a multitude of small particles moving around Saturn in circular orbits. The particles are packed closely together but do not touch, since the shadow cast by the rings is not completely black. At the distance of Saturn the sun's rays cannot relieve the coldness of space, and many of the small particles must be frozen ices. The ring system is a jostling stream of snowballs wheeling around the planet.

The moons of Saturn are probably snowballs as well. Probably in the past one of these moons approached Saturn and came within the Roche limit. Tidal forces on the moon broke it into innumerable pieces which now form the rings. At the present time, the moon Mimas is dangerously close to Saturn, traveling around the outer fringe of the rings. Mimas revolves around Saturn with a period of 22 hours, 37 minutes. The period of a snowball within the Cassini Division would be 11 hours, 18 minutes, 30 seconds according to Kepler's third law. This is exactly one-half of the period of Mimas. No particle could remain for long under these conditions, for every other revolution would find it close to Mimas where gravitational perturbations would occur. The condition is resonant. Mimas has cleared out the snowballs from the Cassini Division and produced a gap. If perturbations in the future pull Mimas within the Roche limit, it too may be disrupted by Saturn to add some more icy debris to the rings.

Saturn, like Jupiter, is a giant planet, with a heavy atmosphere, bright zones, and cloud belts. Markings are not so well defined as on Jupiter, and there is no Red Spot or enigmatic Disturbance. Methane and ammonia bands can be detected with a spectroscope, but the ammonia is weak because of the low temperature. Most of the ammonia has been frozen out to form the crystals in the clouds and the sludge that lies below them. The lower temperature is also responsible for the faintness of the coloration of the cloudbelts. Like Jupiter, Saturn has concentric shells of ice surrounding a central core of rock and iron.

Saturn was the extremity of the universe as recognized by ancient astronomers. Nowadays we recognize two more giant planets, Uranus and Neptune, which although a little smaller, are quite similar to Jupiter and Saturn. Beyond Neptune we find the ninth small planet, Pluto, the iceball, not much bigger than the Earth. Perhaps other planets exist beyond Pluto and occasionally someone announces prematurely the discovery of a new planet "X." Pluto is the god of the underworld, so perhaps if Planet X is ever located we might name it Charon, after the bearded old sailor who ferries dead souls on their last journey across the river Styx; for at these enormous distances from the sun, where gases are frozen and the Earth is but a faint speck, there can be no life in any form.

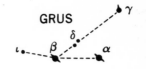

C H A P T E R 15

# THE MOON

OUR NEAREST NEIGHBOR THE MOON IS RATHER NEGLECTED BY modern astronomers. A mean distance of 238,857 miles is too close to the sordid Earth; the worthwhile must surely be at the furthest limit of the telescope. Another excuse has been put forward for neglecting the moon. The German astronomers, Beer and Mädler, made such a precise and detailed map of the surface of the moon in 1837 that further study was unnecessary. Both excuses, although weak, have an element of truth, and we have needed the impact of the space age to revive an interest in the face of the moon.

Johannes Hevelius produced the first good map of the moon in 1647. With a telescope set on the balcony of his house at Danzig he worked through the long night. Frau Elizabeth helped him in the work and continued as an amateur astronomer after her husband's death. Hevelius and his wife must have had long discussions when they chose names for the places on the moon. Scattered over the surface were hundreds of mountain rings or craters. Should they be given numbers or should they be named after astronomers or towns on the Earth? Johannes saw the risks in a personal system; some people were bound to be dissatisfied either because they were left off the moon or because their crater was too small. He therefore named the craters after towns and countries on the Earth. Several mountain ranges were visible and these were given familiar names such as Alps, Apennines, and Caucasus. Large dark areas were seen through the telescope, and Johannes and Elizabeth, thinking these areas were ocean, gave them the name Mare, Latin for sea.

The next important map was produced in 1651 by Riccioli and his assistant, Grimaldi, working in Bologna. Riccioli's map was not very accurate, but it was more successful than previous ones. With more courage, and perhaps a better understanding of psychology than Hevelius, he named the craters after great men. Tycho, Kepler, and Copernicus were there, and many influential people were flattered to find themselves immortalized even though they had never looked at the moon through a telescope. It was true that Galileo and Hevelius had had small features named for them and Riccioli and Grimaldi had chosen two of the largest craters for themselves, but Galileo was dead and Johannes was a quiet man. Riccioli's system for naming the craters was adopted, and nearly all the craters on this side of the moon left unassigned by him have now been named after astronomers born during the last three hundred years. As a compromise we still use the names of mountains suggested by Hevelius.

The photographs of the moon in this book are printed upside down with the South Pole appearing at the top of the page. This is for convenience. When you look through an astronomical telescope you will find the image inverted just as it is in the photograph. The telescope would have to be modified and the image would lose some clarity if it were the right way up. Astronomers prefer to have the clearest view, and it really is no inconvenience always to work with an inverted picture. However, if you wish to see the familiar face of the man in the moon you must turn the book so that south is at the bottom. Then you will see that Mare Imbrium and Mare Serenitatis form the eyes, and Mare Nubium is the mouth. The narrow sea of cold, Mare Frigoris, makes a furrowed brow. The seas are, of course, inappropriately named. It would be better to call them "plains" for there is no atmosphere and no moisture on the moon. There is less moisture on the moon than on Mars. The spectroscope shows no water vapor bands and we do not see a hoar frost forming in the regions of the moon where it is cold. The seas are flat, dry plains of dusty rock bounded at their edges by steep mountain ranges.

The advancement of knowledge does not proceed smoothly, but flows along a rough course, sometimes swirling around in an endless whirlpool. Sometimes you see a fragment of scientific research mushrooming into a heated argument where bad logic and personal prejudices are used as weapons. Ultimately, of course, the feuds die down and there is nothing left but the truth, but sometimes, if the protagonists are strong-willed, the argument will end only when they have been laid to rest. The craters on the moon have caused bitter feeling in the past, and the argument about their origin continues even today. However, the supporters of one side of the argument are elderly and it is only a matter of time.

There are many theories for the origin of the craters. According to one theory, huge blisters formed on the surface of the moon when it was molten and left behind a circular mountain range. This idea was suggested after someone watched bubbles bursting in hot mud pools in volcanic regions. But it is a long stretch from a mud bubble to a blister of rock some hundred miles across. Engineers have shown that the surface tension and strength of the molten rock would not allow such large blisters to form. Perhaps the craters are sink holes where a weakness has developed in the surface of the moon and the material has slumped downward. This idea failed to explain why the craters were exactly circular and how some craters could be embedded in the walls of others. Vesuvius has always made a great impression on the natural philosophers of Europe, and when the small volcanic island of Krakatoa exploded off the coast of Java and the gaping crater was exposed it was clear to everyone that the craters on the moon were extinct volcanoes. The surface gravity on the moon was lower than on the Earth and it was natural to expect larger lunar craters, or so they argued. Prints in old textbooks show jets of molten rock being thrown a hundred miles in the air, to fall back like a fountain around the edge. Anyone who supported the opposing theory, that the craters were blasted in the lunar surface by the impact of meteorites, was clearly wrong. Why, up to the turn of the nineteenth century, the French Academy of Sciences were sure that meteorites did not even exist. Today, by sheer weight of evidence, the meteorite hypothesis is gaining support, but before unfolding the story, volcanic astronomers would wish me to point out that I may be biased, for I have studied meteorites for many years.

Early astronomers wanted to believe in lunar volcanoes and distorted their results to agree with the theory. You can see how the famous Frenchman, Camille Flammarion, drew the Sea of Serenity (Plate 18). In the photograph it looks flat, but Flammarion has exaggerated the verticals, making some of the craters look like enlarged replicas of Vesuvius. Sir John Herschel in England watched the sunrise glinting on a lunar mountaintop, and was convinced that he was looking at an active volcano; such was the strength of the belief. A close look at the photographs, however, shows that the craters are shallow and are not like the lava cone of a volcano. If you stood in the center of Plato, for example, you would see an immense flat plain, and the crater walls would appear as a distant range of mountains, half obscured by the horizon. Ralph B. Baldwin, an American astronomer, has made a careful study of the shape of lunar craters.

The ratio of depth to diameter is what one would expect to find from a study of bomb craters and meteorite craters here on the Earth. If the walls of the craters were pushed in, there would be just enough material to fill up the hole. He concluded that each crater was an explosion pit caused by a violent impact. We shall see later how meteorites are continually falling on the Earth, and they must also be hitting the moon. Every thousand years, on the average, the Earth collides with an object weighing forty thousand tons. Part of the blow is parried by our own atmosphere, but on the moon a crater of some one or two miles in diameter would be produced. Through the long ages of the past, thousands of craters must have been produced on the moon in this way, and it is natural to presume that they are the craters we see today.

The crater named after Copernicus is a showpiece. Situated above Mare Imbrium, near the center of the moon, we look downward into this vast amphitheater. Shadows tell us that the craggy wall is 11,000 feet high and it is 56 miles from one side to the other. After the crater was formed land slides developed on the inner slopes, and a series of giant terraces can be seen where the rock has slipped away. Toward the South Pole you can see Tycho, the magnificent crater and probably the one most recently formed. Like Copernicus it has been blasted into position by the impact of a large meteorite. Baldwin's calculations indicate that a projectile some 2,000 feet in diameter, with a mass of 450 million tons, would be sufficient. From the present rate of fall of meteorites on the Earth, I estimate that the moon would be hit in this manner every 100 million years, but the bombardment may have been more severe in the past. Spreading out from Tycho is a remarkable system of bright rays. Some stretch for more than 2,000 miles around the moon, one passes down through the Sea of Serenity. The rays are formed from dust and debris spewed out from the explosion. The dust has settled on craters, mountains, and seas, and we know that Tycho is younger than any feature marked by the rays. But, argue the vulcanologists, Tycho and Copernicus have a central mountain peak, how can a mound of material appear at the seat of the explosion? Admittedly this is a difficult problem for the meteorite hypothesis. Many other lunar craters show a central peak, particularly the large ones. Small craters on the Earth, from a few feet to a few miles in diameter, do not show a central mountain, nor do craters of a similar size on the moon. Possibly in a large explosion there is a relaxation of the surface after the blow, and when the pressure is released material wells up from below to form the peak. If a crater some fifty miles across is ever blasted on the surface of the Earth we will be quite interested to see what remains, or develops, at the center.

When a crater approaches one hundred miles in diameter it is usually called a walled plain. Ptolemaeus, near the center of the disk, and Plato, at the lower edge of Mare Imbrium, are good examples. The walled plains must have been formed early in the moon's history, because they have been subsequently damaged by more recent impacts which have chiseled out fresh craters on the old floor. A powerful telescope shows many small craters on the floor of Plato and Ptolemaeus ranging in size from a few miles to 1,000 feet in diameter, and a visit to the moon would undoubtedly show innumerable craterlets. Some of the later damage can be seen in the photographs, one or two craters show on the floor of Ptolemaeus and cut into the mountain ring of the old walled plain.

Most astronomers think that the floor of a walled plain is made of lava, but this does not presuppose a volcanic origin, for lava can flow in sheets without forming a volcanic cone. The walled plains are large craters that formed at the beginning of the moon's history, when molten rock existed below a solid crust. A large meteorite was able to dig down sufficiently deep to release the molten rock, which then swamped the floor of the crater. In one of the walled plains, Wargentin, the lava forced its way upward until it became level with the mountaintops, and after solidification formed a large mesa or tabletop mountain.

By studying the floor at lunar sunset and sunrise, scientists have discovered a rough surface where at first glance it appears smooth. The surface darkens very rapidly at sunset because shadows are cast by the microscopic irregularities. We think that the lava flow is very irregular, like the fields of cinders found on the Earth. Some of the volcanic islands in the Pacific are so rough that your shoes are torn to shreds in a few hours as you walk over the surface. Even if the lava flow had been as smooth as glass to begin with, it would now be pitted, scarred, and crushed by the impact of the smaller meteorites that continually bombard the surface.

Professor Thomas Gold of Cornell University holds a minority viewpoint. According to him the floors of the mare are covered with a thick layer of dust, in some places reaching half a mile in thickness. We shall see shortly that there is evidence for a layer of dust on the moon, but not, perhaps, to the depth that Professor Gold suggests. It is, to be sure, easy to imagine a silken covering of dust when you look at a photograph of the moon, but measurements of the reflected light show that the surface is not as smooth as the photograph suggests. Our telescopes are not powerful enough to show the shattered surface. Under high powers, however, we can see innumerable craterlets on the floors of the walled plains, and it is difficult to imagine how these crisp structures could exist in a sea of dust. Also, as Professor Gold admits, it is difficult to explain how Wargentin is brimming over, and why the bright streaks from Tycho are not soon covered over by the drifting dust.

Let us now look at other features of the moon, the mountains and the seas. If you look at the Sea of Crisis, Mare Crisium, you will see an almost circular structure. You must remember that Mare Crisium is not at the center of the disk, and we do not look down onto the sea from above. Rather, we are looking at an angle, and the circular structure takes on the shape of an ellipse, as a saucer does when you look at it from the side. Mare Serenitatis and Mare Imbrium are also circular structures, and if you allow for the rotundity of the moon you can easily trace out the circular outlines. In fact most of the seas are circular areas, though the craters and walled plains have subsequently encroached on the edges of some of them. People who support the volcanic hypothesis are at a loss to explain the seas. Usually they refuse to believe that the outlines of the seas are circular. The problem then becomes much simplified, one has only to explain the occurrence of unconnected mountain ranges like the Apennines and Alps, and this can be done, though without much conviction, by supposing that mountain building occurs on the moon just as it does on the Earth. The meteoric hypothesis can, however, explain the circular outlines quite satisfactorily, and the seas then become the most spectacular regions on the moon. Let us take Mare Imbrium as an example.

Before Mare Imbrium was formed the surface was rough and mountainous, with a few scattered craters. A meteorite, some 10 miles in diameter, struck the surface of the moon a little north of the present center of the sea. The meteorite plunged into the surface, leaving for an instant a clean hole. Momentarily all was peaceful, then the energy was unleashed. The meteorite was vaporized in a blinding flash; the solid crust was lifted and torn away to expose a crater. Debris was shot out in all directions. Gigantic blocks were hurled across the countryside from the seat of the explosion, plowing through mountains and craters on their way. Hundreds of scars can be seen in the mountainous regions surrounding Mare Imbrium. A fine example is the valley of the Alps, a gorge punched through the mountains at the lower borders of the sea. This valley is 83 miles long, 6 miles wide in places, and up to 10,000 feet deep. The crust was folded back to form jagged mountains around the lip of the abyss. The original crater is marked by the Harbinger peaks today, and was some 350 miles across and perhaps 6 or 7 miles deep. Mare Imbrium itself is larger than this, being 700 miles in diameter, and was formed by the subsequent reaction of the moon to this traumatic blow. With an elastic rebound the moon developed a tremendous dome-shaped bulge with the crater perched on top. Twisting and quaking, the great dome crumbled under its own weight. The landslides left behind the precipitous edges that we now see along the Apennine and Alpine mountain ranges. The collapsing dome released lava from the interior, which flowed out to heal the cosmic wound and Mare Imbrium was born.

Astronomers can measure the temperature of the surface of the moon without leaving the comfort of their observatory. All hot bodies send out heat rays in the infrared portion of the spectrum, and the heat rays depend upon the temperature of the body. An open fire warms your body by infrared radiation, sometimes producing a feeling of discomfort if the temperature is high. The radiation can be stopped in an instant by placing a screen between you and the fire. Heat rays are also produced at lower temperatures, and you can feel them by placing your hand near the object, an electric iron for example. Astronomers use a delicate instrument, called a bolometer, to measure the heat radiation, and they can measure with precision the small amount of heat arriving at the Earth from bodies in space. As a simplification we can imagine an astronomer taking the moon's temperature by pointing a telescope and holding a thermometer at the other end.

Working at Mt. Wilson Observatory, E. Pettit and S. B. Nicholson measured the temperature of the full moon. It was 240° F., 28° hotter than boiling water. For two weeks the sun beats down relentlessly on the unprotected lunar surface until the rocks are hot enough to fry an egg. As evening approaches after the long day, the fury of the sun is abated, and at sunset the temperature drops to the freezing point. During the long night the temperature continues to fall as heat is radiated away into the black depth of space. At the low point, the temperature drops to about −234° F., but an exact measurement is difficult because at this low temperature the moon is radiating only a trickle of heat.

During an eclipse of the moon, when the heat of the sun is momentarily blocked by the shadow of the Earth, the moon cools down rapidly. During the course of an hour the temperature drops more than 300° F. Now solid rock does not cool off as rapidly as this; it retains the heat. We say it has a high "thermal capacity." The surface of the moon must be covered with a light dust which is unable to retain a large quantity of heat. A layer of dust cools very rapidly when the heat rays from the sun are obscured, and even if the underlying rocks are still warm the heat does not escape because the layer of dust acts as an insulator. By studying the way the temperature varies on the moon from hour to hour we can surmise what the surface must be like. A layer of dust, not more than half an inch thick on the average, is sufficient to explain the bolometric observations.

The words of Alexander Pope "Hope springs eternal in the human breast," describe our approach to at least two lunar problems. Certain people have cherished the hope of finding an atmosphere on the moon one day. They have also hoped to find some evidence of life, or at least to see some slight changes to prove that our nearest neighbor was not a dead world. Galileo and Hevelius realized that the lunar atmosphere was not exactly the same as the Earth's for no clouds could be seen, but the absence of clouds did not preclude an atmosphere of clear air. In 1790, the German astronomer, Johannes H. Schröter, was sure that he could see mists and vapors lying in the hollows of the craters, and he felt that he proved the existence of an atmosphere by observing a twilight glow along the terminator, or shadow line of the crescent moon. His mists and vapors were undoubtedly imaginary, together with the volcanoes that he saw erupting. Modern work shows a very faint glow from the dark side of the terminator, but it is definitely caused by scattering in our own atmosphere and not by air on the moon. Schröter continued his careful scrutiny of the moon for thirty more years, and began to see signs of smokestacks and lunar factories. His work stopped in 1813 when the French under Vandamme overran his observatory, burning his books, telescopes, and drawings. His life wrecked, Schröter passed away in misery.

Some fifty years later astronomers had found another way to detect an atmosphere. As the moon passed in front of a star it caused an occultation. The star drew closer and closer to a ridge of mountains on the edge of the moon, and then finally disappeared. The occultation was similar to a star setting below the horizon on the Earth, and by looking for refraction, twinkling, and absorption, astronomers hoped to discover an atmosphere. At first the observations were successful; the star appeared to hang momentarily above the mountain range before setting, held there by refraction. But there was a pitfall in the method. The mountain ranges on the moon appear bright when projected against the dark sky, and any measurements of their height are exaggerated. Consequently the brightly illuminated moon appears a little larger than it should, an effect known as "irradiation." The measured diameter of the moon was a little larger than the true diameter, and it was not surprising to find the occultation occurring a little later than expected.

As the problems of each new method of measurement are overcome, the same negative answer appears—the moon has no atmosphere within the limits of measurement. Each new method devised by scientists is more sensitive than the one before, and always the moon has insufficient atmosphere to measure. The most accurate method was devised recently by the Russian astronomer V. G. Fessenkoff. Like Schröter, he looked for the faint twilight scatter, but used a sensitive photometer and a polarizing disk. The polarizing attachment differentiated between light scattered by our own atmosphere and light scattered by the atmosphere of the moon. Fessenkoff again found no measurable air on the moon, and concluded that the moon's atmosphere was less than one ten-millionth as thick as the Earth's atmosphere. Recent measurements with space probes show that it may be even more rarefied than this, perhaps one million-millionth of the air we breathe on Earth.

The second hope is to find life. Schröter's reports of industrial activity were not scorned at the time, and French scientists, with serious intent, asked Louis XIV to construct a telescope 10,000 feet long to show the animals on the moon. When the atmosphere was shown to be too thin to support life as we know it, Flammarion put forward a new ray of hope that persists in some minds even today. At the close of a popular talk on astronomy the lecturer usually has to contend with it. A fish, Flammarion argued, would never believe that it was possible for anything to live without water, in the suffocating dryness of the land, yet the fish would be arguing quite illogically. Similarly how can we say that life cannot exist under extremely primitive conditions just because we ourselves cannot imagine it? With this argument, hope was rekindled, and for a while people still expected to find some form of intelligence.

In the nineteenth century the general public were rather susceptible to arguments of this nature, or, to put it more bluntly, were naïvely gullible. The *New York Sun* carried a long article in 1835 describing observations made by Sir John Herschel with his new telescope. Batmen, bird-men, and bison were "seen" along the shores of the azure blue lunar seas. Their temples and homes were described in great detail, but accounts of lunar behavior, especially between the sexes was propitiously censored. It was clearly a hoax, but not more than one person in a thousand realized the trick. The article was reprinted in pamphlet form and more than 60,000 copies were sold in America alone, some at $3.00 apiece. Later it had a profitable circulation throughout Europe as well. Further repeats of the hoax, however, were not successful and were treated purely as science fiction.

By 1900, although a few people clung to the belief that intelligent beings lived on the far side of the moon, most astronomers would commit themselves only to some low forms of vegetation existing on the crater floors. Plato and Eratosthenes were the most likely spots. The floor of Plato seemed to grow darker as the moon approached the full phase, and this darkening was supposed to be some form of surface vegetation thriving as the sun rose in the sky. But accurate measurements have recently shown that the darkening of Plato is an optical illusion. It is surrounded by the bright Alpine mountain range and it appears to darken because the Alpine range shines brightly in the sunlight. Eratosthenes showed faint gray colorations which seemed to spread over the surface as the lunar day progressed. Soon, no doubt, scientific precision will show that the dusky markings here are just changes in the coloration of the rocks as the sunlight creeps over them.

If there is no life stirring on the moon, then perhaps we can see some changes on the surface, some alteration which will allow us to say our neighbor does not stare down with a changeless gaze. Before photography was invented, there were indeed some notable changes on the moon. When the careful drawings of selenographers were compared, new craters were sometimes noticed which apparently had appeared overnight. Nowadays we have no sure way of checking the observations; the "new" crater could so easily have been overlooked by the first observers. Other craters are supposed to have disappeared. Linné, for example, was described as a "deep crater" in 1823 and 1831, yet in later drawings it was shown as a white spot. Even the drawing of Flammarion with its exaggeration of the vertical scale shows no surrounding wall. Did the crater walls collapse during some landslide or "moonquake," and is the "deep crater" now a pile of rubble? Hundreds of statements have been made during the course of a sometimes hot debate, but nobody has been able to produce convincing evidence for the collapse of Linné.

Minor changes based upon the comparison of sketches must always remain in doubt, and we prefer to rely upon the accurate photographs that are obtainable today. Changes are certainly to be expected. A large meteorite must one day strike the moon and form a crater visible from the Earth, and also our own efforts at shooting at the moon may produce a scar that we can see. Scientists are once again taking an interest in the lunar surface and if any major change does take place it will be noticed immediately.

Hungarian astronomers saw a cloud of dust stir as the Russian moon probe landed near the crater Archimedes, but the probe's crater was invisible. In November 1958 a Russian astronomer, Dr. Nikolai A. Kozyrev, observed a burst of light from the mountain peak at the center of crater Alphonsus. Was it a volcano? The spectroscope showed the presence of carbon atoms, and both Eastern and Western astronomers agreed that the observations were valid. In the United States we think that Dr. Kozyrev saw a gasp of gas escaping through the weakened crust in the floor of a meteoric crater. As far as volcanoes go, one puff does not make a theory. Yet this observation has revived the energies of the vulcanologists, and an argument which yesterday was one foot from the grave may become virulent once again.

CHAPTER 16

# MAN'S VENTURE

CORONA
BOREALIS

THE CALL OF THE UNKNOWN HAS ALWAYS BEEN IRRESISTIBLE TO
man. Now he is making preparations for the exploration of the solar
system, but the first steps in the exploration are quite small by astronomical standards. A few monkeys and mice have been shot a hundred miles or so into the air to be recovered from the Atlantic Ocean.
Russian scientists have placed in orbit around the Earth several dogs,
plants, and other biological specimens. No attempt was made to save
the first dog, "Laika," which died of suffocation in its space capsule.
The dogs "Belka" and "Strelka" were more fortunate because, after
eighteen revolutions around the Earth, a retro-rocket was fired to
bring them back through the atmosphere. Accompanied by forty mice,
two rats, a multitude of insects, and microbe specimens, they floated
down by parachute and made a safe return to Russian territory. Presumably after a routine checkup the entire crew was ready to fly again.

The culmination of the Russian space program came on the morning of April 12, 1961, with the launching of a man. Major Yuri
Gagarin circled the Earth at a height of 150 miles at a speed of
18,000 miles per hour. He survived the ordeal and was anxious to
fly again. In space he found that zero gravity conditions did not
affect him adversely, nor did he complain about the noise of launching, the acceleration, and the heat shock as his space ship re-entered
the atmosphere. We now know that man can function satisfactorily
in space, at least for a few hours at a stretch. In several ways man is
superior to automatic instruments. He is able to make decisions on
the spot and, if necessary, he can alter the program of the flight to
attain maximum advantage. He can also make repairs to the equipment if any malfunction occurs. There is a greater chance of making
a discovery when man himself is in space.

There are many hazards to be faced; at every turn the astronaut risks his life. At the end of the countdown period there is a definite chance that the rocket motor will be blocked or the ignition system will misfire. When this happens the giant rocket is engulfed in flames and the twisted fragments are scattered around the launching pad. The astronaut can be saved only by igniting the escape rocket which shoots him out of the danger area to float down by parachute a mile or so away. If the rocket ignites according to plan, then the astronaut has to withstand the fierce strain of the acceleration for about three hundred seconds. When he achieves orbit and is circling the Earth, these forces disappear and he experiences the feeling of weightlessness under zero gravity conditions. The feeling of weightlessness is quite pleasant for short periods of time; in fact, it seems to be the only pleasant sensation in store for the astronaut. Biologists, however, are not certain what the effects of weightlessness will be over long periods of time. The main functions of the body depend on muscle action and will continue in the absence of gravity, but other reactions may set in, such as space sickness or even insanity. Sickness in a space helmet would undoubtedly prove fatal, and space insanity would be equally horrible.

The astronaut has more dangers ahead when he is circling in orbit a few hundred miles above the surface of the Earth. There is a small but definite chance that he will collide with a meteorite, a massive object of stone or iron moving between the planets. Such a collision would occur at a speed of about fifteen miles per second; death would be instantaneous. Even the smaller meteor fragments would damage his vehicle by eroding the surface like a blast of sand. We, on the surface of the Earth, are protected by the atmosphere. Small meteors are destroyed as they impinge on the air. The atmosphere also shields us from the effects of cosmic rays, charged particles which approach the Earth with the speed of light. Even with the protection of the atmosphere, about eight cosmic rays pass through our bodies every second, and the rate is much greater in space. At the level of eight per second we are safe; each particle damages a number of cells as it strikes us but the body is able to repair the damage. If the astronaut is not provided with adequate shielding, then he will receive an overdose and will become seriously ill with radiation sickness. To make matters worse, there are belts of charged particles which are trapped in the magnetic field of the Earth. Although these Van Allen belts contain particles of lower energy than cosmic rays, it is still difficult to provide adequate shielding. Occasionally the sun erupts with a solar flare, and for several minutes the surrounding space is filled with gamma rays, neutrons, and protons against which it may be impossible to give adequate protection. If by mischance a solar flare does occur during a space flight, there may be nothing we can do to save the astronaut.

The American space program is under the guidance of the National Aeronautics and Space Administration which was formed by Act of Congress in 1958. Long-range plans are necessarily tentative, and it is always presumed that we will be able to overcome obstacles such as the Van Allen belts, the gamma rays from the sun, and space sickness. The reactions of men are being tested in Project Mercury, Commander Alan B. Shepard becoming the first American spaceman on May 5, 1961. The initial explorations of deep space will, however, be carried out with instruments. A standardized rocket, the Saturn, will be modified slightly for each of the different missions. Saturn contains a cluster of motors burning liquid fuel and developing a total thrust of one and one-half million pounds. As designed, Saturn is capable of lifting seven hundred tons, placing a space craft of ten tons in orbit around the Earth, ejecting a three-ton load between the planets, and placing a one-ton capsule with delicate instruments on the surface of the moon. The Saturn rocket is sufficiently powerful to carry an astronaut around the moon and back to the Earth, but it will not permit a landing on the moon with a subsequent return to Earth unless more powerful fuels are developed for the second and third stage motors.

It is perhaps fortunate that our technology is limited, for it is more prudent to send instruments to the moon before we send a man. "Ranger" has the limited objective of placing a seismometer on the moon in 1962. The space craft itself will be smashed but, just before impact, the instrument package will be ejected for a soft landing controlled by retro-rocket. The seismometer will detect tremors caused by moonquakes and meteorite impacts, sending the data by radio back to the Earth. "Surveyor" is scheduled to be placed on the moon in 1963. As its name implies, Surveyor will give us detailed pictures of a particular area on the moon. It will measure the magnetic field, cosmic radiation, and will send back a television picture of the scenery. "Prospector," a roving vehicle, will follow a few years afterward. It will move by command from the Earth over the surface of the moon, greatly extending the survey. Journeys of fifty miles or more are planned with this vehicle, and with a sufficient fuel supply we might be able to guide Prospector across a flat area as large as Mare

Imbrium. Mountain ranges and crevasses will be impenetrable unless the vehicle can be modified to hop from point to point.

The planets also will be explored by instruments before they are visited by man. Venus and Mars, our nearest neighbors, will be reconnoitered by "Project Mariner" between 1962 and 1966. The space craft will pass close by the planet to measure such quantities as atmospheric composition, ionosphere levels, and radiation belts. When the Saturn cluster is fully perfected, the Mariner probe may be sent to more distant planets such as Mercury and Jupiter. By 1966 the National Aeronautics and Space Administration hope to replace Mariner by "Voyager," a project in which a satellite is placed in orbit around another planet. From the satellite, a capsule is parachuted down to the surface. Aided by the Saturn rocket, Voyager has sufficient thrust to place powerful instruments on Mars or Venus. With their aid we will be able to survey the landscape, bore into the surface, listen for tremors, and even search the soil with a microscope for bacteria, spores, and other signs of life.

We would all like to know the answer to the question "Are there other forms of life in the universe?" As we have seen in the last few chapters, the moon is not a very likely place to find life. The planets are equally inhospitable except, perhaps, for Mars where we can already see areas of vegetation through the telescope. The space probe on Mars will tell us a great deal about this plant life and may also introduce us to weird forms of bacteria, viruses, and peculiar insects.

Our primary interest is to find some form of intelligence. We can offer very little hope of finding any intelligent beings on the nine planets from Mercury to Pluto, or their satellites—yet we are still optimistic. The whirlpool theory leads us to believe that the formation of the sun and its attendant planets was not an unusual event. A large number of dust clouds have already been photographed, and we feel sure that many of these clouds will ultimately condense to form another sun and another solar system. The stars themselves are very much like the sun; it is only their great distance that makes them appear faint. Many of these stars must already have planets circling around them, and many of these must be at the correct distance from the star to recreate conditions as we know them on the Earth. Unfortunately our telescopes are not powerful enough to show us these distant planets, but we feel sure they are there. If only one star in a hundred possesses a planetary system, there would be at least a billion planets in our galaxy, the Milky Way. Our galaxy is not alone in space; the 200-inch telescope reveals at least ten billion more.

It would be a very conservative estimate to say that there is one inhabitable planet for every person living on the Earth today.

Will we ever be able to reach these other worlds among the stars? The stars are at immense distances, and at the moment they are beyond our reach. The nearest star, alpha Centauri is 24 million million miles away. We prefer to use a new scale, the light year, when talking of such distances. The light year is the distance traveled by a ray of light in one year. Light can travel from the Earth to the moon in one second, to the sun in eight minutes. In one year it travels six million million miles. The distances of alpha Centauri can therefore be written as four light years. Even if our space craft could travel with the speed of light it would take four years for the astronaut to reach alpha Centauri, and then he might be disappointed to find a dead system. Other stars are at even greater distances, distances which at the moment seem impenetrable.

We can, of course, fall back on speculation and let our imagination travel the distance. Most biologists believe that life will develop from the inert chemicals of the universe whenever the opportunity arises. Thus some form of life is to be expected on every planet which is similar to the Earth. Yet evolution is a very erratic and unpredictable process so we cannot expect to find bodies with exactly the same form as man.

One cannot argue that man is ideally suited to his surroundings and is the final result of natural selection. On the contrary, he appears to have many anatomical defects. His skeleton and muscles are not particularly suited for an upright posture; without modern technology he would suffer from the cold of winter and the heat of summer, and wild animals would decimate his number. If one were to try to imagine a more suitable anatomy for man, his spine should pass through the center of his body to strengthen his upright posture. He should have spare parts, hearts, lungs, and digestive tracts distributed in three cavities around the central spine. An extra leg and extra arm would prevent his being badly incapacitated as he is at present when he loses a limb. His legs might be muscular rods, like the trunk of an elephant, to avoid the problems of joints, with suction pads instead of feet. No, man is not physically perfect, nor can we say he is adapted to his surroundings. Yet he does seem to represent the peak of evolution. The big difference between man and the other forms of life is the special adaptation of his brain. Man is intelligent and is capable of controlling his own environment. By this step forward he is able to use his material resources, he controls the other forms of life and may even be able to affect his own subsequent evolution. Although we do not expect to find life in the shape of man elsewhere, we do expect to find intelligence equal to or surpassing that of man. Intelligence and environmental control seem to be the ultimate form of evolution, whether they be vested in Homo sapiens, a tripod, or even a brain floating around on a stalk.

Science fiction may soon become science fact; speculation has brought us to a point where we have a chance of breaking the distance barrier. We begin to talk of "the principle of instantaneous development." Any species will develop its full capabilities almost as soon as it appears. If any intelligent life does exist on other planets, we expect it to be fully developed right now. Some of these forms of life may have a higher brain power than man and will already have developed a superior technology. We would expect them to understand the nature of light, the principles of radio, and the other facts of science which are part of the physical world. Science cannot remain unknown for long to any active society. These beings must study astronomy and must already have worried about the possibility of other forms of life. We would naturally expect them to search for other life, and they would surely recognize the sun and the solar system as a likely place. We, on the Earth, have developed radio transmitters and antennas to such a degree that it would be possible to send radio signals from the Earth to the nearest stars. Perhaps there are civilizations in space which, although separated by tremendous distances, are communicating with each other by means of radio. Perhaps for the last thousand years or so these civilizations have been beaming signals toward the Earth in the hope that our civilization had developed sufficiently to receive them.

The most likely stars to have inhabited planets within our range are tau Ceti, 61 Cygni and alpha Centauri. These stars are of Type G or K, similar to the sun, and they are all within a distance of eleven light years. Astronomers at the National Radio Astronomy Observatory at Green Bank, West Virginia, are at present monitoring these stars with a sensitive radio telescope in the hope of receiving signals. "Project Ozma," as it is called, is an attempt to seek out other life in a systematic survey which will move from star to star in the neighborhood of the sun. Perhaps we will receive signals, perhaps not—the search is a gamble with unknown odds. Discovery may come suddenly, or there may be several years of work ahead. We are at least making a first attempt to join in the community of the universe that we feel sure exists.

Yuri Gagarin, first in the East    Alan Shepard, first in the West

We do not expect to be able to interpret the signals immediately they are received, for the method of communication will most surely be quite different from anything we have met with on the Earth. Nor will it be possible to set up two-way communications, for even with alpha Centauri it would take eight years to send a message and receive an answer. Rather, we will be forced to use a two-way system in which neither speaker is heeding the other. We will record and attempt to decipher all the signals that come to us, and at the same time we will send back a stream of information to be received years later at the other star. Perhaps at first we will communicate by a series of numbers, to prove that we understand mathematics. Later we may hope to set up a more general communication system with future generations of the Earth learning from our neighbors. Perhaps they will be able to help us with our unsolved Earth problems, perhaps they will tell us how to develop space machines to break the distance barrier. We may one day be guided safely through the void between the stars to undertake *a search for kin*.

# PART IV
# SECRETS OF THE MILKY WAY

Sunspots and the photosphere of the Sun, from a nineteenth century drawing by Samuel Pierpont Langley. (The New Astronomy, S. P. Langley, Houghton Mifflin)

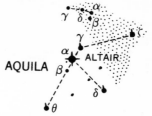

# THE POPULATION
# OF STARS

A STAR IS RATHER DISAPPOINTING WHEN VIEWED THROUGH A TELE-
scope. It appears quite bright, but you can see no more detail than
with your eye alone. Sir William Herschel and his son were obliged
to shade their eyes when the 48-inch reflector was pointed toward a
bright star like Sirius, for the star would dazzle them by its brilliance,
causing night blindness for half an hour or so. A telescope certainly
increases the brightness of a star by collecting a large amount of light,
but the star will never show as a disk, because it is so far away. To see
more detail on the stars, we would need a giant telescope to provide
us with the necessary resolving power. We would need a mirror one
mile across to show the stars as a disk. Even then, the view would be
indistinct because of the disturbances in the Earth's atmosphere which
cause the image to dance and shimmer. We are limited, we are frustrated by the gulf that separates the stars from the Earth, and we
see no more than the ancient stargazers. The secrets of all the stars
are hidden in a fiery point of light; all stars except one—the sun.
Before exploring the stars in the Milky Way, we should look at our
own star, for the sun will act as a guide.

The sun has a bright edge, and when it is setting on the horizon it
is easy to imagine that it is a solid disk. However, it is not solid, it is a
glowing ball of gas. The bright surface is called the photosphere, or
"sphere of light," and is a region where the gas becomes opaque, ob-
structing our vision. We cannot see below the photosphere. There is
still gas present above the photosphere; in fact the sun has a semi-
transparent atmosphere. The lower layer of the atmosphere is hot and
glows with a dull red light. It is called the chromosphere, meaning

"sphere of color." Usually we cannot see the chromosphere because the brilliant photosphere dazzles our vision. When the moon covers the photosphere during an eclipse of the sun, the chromosphere comes into view, shining like a crimson ring around the moon. Also during an eclipse we can see the outer atmosphere of the sun, the corona, which shines with a pale green light. The veil-like corona is a rarefied gas, fluorescing in the sunlight. Atoms of iron, neon, and other elements absorb a portion of the sunlight, hold it momentarily, and then send out the energy once again. Each atom, as it fluoresces, sends out light of a distinct color. Solar energy is thus absorbed and re-emitted with the trademark of the atom. A spectroscope splits up the light of the corona into the various colors, and once these colors have been separated we have the answer to the mystery of its light. Unfortunately astronomers were rather slow in their detective work. For nearly fifty years the green lines in the corona were supposed to be due to a new element, unknown on the Earth. It was called "coronium." Year by year chemists filled the gaps in the table of elements until all ninety-two elements had been found, and there was no room for coronium. The astronomers' embarrassment was relieved when the Swedish scientist, B. Edlén, showed that the green lines were produced by atoms of ordinary iron which were stripped of electrons. Normally an ion consists of a nucleus within a cloud of twenty-six electrons, but at high temperatures some of these electrons escape. The iron atoms in the corona have lost ten electrons, and this occurs at a temperature of several million degrees. At first some astronomers were skeptical about the high temperature in the corona but it has been confirmed by other methods. For example the electrons torn from the iron atom send out radio signals, and from the strength of the signals we again find a temperature of several million degrees.

The corona and the chromosphere are heated by explosions from below. The photosphere is a seething inferno where mushroom-shaped clouds rise to the surface with a load of searing heat. Through a powerful telescope you can see millions of bright cells in the photosphere. Each one is like a giant hydrogen bomb, spreading over five hundred miles of territory. These upheavals pound incessantly on the base of the chromosphere and corona, and the layers become heated by the blows. Sometimes the photosphere erupts with unusual violence, and then material punctures its way through the chromosphere out into the corona. A stream of incandescent gas rushes for thousands of miles through the atmosphere of the sun. As it moves it is guided by magnetic lines of force, following a curved path out to the corona and back to the photosphere. We see the glowing gas more easily when the glare of the photosphere is obscured. During a total eclipse of the sun bright tongues of gas, called prominences, project from the edge of the sun. Imaginative people sometimes see a prominence take the shape of a dinosaur, a prehistoric lizard, or other weird things.

If you follow the prominence down through the sun's atmosphere toward the surface, it leads to a region of disturbance. Most prominences begin and end at the edge of a sunspot, the dark blemishes first seen by Galileo. The dark spot itself is not a storm region but a region of quiet, a cool patch isolated from the surrounding photosphere by a strong magnetic field. Around the spot, however, the sun is in violent upheaval. Energy from the interior of the sun is pouring out around the edge of the spot, causing explosions and ejection of material. Sometimes the explosion is so violent that a portion of the photosphere is blown off, and leaves the sun completely to move between the planets as an ionized cloud.

The sun is continually in action, squandering a tremendous amount of energy. A small part of this energy falls on the Earth. It is absorbed by plants which supply us with food, it is preserved in the coal seams which give us fuel, and it supplies the heat which maintains the warmth of the ocean. We therefore have an interest in the energy of the sun, for if it should cease we would die. The energy is released by atomic fusion, deep below the photosphere. Our view is blocked by the glowing layer of hydrogen, the so-called surface, and our telescopes cannot penetrate to the interior of the sun where the energy is produced. At this level the sun becomes unobservable, and our nearest star can tell no more than the other distant points of light. It would, of course, be quite impossible to explore the interior of the sun by sending a space ship from the Earth. Even if the space ship could pass rapidly through the corona and chromosphere, the photosphere itself with its temperature of 10,800° F. would cause the space ship to vaporize. But we can explore these inaccessible regions by another method. Theoretical physics is now a powerful tool, and a scientist can now explore the interior of the sun and stars with a computing machine and the laws of physics.

At the start of the journey into the interior, astrophysicists assume that the sun is balanced. Every cloud of gas is held in position by equal forces pressing on all sides. At any chosen depth there is a downward force. This is caused by the pull of gravity, and a wisp of gas down there has to support the weight of gas above. The wisp is supported by an upward force from below. Part of this force is supplied by radiation pressure, and part by gas pressure. Light and other forms of energy continually flow outwards from the center of the sun, and the gas particles tend to float in the brilliant stream. Gas pressure is caused by the collision of minute particles, each collision producing a small force. When the gas is compressed, more collisions occur, more force is exerted, and we say the gas pressure has increased. The gas pressure also increases as the temperature increases. Then the particles move around more rapidly, more collisions occur, and a greater force is produced.

The astrophysicist has to explore the interior of the sun step by step, proceeding at first by a process of guesswork. From the photosphere he moves down several miles, and calculates the load of the overlying material. He then chooses a temperature which will produce sufficient gas and radiation pressure to balance the downward force. He then repeats the process, moving step by step till he reaches the center of the sun. Although the calculations are laborious when made by hand, they can be carried through in a few minutes with electronic computing machines. Only one solution can be correct. The guesswork solution has to be checked to see whether or not it gives the correct mass for the sun and allows for a uniform flow of energy from the center to the surface. If these conditions are not met, the solution is incorrect, and the calculation must be repeated with a different guess for the temperature steps. The process can, at times, become exasperating, but usually a solution can be found in the end. The astrophysicists are very persistent. As Dr. Martin Schwarzschild of Princeton said, "The sun has to solve these equations in order to qualify as a star. If the sun has solved them, so will we!"

Dr. Schwarzschild's latest calculations give a temperature of 27 million degrees Fahrenheit for the central regions of the sun. The calculations for other stars show that they also have high temperatures at the core, so the sun is a typical star in this respect. The high temperatures are a clue to the tremendous output of energy from the sun. Year after year billions of kilowatts are squandered into space, and we on the Earth receive only a tiny fraction of this energy. The energy is released by nuclear fusion as in a hydrogen bomb. Protons of the hydrogen nucleus collide with tremendous speeds because of the high temperature. Four protons coalesce to form the nucleus of the rare gas helium. While the protons are joining together, a small fraction of the material disappears. If the four protons together weigh 400 units, the helium nucleus weighs only 397. About 1 per cent of the matter has disappeared; it has been annihilated. Einstein has shown that when a small amount of material is destroyed, a large amount of energy takes its place. If we could convert a pint of water into energy we could supply all the power needed on the Earth each day for lighting, heating, and heavy industry. Thermonuclear fusion is the most efficient process we know for creating energy. Nature has chosen it as the power supply for the sun and the stars.

When an astronomer turns from the sun to the stars his problem is a little more difficult. He cannot see any details, and his sole source of information is the coloration of the light. With a spectroscope all the various colors are displayed side by side in intricate detail. Some stars show a continuous gradation of color through the spectrum from deep red to blue, while others have fine absorption lines where certain colors have been absorbed in the atmosphere of the star. Some stars have bright emission lines, shining with a blend of a few distinct colors. We know that the continuous spectrum of the sun is generated at the shining surface, or photosphere, and we presume that the continuous spectrum of a star is also produced from an incandescent surface. The stars which emit bright lines have a hot, rarefied atmosphere, like the corona of the sun, where the distinct colors are produced. The dark absorption lines are removed from the continuous spectrum by atoms and other particles suspended in the chromosphere of the star, and by analyzing the dark absorption lines we can identify the various elements, making a rather exact chemical analysis.

When all the colors are added together, as in the human eye, we measure the total intensity of light from the star. This brightness is measured in units of magnitude. To get a true comparison of the brightness of stars, however, we must be careful to allow for the effect of distance. Two stars which appear equally bright in the sky might be quite different if we could visit them with a space ship. One star might be faint and near to the Earth, the other star might be brighter and further away. Nearby stars, of course, tend to appear brighter to us because of their proximity. If a star is brought from a distance of ten light years to a distance of one light year from the Earth, then its apparent brightness will increase by one hundredfold, or five magnitudes. Thus when comparing the brightness of stars, astronomers are forced to allow for the effects of distance, and the brightness of all stars is reduced to a standard distance of thirty-three light years. When the correction for distance has been applied, we have found the absolute magnitude of the star, and have a true measure of its brightness. The absolute magnitude tells us how bright the stars would appear if they were all lined up at a standard distance of thirty-three light years.

On a clear moonless night you can see more than two thousand stars, and with a telescope the number jumps into the millions. The work of the astronomer would never end if all these stars were different. If stars showed as many individual traits and variations as people, for example, a complete survey would be impossible. Fortunately the millions of stars can be arranged in eight broad classes, according to their spectral type or color. We use letters of the alphabet to distinguish between one star and the next, but there was much argument, discussion, and changing of minds before the system was finally established. The letters have therefore finished up in some disorder:

O  B  A  F  G  K  M  N

Each letter represents a distinct class of star, easily identified from its spectrum. There is as much difference between an O star and N star as there is between a man and a mouse. Although the letters are jumbled, the classes are firmly established and are learned by each succeeding generation of astronomers. To aid the memory some professors suggest the mnemonic "Oh be a fine girl kiss me now."

TABLE 3. CLASSIFICATION OF STARS

| Spectral Type | Photosphere Temperature °F | Color | Sample Star |
|:---:|:---:|:---|:---|
| O | 100,000 | Blue | Orion's sword |
| B | 45,000 | Pale blue | Spica |
| A | 20,000 | Blue-white | Sirius, Vega |
| F | 13,000 | White | Procyon |
| G | 11,000 | Yellow | Sun, Capella |
| K | 9,000 | Pale orange | Aldebaran, Arcturus |
| M | 6,000 | Orange | Betelgeuse, Antares |
| N | 5,000 | Red | None for naked eye |

Fifty years ago when the spectral classes were being arranged in order, astronomers did not realize the significance of the series. We now know that the difference among the eight classes is entirely one of temperature. The O stars have extremely hot photospheres with temperatures of 100,000° F., the B stars are a little cooler at 45,000°, and the temperature decreases until we find the coolest stars, the N stars with photospheres at 5,000° F. Of course these classes are broad and many stars fall at the boundary between two classes. Each class is subdivided into ten subsections, a star near the boundary between G and K being a G 9 star. Our sun has a photosphere temperature of 10,800° F. and is a G 2 star. The temperature of the star depends upon its bulk. If the sun were ten times as massive, more energy would be released in the interior, and its surface would rise to a temperature of 100,000°. The sun would then be an O star. If the

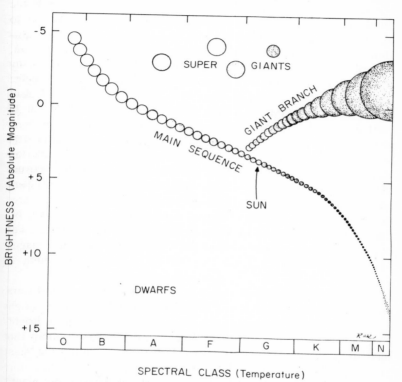

Fig. 25.    The Hertzsprung-Russell diagram showing the grouping of stars according to brightness and spectral class

mass were one-tenth as large, the surface would be cooler, and the sun would be an N star. You can see the differences in the stars for yourself without a telescope, because the color depends upon temperature. The hot B stars are pale blue, F stars are white-hot, and intermediate stars, like the sun, appear yellow. The cooler stars glow with an orange or dull red color. A fine example of a cooler star is Betelgeuse in the shoulder of Orion. Colors, of course, are subjective, depending to a great extent on your eyesight. Also, the eye loses all sensation of color when the stars are very faint, so only stars of first magnitude are sufficiently bright to give a color impression. The colors listed in the table are my own impressions, and if you look at these stars yourself you might disagree to some extent.

The temperature of a star also controls its brightness. An A star is one hundred times brighter than a G star, and a G star is one hundred times brighter than an M star. The relation between brightness and temperature was first noticed by the Danish astronomer Ejnar Hertzsprung and the American astronomer Henry N. Russell. In 1913 Russell arranged all the known stars in a special diagram. Each star was set at a certain distance along the page according to its spectral class and at a height corresponding to its absolute magnitude. Russell was quite surprised to find that the many thousand stars that he plotted formed a narrow line, a sequence. Class B stars were very bright with absolute magnitudes of $-2$, and the cool M stars were much fainter with absolute magnitudes of $+12$. The line of the stars was called the main sequence and showed a clear relationship between the various spectral classes. From a study of the myriads of stars came an orderly array of points; from observational chaos order appeared in the population of stars. The sun is a member of the crowd, occurring in the lower half of the main sequence. If the sun were taken out to a distance of thirty-three light years, it would be fifth magnitude, and it would be lost among the many stars on the limit of visibility.

To the right of the main sequence we find a second group of stars. Here some stars of Type K and M are many hundred times as bright as the stars on the main sequence. Because of their excessive brightness, members of this group are called giants, and the pattern that they form in the Hertzsprung-Russell diagram is called the giant branch. A few stars are found shining ten or a hundred times more brightly than the giants. These brilliant stars are called super giants, and occur with all spectral types from B to M. A few stars occur below the main sequence because they are several thousand times fainter than ordinary stars. In view of their faintness, these stars are called white dwarfs. Several years ago stars in the lower half of the main sequence were also called dwarfs, but since this region includes the sun, astronomers try to avoid this name with its stigma of inferiority.

This orderly array of characteristics was found by observing stars in the sun's neighborhood. It was the first grouping to be discovered, and stars within the group are known as Population I stars. During World War II, the subdued lights of Los Angeles permitted Dr. Baade to study more distant groups of stars. From his work he found a second population of stars whose members produced a slightly different pattern in the Hertzsprung-Russell diagram. In Population II, there is an absence of stars in the upper level of the main sequence, in spectral classes O, B, and A. Also the stars on the main sequence are about one-half as bright as their Population I counterparts. We now know that Population I stars are a minority group in the universe, and that Population II stars predominate. There is strong segregation, and stars of one population are seldom found amongst members of the other. The difference between the two populations seems to be one of fecundity. The sun belongs to a group where new stars are continually being produced to replace the older stars. In Population II, no new stars are appearing; the population is not being replenished. If Providence does not intervene, every cloud of Population II stars is doomed to extinction.

CHAPTER 18

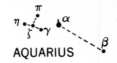

AQUARIUS

# BETWEEN THE STARS

THE PALE BAND OF THE MILKY WAY SPREADS ACROSS THE SKY, running through the sparkling constellations of Cygnus and Aquila. For northern observers the Milky Way passes overhead during the evenings of the late summer. If you move out into the country away from the glare of city lights you can see the white patches joining and merging to form a continuous arch. If you look at the Milky Way with binoculars you will repeat the discovery of Galileo. The Milky Way is the hazy glow from millions of faint stars, which cannot be seen separately by the naked eye. The Milky Way is a system of one hundred billion stars, called the local galaxy. The center of the galaxy is in the direction of the constellation Sagittarius, and the sun and all the other stars are whirling around this center, like a gigantic solar system. As they move, the stars form into long, curving arms. If we could view the galaxy from the outside it would appear as a spiral wheel, suspended in the darkness of space. It is so large that light would take eighty thousand years to travel from one side of the wheel to the other. To travel through the thickness of the wheel, light would take fifteen thousand years. Our sun is embedded in one of the spiral arms some thirty thousand light years from the center of the galaxy. We, on the Earth, cannot see the full splendor of the galaxy, because we are within it. We see the wheel edge-on and the spiral arms are superimposed to form a single band in the sky. Astronomers have for many years probed the Milky Way with telescopic cameras to see the stars and other objects that form the nearby spiral arms.

The stars of Population I are scattered along the spiral arms in vast clouds. All classes of spectral type are mixed together; we can, for example, find any type of star, giant or dwarf, in the neighborhood of the sun. Photographs of the Milky Way give us the impression that the stars are closely packed together. This is an illusion, for the image of the star exaggerates its size. The average separation between stars in the spiral arms is about four light years, twenty-four million million miles.

At first astronomers thought that the space between the stars was empty, but it is not. The spiral arms are filled with a tenuous gas. In places the gas has collected together to form clouds, and even between the clouds the gas still exists in a rarefied state. A faint fluorescence of a deep red hue has been detected from the clouds, showing that the gas is hydrogen. The faint red glow can be traced with very sensitive instruments between the clouds for most of the length of the Milky Way. The brightness of the glow tells us how many atoms of hydrogen there are in a cubic inch. The number varies from several thousand to a lower value of ten. Thus no space in the galaxy is completely empty. If you search for a place where you would be alone, you would always have to tolerate the presence of ten hydrogen atoms in every cubic inch.

The clouds of glowing gas are spectacular objects in the sky. One of the most impressive clouds is the great nebula of Orion, which spreads around the stars in Orion's sword. The cloud can be seen with binoculars or a low power telescope, but the best view is given by a long exposure photograph. At the center of the nebula are four Class O stars, which appear to the naked eye as a single star, the middle star of the sword. There are many other O and B stars scattered through the cloud, and the ultraviolet radiation from these stars is causing the gas to fluoresce. Hydrogen, oxygen, and nitrogen in the cloud absorb a portion of the starlight, and send it out once again with a different color. If the stars were not present in the cloud, then the gas would not fluoresce and would remain invisible to our eyes. It would be much more difficult to detect.

If we could place the solar system in the Orion nebula, we would be dwarfed by comparison. The glowing cloud is twenty-six light years across and the entire solar system would appear as a tiny pinpoint on the photograph. Our lives would not be very much different in the nebula, however. The night sky would glow with a faint, pale green, but the nebula would be too rarefied to affect the Earth's atmosphere. Astronomers would complain of the glare, but life would otherwise be normal.

The pale green color, which is so characteristic of gaseous nebula, was difficult to explain. Physicists had never detected this green spectral line from any of the known elements in the laboratory. Astronomers began to talk about a new element "nebulium," a gas which existed only in the nebulae. Nebulium, however, like the hypothetical coronium in the sun, was found to be an ordinary chemical, under unusual conditions of excitation. Dr. Ira S. Bowen, director of the Mt. Wilson and Palomar Observatories, showed theoretically that the green line is produced, under exceptional circumstances, by an oxygen atom which has lost two electrons. The emission can take place only if the oxygen does not suffer a collision. If a collision occurs during the moment of fluorescence, the green line is not produced and the radiation is emitted at a different wave length. The line was called a "forbidden line," because it is impossible for the emission to take place from oxygen in the laboratory. In the laboratory we can never reduce the gas pressure sufficiently to prevent a collision between atoms. Even with the best laboratory vacuum, the oxygen is always interrupted during the emission process. In a gas cloud in space, however, the particles are well separated and oxygen emits the green line without disturbance.

No gas can escape our notice if it is near the giant stars of Class O or Class B, for the intense radiation tears an atom apart, causing it to reveal its presence. Hydrogen, within a distance of two hundred light years from an O star, is split into protons and electrons. The hydrogen has become ionized, and the O star can be found at the center of the sphere of broken atoms. This sphere glows in a manner similar to the gas in the Orion nebula. Occasionally a proton and an electron combine to form a hydrogen atom, and during the process light is emitted at the hydrogen wave length as the electron, step by step, approaches the proton. But the formation of the atom is only momentary; almost immediately it is ionized once again by the radiation from the central star. Thus the giant star illuminates an enormous sphere of gas around it, and appears even larger than before.

Not all O and B stars are enveloped in interstellar gas, and without the gas the stars do not normally develop a glowing domain. A few stars, however, have thrown off a shell of gas in the past, and this gas shines today as it moves outward from the star. White dwarfs with a high surface temperature sometimes do this, and we then find a glowing shell enclosing a faint star. Through a telescope the nebula shows as a small disk and can easily be mistaken for a planet. Because of this they are called "planetary nebulae," but, of course, apart from the appearance, they have no relation to the planets in the solar system.

They are not solid objects and do not move from month to month against the background of stars. Professor Donald H. Menzel of Harvard and Lawrence H. Aller of Michigan University have helped us understand the true nature of these objects.

There is a fine planetary nebula in the constellation of Aquarius, photographed by Walter Baade at Palomar Observatory. A shell of gas is expanding with a speed of fifty miles a second, and the original explosion or ejection took place about twenty thousand years ago. The central star is a dwarf, and appears faint on the photograph because most of its light is radiated in the ultraviolet. This radiation is intense, blowing the gas outwards with the wind of radiation pressure. The wind is blowing away the atmosphere of nearby stars. You can see how "comet tails" have formed from the material, pointing outwards from the central star. The entire illumination of the gas ring is caused by the hot dwarf at the center which appears so inconspicuous on the photograph. If we could look at the planetary nebula with ultraviolet eyes we would see the star in the center in its true brightness, shining like a lighthouse in the mist.

Although the planetary nebula in Aquarius looks like a flattened smoke ring, it really has quite a different shape. If you look carefully at the photograph (Plate 25) you will notice that the inner hole of the smoke ring is brighter than the sky surrounding the nebula. This is one indication of the spherical form of the shell. In the three-dimensional model, the glowing gas would curve upwards from the page, arching over the central star in a dome. As we look down on the spherical shell, the gas is thicker at the edges, and therefore shines more brightly. We have another argument to support the idea of the spherical shell. There are many ring-shape planetary nebulae in the sky. If the ring were indeed a flat smoke ring, we should expect to find at least some of these rings set edgewise to the Earth, to form a line or ellipse. Not one of the planetary nebulae show any effects of tilt, and we see a disk or smoke ring in every case.

In 1904, the German astronomer, J. Hartmann, was puzzled by the star delta Orionis. Hartmann knew that the star was a blue B star, showing very few absorption lines in its spectrum. Yet there was one absorption line, produced by the element sodium, which did not seem to belong to the star at all. In the following years other mysterious absorption lines were detected in starlight, and there was much discussion as to the cause. The calcium absorption line was found in the spectrum of several stars in the constellation of Orion. The spectrum of the eight classes from O to N are quite different from each other, yet the calcium line stood there in the same part of the spectrum whatever the class of the star. In 1909 the American astronomer V. M. Slipher solved the mystery. A cloud of interstellar gas exists between us and the stars, and the gas absorbs the same characteristic color from the light of each star. The interstellar gas had revealed its presence by disturbing the light of the background stars, and by tracing the blemish in the spectrum from star to star, astronomers could map out the extent of the cloud.

The gas contains a large number of elements: calcium, sodium, potassium, and iron. In fact if any element is capable of absorbing light when in a gaseous form, it shows up. Presumably, elements without absorption lines are also present, even though we cannot detect them. The gas seems to be composed of the same mixture of elements that form the atmosphere of the stars. In addition we find combinations of two or more atoms in the form of a molecule. Molecules of carbon plus nitrogen, carbon plus hydrogen, and oxygen plus hydrogen are often found. The constituents of the gas make an explosive mixture. Sodium reacts violently with hydrogen, and the molecules of carbon plus hydrogen would explode by themselves, without the addition of other elements. An explosion is prevented by the rarefied nature of the gas. When the number of atoms is no more than a thousand per cubic inch, then collisions between atoms are very infrequent. When a collision between two explosive atoms does take place, the violence of the reaction is dissipated in the surrounding void. Thus the chain reaction that runs through a compressed stick of dynamite cannot occur, and the interstellar gas is rendered harmless.

Large aggregates are gradually built up by the collision between the atoms. Chemical compounds appear in the form of particles, perhaps crystals, where several million atoms have joined together. We have no way of telling the exact composition of the particles that form in space, because after the atoms are joined together in a block, they no longer absorb light of a characteristic wave length. We presume that the particles are made of solid fragments, like sand (silicon dioxide), and of frozen ices, like water and carbon dioxide. Although we cannot find out exactly what the particles are made of, we know they are present. The interstellar dust grains form immense clouds, obscuring the light of the stars behind them.

When you first look at a photograph of the stars in the Milky Way, you imagine that the stars are grouped together. In reality the stars of the Milky Way are distributed much more uniformly than they appear in the photograph. The dark patches in the Milky Way are not a window through which we see the space beyond the stars. Instead, the dark areas are clouds of interstellar dust. The Coalsack is the best example of an obscuring cloud, but we cannot see it in the Northern Hemisphere, for it is situated near the Southern Cross. But we, in the North, can see a dark rift in the center of the Milky Way near the constellation Aquila, where a number of dust clouds are superimposed. The dust clouds are scattered around the spiral arms of the galaxy, and form a flattened disk. If we could view the edge of the galaxy from the outside, the dust would appear as a dark lane running through the middle.

The dust in space is a great hindrance to an astronomer, because it obscures his view. The clouds are located in the spiral arms where the most interesting objects are to be found. The astronomer can see only the portion of the spiral arm in which the sun is located, and the view is restricted in the arms on either side to a distance of some fifteen thousand light years. In particular the central nucleus of our galaxy, north of the tail of Scorpio, is completely obscured. If an astronomer wishes to explore to greater distances, he has to point his telescope away from the plane of the Milky Way, in the direction where the layers of dust are not so thick, but even where the dust does not block our view completely, it still causes trouble. Starlight becomes reddened as it passes through the clouds. The color change is due to the scattering of blue light by small particles, so that the red wave lengths of the spectrum predominate. The dust is acting like a red filter interposed between us and the star. A similar effect takes place in our own atmosphere when the colors from the sun are scattered by terrestrial dust particles. At sunset the red glow of the sun is caused by the longer wave lengths which have been able to penetrate through the layers of dust near the horizon. The shorter blue wave lengths have been scattered to the side and do not reach our eyes. During the day you can see the blue wave lengths quite easily, as they are scattered by the particles overhead to form the blue of the sky. If the atmosphere were removed, the sky would be dark, for there would be no particles to scatter the blue light from the sun.

By measuring the amount of reddening in starlight we can calculate the size of the dust particles in space. The particles are about one thirty-thousandth of an inch in diameter. The reddening also tells us the number of dust grains in a certain volume. There are, on the average, about one hundred of them per cubic mile. By earthly standards the dust pollution in space is not very great. The Earth's atmosphere carries millions of particles per cubic mile—fragments of rock, industrial smoke, and pollen. Yet the cosmic dust has an appreciable effect on a beam of starlight for the distances in space are immense. By comparison, the journey of starlight through our atmosphere is quite short. Thus the sprinkling of cosmic dust causes more trouble to the astronomer than the terrestrial smoke and haze.

In one or two areas of the sky we find relatively small clouds of dust. These can be seen only when they are projected against a bright background, such as an emission nebula. In the photograph of the bright nebula in Serpens, you can see many black specks, globules of dust. Each globule is small by cosmic standards, no more than one or two light years across, not much bigger than the domain of the solar system. Within the globules the dust particles are packed more closely than in the larger dust clouds. It seems as though a cloud of dust is being compressed into a small volume of space. We have so far been unable to see through a globule to obtain a measurement of the reddening of the light, and so it is difficult to tell how dense the cloud really is. We think that the dust particles may be packed as closely as the dust in our atmosphere, with many hundreds of particles in a cubic inch. Later, we shall see how these black specks in the photograph are critical in our theory of the evolution of the stars.

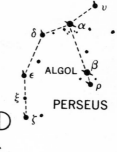

CHAPTER **19**

# TWINS AND
# MULTIPLETS

THE STAR IN THE MIDDLE OF THE HANDLE OF THE BIG DIPPER IS double. If you look with the unaided eye you should be able to see the bright star Mizar, and a fainter star Alcor, nearby. If you cannot see Alcor then you are either living too near the city, or you are in need of glasses. Although Alcor was rated as a test for eyesight by the Arabs some five hundred years ago, it is magnitude 4.5, and a person with normal eyesight should see more than a thousand stars fainter than Alcor. The two stars are one-fifth of a degree apart in the sky, which is quite wide. A person with 20-20 vision should be able to resolve the star epsilon Lyrae, two degrees east of Vega, where the components are less than one-twentieth of a degree apart.

Double stars are sometimes a chance alignment where two stars appear in the same direction, but one star is much farther away than the other. Double stars of this type would appear to separate if we moved from the solar system and looked at them from a nearby star. These unrelated stars, called "optical doubles," are of no special interest to the astronomer. If, however, the stars are at the same distance from the Earth, we are sure that they must be close together in space. Each star is then affected by the gravitational field of its companion, and the two stars revolve about a common center of gravity. Doubles of this type are of great interest to the astronomer, and are called "binary stars."

Alcor and Mizar form a visual binary. Alcor is within the gravitational field of Mizar, about thirteen thousand astronomical units away, and is moving in an elliptical orbit according to the three laws of Kepler. This binary has one of the widest separations known, and if the stars have a mass that is not much greater than the mass of the sun, Alcor will take a million years to make one journey around Mizar. This orbital motion, of course, is too slow to have shown itself yet, but other binaries are closer together and the movement can be seen from year to year. The star Castor, alpha Geminorum, is a binary with an average separation of 70 astronomical units, and the fainter star moves around the primary with a period of 380 years. Castor was one of the first double stars to be recognized as a true binary. When the first telescopes were turned toward it in 1770, the stars were well separated. Now, one-half a revolution later, the companion is quite close to the primary and is difficult to see. Some visual binaries have periods that are close to the period of the Earth. The binary Wolf 390 is a twin system where the stars revolve around a common center in 1 year, 8 months. The stars are about one astronomical unit apart, and the laws of Kepler and Newton show that the mass of each star is about one-half of the sun's mass.

Sometimes one of the components in a binary system is too faint to see. Then we have the odd occurrence of a star moving in an orbit without a companion. Sirius, the brightest star in the sky, is an example of a star with an unseen companion. After several years of observation, F. W. Bessel, at Königsberg, noticed that Sirius was moving in a wavy line. He concluded that Sirius was being deviated from a straight-line path by a companion star, and he was able to calculate an orbit. The announcement was made in 1844, and of course some people doubted the result, applying the adage "seeing is believing."

The doubt continued until 1862, when Alvan Clark, a telescope maker in Cambridge, Massachusetts, was commissioned to make a large telescope for the University of Mississippi. The lens was to be eighteen and one-half inches in diameter, three and a half inches larger than the Harvard telescope, which at the time was the largest in the world. For several months the glass blank was ground and polished with extra care. At night it was stored in a fireproof safe, and, as an extra precaution, Clark had a special alarm installed by his bed. At last the lens was ready to be tested. Its maker mounted it in a rough tube and pointed it at Sirius. He saw a double image. In a moment of dismay he thought there was an imperfection in the lens, but the second image turned out to be the companion predicted by Bessel. The companion has since proved to be a remarkable star, a white dwarf. It is very compressed so that, although it is faint, it has a large mass and is capable of swinging Sirius around in an orbit. The remarkable lens never reached Mississippi, because of the Civil War.

It was mounted at Dearborn Observatory, near Chicago, instead.

Sometimes two stars are separated by less than a tenth of a second of arc, and then they cannot be resolved in the most powerful telescope. If it were not for the Doppler effect, the binary nature would go undetected, and we would count the star as single. As the stars revolve around the common center, there is a position where one star is approaching us and the other star is receding. At this time the spectral lines of the approaching star are displaced slightly toward the blue, and the lines from the receding star to the red. Thus the spectral lines of a twin system appear double twice during each revolution. By measuring the slight displacements of the line accurately, astronomers are able to measure the speed of each star. Knowing the speed and the time taken for one revolution, they can calculate the distance around the orbit. It might seem that we can measure the orbital motion of binary stars without ever seeing them individually, but there is one snag. If we are looking directly down on the orbits, then both stars are always moving at right angles to the line of sight. Even though they are moving around a common center, they always keep exactly the same distance from the Earth. Under these conditions there is no velocity component in the line of sight, and the spectroscopic method fails. In fact the Doppler shift depends very much on the angle of tilt of the orbits, and yet this angle of tilt cannot be determined. Faced with this problem the astronomer takes a gamble, and assumes that on the average the angle of tilt is forty-five degrees. He has a considerable chance of being wrong with any particular binary, but in statistical problems, where he deals with the average of a large number of binary systems, his answer will be correct.

A spectroscopic binary holds the record for speed. The two stars which form DQ Herculis revolve with a period of only 4 hours, 39 minutes. The two stars must be so close that they touch each other. Perhaps they form a double teardrop, a Siamese twin among the stars.

Some astronomers have devoted their life to the measurement of double stars. The American amateur, S. W. Burnham, measured double stars every clear Friday and Saturday night for a period of over twenty years. With his six inch lens, made by the Clark brothers, he prepared a catalogue of 1,290 doubles, which forms a valuable reference for astronomers today. At the present time more than 23,000 visual binaries and 1,000 spectroscopic binaries are known. From a careful study of our neighborhood in the Milky Way we think that at least one star in two belongs to a binary system. Twin stars seem to be a common occurrence.

There are many cases of multiplets. The system of Alcor and Mizar is a good example. With the naked eye we see Alcor and Mizar separately as a wide visual double. It was certainly one of the first doubles to be seen by early man. The star Mizar itself was the first star to appear double through a telescope. The Italian, Riccioli, made this discovery in 1650, announcing that Mizar had a faint companion. The bright component of Mizar is also a spectroscopic binary, the first to be discovered by this method. In 1889, the American, E. C. Pickering, noticed that the spectral lines were doubled every 52 days, and the stars therefore revolved with a period of 104 days. Thus we now know of four stars in the group. The brightest component of Mizar is a twin system, unresolved by the telescope. Around this twin circles the telescopic component of Mizar, with a period of 3,000 years, while Alcor revolves around the trio with a period of about 1 million years.

The star epsilon Lyrae is a double-double. The two stars visible to the naked eye are each resolved in the telescope. Each pair revolves independently like an ordinary visual binary, and one pair revolves slowly around the other pair. Castor is a sextuplet. Each of the two stars seen in a small telescope is a whirling twin. Another faint twin system has been found moving in a large orbit around the four at the center. Multiplet systems always seem to form pairs, and if there is an odd star left over, it circles around the pairs in a large orbit. We have never found two or more stars revolving around the same primary, like the planets in the solar system.

On rare occasions, one binary star sometimes passes in front of the other, obscuring the light of its companion and causing an eclipse. An eclipsing binary gives us a wealth of information, because if an eclipse occurs, we must be looking edgewise to the orbit, and the tilt is known. The shift of the spectral lines gives us the exact shape and size of the orbits, and the mass of each star can be found precisely. In addition, as the star is eclipsed we can find out its size, shape, and surface brightness. An eclipsing binary is indeed a fortunate occurrence.

Sometimes observations with the naked eye are sufficient to yield important facts. The star Algol, in Perseus, for example, was known to vary its brightness when John Goodricke, at the age of nineteen, decided to make some systematic measurements. He watched the variation of brightness for eleven nights in 1783, and noticed that Algol grew faint every sixty-nine hours. The star remained dim for a surprisingly short period of time, seven hours, and Goodricke correctly suggested that Algol was being eclipsed by a large companion. By his simple stargazing, he was the first to discover a binary star. Unfortunately he was never recognized for this discovery, and the credit went to Sir William Herschel, twenty years later. Perhaps a black spot on Algol could cause the diminution of light as the star rotated, and so the evidence for a binary star was not conclusive. Nevertheless John Goodricke was given polite attention. He finished

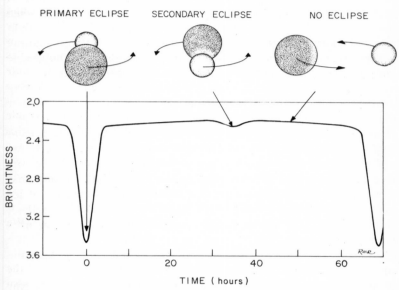

Fig. 26. Algol, eclipse followed by eclipse

his observations on May 3, 1783. On May 12, he mailed a letter from York to the Reverend Anthony Shepherd, who was a fellow of the Royal Society at Cambridge. From Cambridge the letter was taken by the first available stagecoach to London, and was read before the members of the Royal Society on May 15. Thus within nine days the scientific paper was written, within three days it was read before the learned society, and within three months it was published in the volumes of the philosophical transactions of the Royal Society. We seldom find such speed today.

Astronomers with accurate instruments can follow the variation of brightness hour by hour. A curve which shows the variation of magnitude is called a "light curve." The light curve of Algol shows the sudden eclipse, lasting no more than seven hours, as the dull companion moves in front. The bright star is not totally obscured, and some light shines over the top during eclipse. The exact shape of the minimum in the light curve tells the astronomer the diameter of the stars, and how much of the bright star is covered. We can therefore draw a picture to show how the two stars appear at various times through the cycle. There is a simple law in eclipsing binaries which cannot be broken—if Star A eclipses B then Star B will eclipse A. If we call the dull component of Algol A, then A is in front of B when the brightness decreases. Midway between the minima the bright star A eclipses the faint one B. This produces a secondary dip, midway between the primary ones. The secondary eclipse is scarcely noticeable with the eye, because the change of brightness is less than one-tenth of a magnitude. From this we conclude that the companion is glowing with only a feeble light. Between five hours and thirty hours after the primary eclipse we are observing the light from both stars without obstruction. The combined light from the stars of Algol should remain constant during this time, but the light curve on the contrary shows a slight increase. This increase is due to light reflected from the surface of the dull star. The side facing the bright star is heated and glows, giving it the appearance of a half-illuminated moon. We see the fully illuminated hemisphere just before the secondary eclipse, when the reflection increases the brightness by one-twentieth of a magnitude.

Sometimes one star is very much smaller than another, then the small star is unable to eclipse its large companion. The small star makes a transit across the bright disk. The combined light of the pair remains constant, and the primary minimum shows a flat bottom. When the small companion is in turn eclipsed it is totally obscured by its companion. The secondary minimum is also flat-bottomed, because during this time we are receiving the light from the bright star alone.

Some binaries, like DQ Herculis, are almost touching. Each star heaps up the material on the other, until the pair is pulled out of shape. The stars become elongated, and if they are members of an eclipsing binary system, the light curve is distorted. Beta Lyrae, the star six degrees south of Vega, is a fine example. The brightness does not remain constant between eclipses. After eclipse the stars revolve around the common center, and turn broadside on to the Earth. As they turn, more and more of the surface is brought into view, and the shape of the light curve is directly related to the shape of the stars.

There are some extra lines in the spectrum of beta Lyrae which result from the extreme closeness of the stars. At the point where the stars are nearly touching a continual stream of gas is leaving the bright star and swirling off into space. The bright star is losing gas at a rate of one billion tons per year, and there seems to be no replenishment. The gas is continually streaming outward in a spiral to join the clouds of interstellar gas. Astronomers wonder how long this process will last. If the rate of loss is maintained, the stars will have disappeared within three hundred thousand years. But we expect something to happen long before then. Perhaps the stars will slow down in their revolution, moving further apart so that this vigorous interaction will cease.

# CHAPTER 20

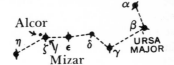

# CLUSTERS

SO FAR AS WE CAN TELL THE SUN IS ALONE IN SPACE. ALPHA Centauri, a triplet system, is our nearest neighbor. The average separation between the stars in a spiral arm is 8 light years. Alpha Centauri is 4.3 light years away, a little closer than the average, but not close enough to affect the motion of the sun by its gravitational field. In some regions of the Milky Way we see several hundred stars closely packed together with an average separation of about one light year. This is close enough for gravitational effects to occur, and the stars hold together as a group. The group is really a multiple star, but since the individual stars are not moving in a simple orbit, we prefer to use another name. We call them a galactic cluster.

Our galaxy must contain thousands of these clusters. We can see more than four hundred in the spiral arms near the sun out to a distance of ten thousand light years, and then our view becomes obscured by interstellar dust. The nearest cluster is in the constellation Ursa Major. The seven stars of the Dipper (excluding the stars at either end) and many fainter ones nearby form a stable group. These stars are moving together through space toward the constellation Draco, and will survive as a unit for many millions of years to come. Many of the fainter stars in Taurus the bull also form a cluster, and they are moving toward the constellation Orion. The stars of Taurus and Orion will appear to merge in about half a million years if the present rate of movement continues.

About ten degrees northwest of Taurus you can see another galactic cluster called the Pleiades, the seven sisters, or the "Micro-Dipper." A person with normal eyesight can see six stars in the group, and we are told by the ancient stargazers that the seventh star deserted the group, moving over to become Alcor, the companion of Mizar.

This is purely a myth, of course, as Alcor is moving along with Mizar and has almost certainly been a member of the Ursa Major cluster since it first began to shine. Binoculars will show many more stars in the Pleiades and, with photographic surveys, astronomers have already identified more than 250. It is interesting to compare the Big Dipper with the Pleiades. The clusters have approximately the same size but one is further away than the other. The bowl of the Big Dipper is 10 degrees across, whereas the bowl in the Pleiades is about ¾ of a degree across. As we look at the two clusters in the sky we would infer from the apparent size that the Pleiades were 13 times more distant than the Ursa Major stars. Accurate measurements confirm this estimate, the distances are 410 and 32 light years respectively.

If a cluster is much farther away than the Pleiades we cannot see it clearly with the naked eye. In the constellation of Cancer, the crab, there is a hazy patch of light called the "Beehive." Through binoculars, the hazy glow becomes a mass of stars and you are looking once again at a galactic cluster. Some clusters are very distant, and even in a telescope we see them only as a faint glow. Many other clusters must lie beyond our reach, lost in the distance and obscured by dust.

Galactic clusters are composed of stars of Population I, containing the bright, but short-lived, O and B stars. The clusters are always found in the plane of the galaxy, embedded in the spiral arms. The arms are filled with interstellar gas and dust, and this material infiltrates into the cluster. We believe that the stars in any particular cluster are all of the same age, and that they formed as a group from a single cloud. A typical galactic cluster is thirty light years across, and contains five hundred members. After formation the cluster moves along within the spiral arm, sharing in the general rotation of the galaxy, and the members keep together by mutual attraction. There are disturbing forces, however, which slowly break up the cluster. Differential rotation is the most serious of these. Some members of the cluster are closer to the galactic nucleus than others. The members on the inside track must move faster to balance the stronger pull from the nucleus of the galaxy. Thus after billions of years have elapsed, the cluster becomes elongated, until finally the aging stars are dispersed along the spiral arm.

When clusters form away from the spiral arms their shape is quite distinctive. The stars form a compact, round cloud which we call a globular cluster. The photograph shows a typical globular cluster in the constellation of Hercules. It is about four times as big as a galactic cluster, with a diameter of 120 light years, and contains many more members. Thousands of stars merge together at the center to become lost in the glare. We cannot count the stars in the cluster, nor can we measure the average separation. We can, however, obtain an estimate of the number by measuring the total brightness. The absolute magnitude of a globular cluster is −9, some 500 thousand times brighter than the sun. We presume therefore that the cluster contains about half a million stars. At the center the stars are about one-quarter of a light year apart, about as close as some of the visual binaries in the spiral arms. If the Earth were in a globular cluster, we would see a thousand stars brighter than Sirius, and the crowded constellations would shine on the landscape like moonlight.

Globular clusters are not found in the spiral arms. They are usually found above and below the plane of the galaxy, within a distance of ten thousand light years from the nucleus. More than a hundred globular clusters have been photographed and perhaps an equal number remain hidden. They form a spherical cloud around the nucleus—a cluster of clusters.

Like galactic clusters, we think that the stars in a globular cluster have formed at the same time. There is very little dust in the regions away from the spiral arms, and the stars in globular clusters are therefore all members of Population II. In the globulars we find no young stars of spectral type O and B, and we presume that these stars burned out a long time ago. Unless a fresh supply of dust is added to a globular, we expect the stars eventually to burn out, leaving no visible trace. If new stars are to be born in a globular cluster, the cluster will have to dip down into the spiral arms in a long elliptical orbit, where the supply of dust can be replenished.

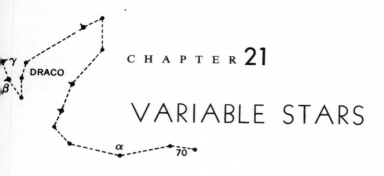

# VARIABLE STARS

ALGOL DECREASES IN BRIGHTNESS EVERY THIRD DAY, BUT ALGOL IS not really a variable star. The two components in the system shine with constant brightness, and the fading is produced by the accident of an eclipse. John Goodricke discovered the regular variations of Algol in 1783 and then, in the following year, discovered two stars which are true variables. They were delta Cephei, and eta Aquilae. In his short life, Goodricke did more for the astronomy of variable stars than any previous observers. Yet he was an amateur and was handicapped by deafness and an impediment in his speech. He died in 1786 at the age of twenty-two.

Delta Cephei has proved to be a member of an important group of variable stars that are found throughout the universe. Members of the group are called Cepheid variables, though of course they are not restricted to the constellation Cepheus. The variation in brightness is caused by a rhythmic expansion and contraction of the star. It is pulsating like a large jellyfish. We do not know exactly how the oscillation started, nor do we know the controlling forces. The movement seems to be affected in some way by the mass and size of the star, for the larger stars have a slower variation. Delta Cephei, for example, has an average brightness of −3, and varies its light by half a magnitude once every six days. A brighter Cepheid, with a magnitude of −4, has a period of 20 days, while fainter Cepheids vary every day or so. Astronomers have found a definite relation between the brightness and the period. Of course, in talking about brightness we have referred all the stars to the standard distance of 33 light years. Although delta Cephei is a giant star, it is at a distance of 1,000 light years and we see it in the sky as a faint, fourth-magnitude star. This connection between brightness and period of oscillation is a very important one for the astronomer. It is called the "period luminosity relation," and we will see later how it helps the astronomer to measure distances. It gives him one of his most accurate yardsticks.

Cepheid stars are giants of spectral type F, G, and K. They are found in a small area of the Hertzsprung-Russell diagram, and most stars within this area are Cepheids. The Cepheids occur in a sparsely populated region of the diagram, and therefore are a rare type of star. The sun has the spectral class of Cepheids, Class G, but it is

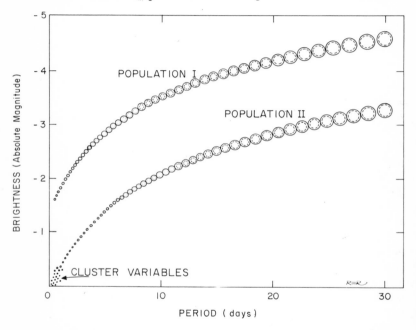

Fig. 27.   Period-luminosity relation for Cepheid variable stars. The large stars pulsate more slowly than the smaller stars.

not one of them, because of its position on the main sequence. If the sun were a Cepheid, the photospheric temperature would change by several thousand degrees every week, and living on the Earth would be uncomfortable, if not impossible.

The star Mira marks the eye of the whale in the constellation Cetus. It is another type of variable star—Stella Mira means the wonderful star. For two months it shines as a third-magnitude star, and then it fades away. Through a telescope you can still see Mira as it changes from a fifth- to a tenth-magnitude star. The star stays faint for several weeks and then increases in brightness again, reappearing as the eye of the whale after a period of eleven months.

Mira is a long period variable of spectral type M, on the giant branch of the Hertzsprung-Russell diagram. There are many stars in the sky with a variation like Mira; in fact the majority of Class M and N giants are long-period variables. The variation in brightness is due to a pulsation, similar to that of the Cepheids. Instead of a

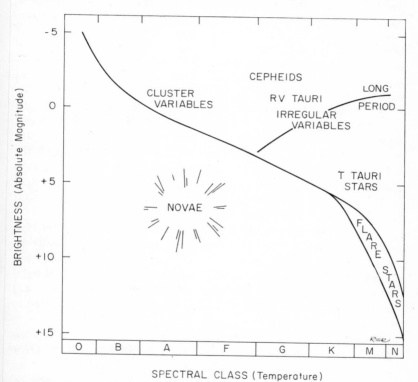

Fig. 28. The Hertzsprung-Russell diagram showing the location of variable stars. Each type of variable has a well-defined brightness and spectral class.

variation of half a magnitude, however, the long period variables change in brightness by seven magnitudes, a six hundredfold decrease in brightness. As with the Cepheids, we do not have an exact theory to account for the behavior of the star. The change in brightness is too great to be accounted for by pulsation alone. At the minimum brightness, astronomers have found absorption lines from molecules of carbon. These absorption lines give us a partial explanation for the extreme faintness of the star. As the star cools, particles of carbon condense in the atmosphere of the star, obscuring some of the light. Mira at these times is hidden by a blanket of soot.

The sun, like other stars on the main sequence, is not variable to any great extent. The sun's brightness has been accurately measured for the past fifty years, and the output has been constant to within 1 per cent, or less than one-hundredth of a magnitude. The rhythmic pulsations are confined to the giant stars, and of these the red giants show the greatest variation. At the red end of the main sequence, however, we do find some slight variations, though there is no regularity as with the giants. M stars and N stars on the main sequence occasionally increase in brightness by a magnitude or more. They are called "flare stars."

We think that the sudden flare is caused by a cloud of dust falling into the photosphere of the star. The M and N stars are cool and faint and the radiation pressure from their light is small. If the star moves into a region of interstellar dust it will inevitably absorb the material. On the other hand, brighter stars, between spectral type K and O, are hot, and a large quantity of light is emitted. This light is strong enough to sustain a radiation pressure which prevents dust from falling to the surface of the stars.

A little to the right of the main sequence, we find a very rare type of star called a "T Tauri" variable. The spectral type is usually K, M, or N, and the star is a little brighter than its main sequence counterpart. T Tauri stars are very irregular in their emission of light, and give the impression of a continuous sequence of flares. We will see later how T Tauri stars, and other variables, fit into our picture of stellar evolution.

Although we can see more than two thousand stars in the constellations, there are millions of stars which are too faint to be seen. Once every year or so, one of these inconspicuous stars suddenly increases in brightness. Within a day it rises from mediocrity, changing by twelve magnitudes to become a first-magnitude star. For a day or two the star alters the shape of the constellation, and anybody who has done a little stargazing will notice it quite easily. The discovery of a "new star" or nova should be reported by telegram to an observatory, for these objects have great interest for astronomers.

Before the change a nova is a white dwarf star with a diameter not much bigger than the planet Jupiter. The transformation takes place in a few hours. The photosphere begins to expand, and a hot shell of gas moves outward with a speed of one thousand miles per second. The expanding shell is the cause of the brightness. As the heated gas moves out into space it produces bright emission lines at the characteristic wave length of hydrogen. After a day or so, the gaseous shell begins to cool and the emission decreases. Finally the gas shell, although still spreading into space, becomes invisible, and the star returns to its original state.

Novae are, of course, extreme examples of a variable star. At first it was thought that a nova was a unique occurrence, but we now have evidence to show that a nova can repeat. A star in Corona Borealis appeared as a nova in 1946, in the same position as the nova of 1866. Some novae have recurred as many as four times in the last fifty years. We are able to say, with a modicum of truth, "once a nova, always a nova."

J. P. Manning Prentice, an English amateur, discovered the famous nova DQ Herculis. It appeared at Christmas 1934 and was visible to the naked eye until March of the following year. Most novae fade by five magnitudes within a period of a week, but DQ Herculis shone with constancy for over a month. After six months there was a sudden decrease in brightness, but the nova made a faint recovery within a year. Since 1935 the nova has been slowly fading again, but it will take about forty years to return to its original state. DQ has since been found to be an eclipsing binary with the remarkably short period of 4 hours, 49 minutes. The nova and its companion are so close that they touch. The nova itself is a compressed white dwarf and material from the companion seems to be passing across to fall on the nova. Some astronomers think that this nova may erupt periodically when a sufficient amount of material has passed from one star to the other. They talk of irritation building up, until the nova shakes off the load in what seems to be a cosmic sneeze.

There is one thing more spectacular than a nova, and that is a supernova. Instead of just loosing the outer shell, the explosion of a supernova engulfs the whole star. A supernova appears about once every three hundred years, when for a few days, the star shines with a light which rivals the entire galaxy. The astronomer is not limited by distance; he can see the supernova even if it occurs on the distant spiral arms, because the intense light penetrates the clouds of dust. Unfortunately a supernova has not occurred in our galaxy since the telescope, spectroscope, and other instruments have been available. The last two supernovae came along at the time of the Renaissance. We must wait for a modern supernova to appear before we can tell what type of star disintegrates in this manner, and what happens during the explosion.

About one degree to the northwest of zeta Tauri, the left-hand tip of the horns of the bull, we can see a faint patch of light. The shape vaguely resembles a crab from which it takes its name. The Crab nebula is M 1, the first nebula noted by Charles Messier in his famous catalogue. Photographs taken several years apart show that the nebula is a cloud of gas which is expanding year by year. If we work backwards in time, the cloud of gas would have been a single point about nine hundred years ago. Something must have happened in this region of the sky about 1100 A.D.

At this time Europe was lost in the Dark Ages, nobody noticed events in the sky, and, of course, North America had not been settled. Fortunately for astronomy, the people in China were very observant. Imperial astrologers noted the movement of the planets and any unusual change in the constellations. The observations were necessary for the preparation of horoscopes for the emperors of the various dynasties. To keep a check on the accuracy of the predictions, the horoscopes were written out by the scribes in the Bureau of History, and we can still read these records today. In the *History of the Sung Dynasty* by To-To we read: "In the first year of the period Chih-ho, on the day Chi-chou of the fifth moon, a guest star appeared near Tien-Kuan." Tien-Kuan is a group of stars near zeta Tauri, and from the Chinese calendar system the date given corresponds to July 4, 1054, A.D. By a guest star the Chinese astronomers meant a nova, and they stated further that the star remained visible in this position for two years before finally fading away. The star was visible by day as well as by night, and this would be possible only if it were brighter than Venus, magnitude $-4$. Thus we find an agreement in position in the sky, and also in the date of occurrence. We are sure that the Chinese record refers to the explosion that has produced the Crab nebula.

We can even extract information from the horoscope. The chief astrologer of the Sung dynasty, Yang Wei-te, forecast good times ahead. This was because the guest star was yellow on August 27, the color of the Imperial Emperor. Later, in February 1055, the star apparently changed from yellow to an unfavorable red color, for over in Peking the astrologer predicted that the Emperor of the Liao dynasty would die. Strangely enough, the horoscope came true, the Emperor died within five months. The good omen for one Emperor, and the bad omen for the other were of course no more than shrewd guesswork. Personal influence of the astrologers, in their capacity of advisers and physicians, was certainly much stronger than the influence of the supernova! Yet the description of the change of color from yellow to red tells us of changes in the spectrum of the star. Perhaps it was due to the cooling of a superheated ball as in the explosion of a hydrogen bomb, or perhaps it showed a decrease in atomic excitation. Maybe we will find the answer to these questions when the next supernova blows up.

We know of five other supernova in our galaxy. They occurred in A.D. 185, 369, 1006, 1572, and 1604. The brilliant star observed so well by Tycho Brahe in 1572, was certainly a supernova because of its brightness and length of visibility. Tycho's star appeared in his youth and gained him the recognition of the King of Denmark. Because of his thorough study of the supernova, Tycho was provided with the observatory of Uraniborg where he devoted his life to the observation of planets.

The last supernova appeared in 1604, while Kepler was working on his planetary laws. To appreciate the impact of the third supernova, we must remember that mysticism and astrology were still important subjects in 1600. Kepler himself still interpreted the behavior of his relatives, particularly his wife, by the movement of the planets from one sign of the zodiac to the other.

By the summer of 1604, a great conjunction was beginning—the most important planets in the sky, Jupiter and Saturn, were approaching one another. The conjunction was to take place in the sign of the zodiac called Sagittarius, a member of the powerful fiery trigon. This sign, in 1604, was located just below the constellation of Ophiuchus, at the lowest point of the ecliptic. This celestial event was known to repeat every 804 years. The previous one came at the height of the career of Charles the Great, the cultured Emperor of Europe. Previous to that, the conjunction had signaled the birth of Christ. By October 1604 the excitement was intense because Mars, the planet of war, had also moved into the sign of Sagittarius, and Jupiter, Saturn, and Mars came together in a brilliant triangle. At the climax, on October 11, a supernova appeared just above them in Ophiuchus, sparkling in all the colors of the rainbow and outshining the planets.

Kepler was summoned by the Emperor Rudolph to interpret the omen. Some astrologers talked of the coming of the Day of Judgment, others of the overthrow of the Turkish Empire, or the birth of a great new king—"Nova Stella, Novus Rex," they said. Kepler could find nothing significant in the conjunction, however, and the horoscope presented to the Emperor was vague. He was, at the time, absorbed in the analysis of Tycho's observations, and was beginning to look upon astrology with distaste. The wonder of the solar system was unfolding in his calculations, and it was not to be defiled in a horoscope. Kepler stated politely that he was not appointed as a public prophet, but was a mathematician whose duty was to analyze the work of Tycho Brahe. If any great development on the Earth was foretold by the stars, we would recognize it today in the work of Kepler himself.

C H A P T E R **22**

# A STAR IS BORN

When Dr. Russell discovered the main sequence of the stars in 1913, astronomers began to wonder about the evolution of the stars. A few astronomers thought that a star began as a faint, cool N star, and then, by a process of accumulation, moved up the main sequence becoming larger and hotter until it finished as a brilliant O star. The majority, however, talked of an evolution down the main sequence, with each star ending its life as a cool red dwarf. In the beginning, they suggested, a star appeared in the sky as a large glowing ball of gas. At first it was extremely hot, but gradually energy was radiated into space, making the star become smaller and cooler. The arguments continued for thirty years, but very little progress was made because some important parts of the picture were missing.

The study of stellar evolution is difficult because the Hertzsprung-Russell diagram shows us the stars for only a brief instant in their history. It is as though you were given a snapshot of a crowd of people and from the photograph you were asked to describe the life story of a man. The photograph shows children and grownups, dark skins and white. Does a man develop from a child, or is a child the last fragment remaining as a man is worn away? Does the skin color remain constant, or does it darken with age? To answer these questions correctly you would need to see a complete set of photographs. Even if astronomers work for a billion years they will not obtain a complete set because the average star changes very slowly. Within the last few years, however, some new facts have been discovered which help us understand the lives of the stars when we look at the snapshot. The story is not yet complete, and the facts already known have been discovered at different times and not in a logical order. From the mosaic, I will try to present a biographical sketch of a star as it is seen by astronomers today. As an example I will take a typical star, of Class G 2, like the sun.

The star condenses from a cloud of gas and dust—the dark globules we see projected against a bright nebula. The force of gravity draws the dust and gas together, and interstellar matter falls in toward the proto-star. Energy is released by the falling material, and the proto-star becomes warm and then hot. At a certain instant in the

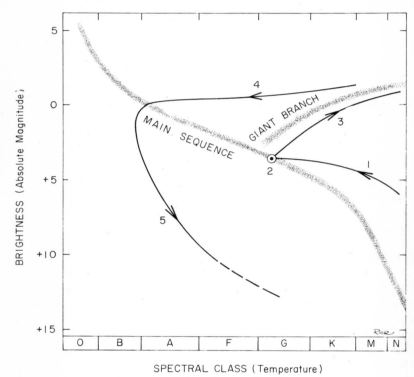

Fig. 29.    Evolutionary track of the sun

development, the energy of contraction is great enough to cause the proto-star to shine with a dull red glow. We do not know exactly how long the contraction lasts, but it may take about a million years, which is short period of time in the life of a star. The contraction energy is released quite quickly and the star changes from dull red to orange and then yellow as it grows hotter. The color change and temperature change mean that the star is changing its spectral class from N through M and K to G. The star moves toward the main sequence along Path 1 as shown in the Hertzsprung-Russell diagram. Thus stars do not progress up or down the main sequence, they move into the main sequence from the right-hand side.

We can see a few stars in the sky which are in this proto-star stage at the present time. They are very rare, because the process does not last long. These stars are called T Tauri stars, and their light varies irregularly. Dr. George Herbig, of Lick Observatory, has taken three photographs of stars in the process of formation in the Orion nebula. Between 1947 and 1954 three or four new stars appeared. One of the brighter stars in the first photograph shows a new companion in the second photograph. The transition from a dark dust cloud to a luminous star has taken place within the short space of seven years. In 1959 the new stars had developed still further.

The new born star releases energy as the material falls together. The temperature at the center of the star rapidly increases until it reaches 10 million degrees Fahrenheit. Nuclear physicists have shown that nuclear fusion can take place at high temperatures. Hydrogen is the simplest element in the universe, and in the fusion process hydrogen nuclei combine to form the heavier elements. At a temperature of 10 million degrees heavy hydrogen is produced, but for the formation of new elements, the temperature at the center must be even higher. The fusion of hydrogen to make heavy hydrogen in the T Tauri star gives the star a new supply of energy, nuclear energy, and the contraction process begins to slow down. Calculations show that the contraction will stop when the central temperature reaches 25 million degrees Fahrenheit. At this stage the star has reached Position 2 on the diagram. It has arrived on the main sequence.

With a central temperature of 25 million degrees the star can make use of a very efficient source of energy, the fusion of hydrogen to make helium. The reaction is steady, and can continue for a long period of time, until most of the hydrogen at the center of the star is consumed. We estimate that the sun has been on the main sequence for six billion years and will remain there for another six billion. I have already described the steady condition in an earlier chapter. The gravitational pull is balanced by gas pressure and by the pressure of the escaping radiation.

Because a star spends so long in a condition of equilibrium, most stars are found in this stage when we take our snapshot. Stars move rapidly toward the main sequence, and most of them will be found there whenever we make a survey of brightness and temperature. If the original globule of gas and dust is small, the star takes up a position at the lower end of the main sequence. It becomes a faint cool star of Class M or N. If the globule is more massive, the proto-star will develop into a class G or K. The largest globules produce the stars at the top of the main sequence, the brilliant O, B and A stars. Temperature within the larger stars is higher than the temperature within the sun. When the central temperature exceeds 40 million degrees Fahrenheit, the nuclear reactions become violent. Hydrogen is fused directly into helium, as in the sun, but in addition the carbon cycle can take place. The carbon acts as a catalyst, speeding up the conversion of hydrogen into helium. As a result these stars burn more rapidly, shine with a greater intensity, and have a lifetime that is shorter than the sun's. Calculations show that an O star stays on the main sequence for about ten million years, whereas the sun will remain there for at least ten billion.

As the star burns on the main sequence the interior contains the seed of its own destruction. Helium is produced and forms a dead core at the center, clogging the furnace. At first the helium core is no more than a mile across, but during the course of ten billion years the core spreads until it occupies one-tenth of the star's interior. There is no stirring action to break up the core, and although the center is hot, there is no hydrogen left to burn. After twelve billion years or so, the core has grown so large that it fills the hottest regions of the interior, normal fusion ends, and the star leaves the main sequence.

The third stage of evolution gives no warning of the final decline, for the star grows larger. It becomes a red giant. When no more energy is released in the core, there is no outflow of radiation to prevent the core from collapsing. It therefore begins to contract as the dust globule did some twelve billion years previously. The core, however, is much more compressed than the dust cloud, and releases much more energy. The energy of contraction heats the upper layers in the star and they begin to expand. The star becomes bloated, increasing its size by a hundredfold. In six billion years' time the sun will reach this stage. It will grow in size until the surface reaches the planet Mercury. The photosphere will cool slightly, changing from yellow to red, but the increase in size will compensate for the slight lowering of temperature. From the Earth we would see the sun swell into a red ball of fire. At sunset the disk would extend from the horizon to a point halfway up the sky, and during the day the heat would be intense. At this stage the oceans will boil away, the atmosphere will escape, and most of the rocks at the surface will melt. The Earth will then become a lifeless inferno, similar to the proto-planet stage in the beginning.

The core of the red giant is growing hotter by contraction, but nuclear fusion will not occur in the helium unless the temperature reaches 200 million degrees. Fusion is still going on within the hydrogen shell, for the contraction energy heats up the layers around the core. The burning shell slowly eats its way toward the surface, and the helium produced by the fusion sinks down to enlarge the dead core. A critical condition is reached when the core contains one-half of the mass of the star. Then the star is at the topmost point of the giant branch, with maximum diameter and brightness. Once again the behavior of the star is controlled by events taking place within a small region at the center.

The center heats up to a temperature of 200 million degrees Fahrenheit as the star reaches the climax at the top of the giant branch. Physicists have shown that at this temperature the dead core itself can be used as a fuel. Helium nuclei can fuse to form carbon, with the release of further energy. As soon as the furnace is relit, the outflow of radiation prevents the contraction of the core. The outer layers settle down, and the star returns to a more normal size. The gases at the surface become more compressed and there is a slight rise in temperature, which changes the color of the photosphere from red to yellow. The star moves along Path 4 in the Hertzsprung-Russell diagram.

We do not know much about this stage of development. The evolution probably takes place rapidly, and the star becomes somewhat unstable. You will notice that Track 4 passes through the area on the diagram in which we find Cepheids and other variable stars. The process of shrinking does not occur smoothly, and rhythmic oscillations seem to develop. The star recrosses the main sequence at magnitude zero, spectral class A. It can be distinguished from an ordinary main sequence star, however, because the pulsations are still continuing. They are now occurring quite rapidly with a period of a few hours, and it has become what we call a "cluster type variable."

Stage 4 is a very important one for planets and for life. The helium core develops extremely high temperatures, perhaps approaching 10 billion degrees, and many fusion processes can take place. The American physicist, William A. Fowler, and his associates, think that all the heavy elements are formed at this stage. The star becomes a factory in which the ninety-one elements in the atomic table between helium and uranium are made. Oxygen for our atmosphere, iron for our blood, and carbon for the Earth's vegetation are formed. Every atom in your body, save perhaps the hydrogen, was made in the core of a giant star.

The process is not very efficient, however. If a star begins as a cloud of hydrogen, not more than one atom in a thousand will have been converted into a heavy element when the process is over. An enrichment of one part in a thousand is produced by the first generation, but it seems likely that the process can continue. If the material from the first generation is re-formed in a second star, then we will finish with two heavy elements per thousand, and the third generation will be further enriched. A spectroscopic analysis of the sun indicates that about three atoms per thousand are heavy ones, and from this we conjecture that the sun is a third-generation star. It is certainly a member of Population I, the younger stars which are continually forming from the gas and dust in the spiral arms. The dust itself has already been enriched in heavy elements and the concept of the sun as a young star makes sense.

On the other hand, the stars of Population II seem to be first generation stars. They are found in globular clusters where there is very little dust, and where the young O and B stars are not forming at the present time. A spectroscopic analysis of Population II stars indicates a deficiency in the heavy elements, and they seem to contain no more than one heavy atom per thousand of hydrogen.

We find the greatest concentration of heavy elements not in the stars but in the planets. We have already discussed the remarkable process by which the original cosmic mixture collected together to form a proto-planet, and how the mixture was further enriched by the evaporation of hydrogen and lighter gases in the glare of the primeval sun. If our conjectures are correct we would not expect planets to form around a first-generation star. The stars of Population II will therefore not have planets, or at least planets like the Earth. If planets do form near Population II stars, they will be large spheres of frozen hydrogen, icebergs without any solid inclusions.

The astronomers are talking about the birth and rebirth of stars, and of course, this raises the question "How is the material from a dying star dispersed, so that a second star can form?" The fifth track seems, at first sight, to be a journey to extinction. The heavy elements in the helium core clog the furnace, slowing down the nuclear reactions. By this time the core occupies more than 80 per cent of the star's interior, and only a thin coating of hydrogen remains around the core. The supply of hydrogen fuel is almost exhausted, and the core itself ceases to burn. Once again a contraction sets in, and gravity causes the star to become more and more compressed. Ultimately, in the white dwarf stage, there is no space left between the particles, and the compression can go no further. A cubic inch taken from a white dwarf would weigh several tons. If a cube of this degenerate material were placed on a table, it would crash through the table and the floor to burrow into the Earth. Astronomers call the white dwarf region of the Hertzsprung-Russell diagram the stellar "graveyard." In this compressed state there seems to be no hope of recovery for the star. It will gradually cool and unless something else happens it will become a cold, dark cinder in space.

Again there is no certainty in the theory, but we think that the dispersion takes place in the fifth stage, during the formation of a white dwarf. We know the stars do not approach the graveyard quietly. White dwarfs occasionally flare up to produce a nova. A portion of the outer layer is blown off into space, and here at least we have one mechanism for redistributing the rich material of the aging star.

Professor Subrahmanya Chandrasekhar, of the University of Chicago, has investigated mathematically the extreme state of a white dwarf. If the mass is greater than 1.4 solar masses, then the internal pressures reach a critical limit. It is just as though the particles were compressed to the point where they were touching. An exact analysis, using the theory of relativity, shows that it is impossible to compress material beyond this point. Yet if the mass were greater, this condition would be encouraged. We presume that white dwarfs cannot exist if their mass is greater than the critical value, and indeed, no white dwarfs have been found in this condition. If a star is approaching a white dwarf stage with an excess of mass, then something must happen to dispose of the excess. Perhaps under the extreme pressures the whole star explodes, and we see a supernova. We can only check the suggestion when a modern supernova is observed, and the prenova can be seen in our present photographs. Certainly a supernova is the most efficient mechanism we know for spreading the enriched materials into the breeding ground of the stars—the dust clouds in the spiral arms.

As the research proceeds we are encouraged to think of the evolution of stars as a continuous process. In some way the material of a white dwarf is made available for the next generation of stars. There may be a sixth track in the Hertzsprung-Russell diagram, linking the white dwarfs with the T Tauri stars and completing the cycle. But if such a track exists, it is not known at present. It remains as one of the undiscovered *secrets of the Milky Way*.

# PART V
# BETWEEN THE PLANETS

Flammarion's proposal for launching an artificial satellite in the late
nineteenth century. (*Popular Astronomy*, Camille Flammarion, Appleton-
Century-Crofts, Inc.)

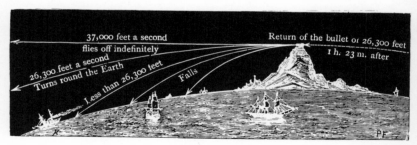

37,000 feet a second
flies off indefinitely

26,300 feet a second
Turns round the Earth

Less than 26,300 feet

Falls

Return of the bullet of 26,300 feet
1 h. 23 m. after

PF

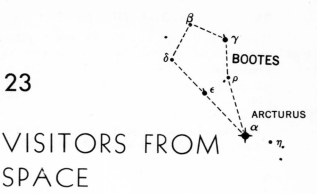

C H A P T E R **23**

# VISITORS FROM SPACE

NOT MANY PEOPLE HAVE SEEN A METEORITE REND THE SKY AND strike the Earth. Fortunately, large meteorites have never fallen near our modern centers of population such as New York and London. The Biblical towns of Sodom and Gomorrah were almost certainly destroyed by means of a meteorite, and if the punishment was chosen to fit the crime these townships must have been hotbeds of evil. Lot's wife was turned to salt, or perhaps more correctly ashes, in the flash of the cataclysm. This indicates a brightness several times more intense than a hydrogen bomb. In the present century we have had several visitors from space that have produced effects similar to the destruction of Sodom and Gomorrah, but fortunately the wrath has been spent on uninhabited portions of the world.

Scientists today are still investigating and writing about the great Tunguska meteorite which fell at 7:30 A.M. on June 30, 1908, in the desolate swamps of northern Siberia. The people within a radius of four hundred miles saw and heard a tremendous explosion. Eyewitnesses spoke of a brilliant object moving overhead from the southeast, dropping sparks and leaving behind a trail of smoke. As it hit the ground, the meteorite exploded with the violence of many hydrogen bombs, producing a pillar of fire and smoke such as that described at Sodom and Gomorrah.

The sound of the explosion could be heard seven hundred miles away, and many people and animals were knocked over by the blast of air. An inhabitant of the Vanovara Trading Post, some forty miles to the south of the fall, describes how he was sitting quietly outside his house when he experienced the effects of a searing heat. He was lifted from his seat and thrown several yards, a little ruffled, but grateful to be still alive. Earth tremors then followed, houses shook, windowpanes were broken, and household objects began to move and fall. An engineer on the trans-Siberian railroad stopped his train because he feared that it would be thrown off the tracks by the heaving and shaking earth. It was clear to all that a catastrophic event had taken place to the north, but people were unable to penetrate into the swamps to find out what had happened.

Nineteen years later the first scientific expedition led by L. A. Kulik broke through to the Tunguska River valley to view the destruction. Over an area larger than New York and her suburbs, trees had been knocked over and charred by the searing heat. In many areas forests had been completely obliterated. Reindeer and other wildlife living in the area must certainly have perished during that brief instant nineteen years previous.

Kulik and the other scientists were surprised to find no large crater in the area of destruction. Although the original object was estimated to have weighed a million tons, it must have disintegrated in an explosion at the surface, or else the living swamp had healed over the wound in the ensuing nineteen years. A large number of small water-filled holes were noticed all over the area but very careful work showed that these were not meteorite craters but were natural formations created by the heaving of the ice below the surface. This region was sufficiently far north to be permanently frozen below the surface. In fact Kulik and his associates made some of the very first studies of the phenomena of permafrost. In the summer, the layer above the frost turns to mud which becomes more and more slimy as sphagnum moss grows. A hummock of moss develops until subsequent freezing and thawing breaks a sinkhole at the top, forming a slimy lake. The Tunguska fall hardly rates as a tourist attraction, but it is still of great interest to meteoritic scientists.

The second largest meteorite to fall this century also chose the inaccessible Taiga of Siberia. About seventy tons of iron rushed through the air and crashed into the Sikhote-Alin mountain range, a few hundred miles north of Vladivostok. The time was 10:35 A.M. on February 12, 1947, a period when cold war tensions were developing. If the meteorite had landed in Moscow or Washington, either side might have swiftly retaliated.

An aerial reconnaissance showed that the forest had been laid waste over a region two miles long and one mile wide. A scientific expedition set out overland under the direction of Dr. E. L. Krinov who had been on the earlier expeditions to the Tunguska fall. After many hardships the expedition finally arrived at the Sikhote-Alin Mountains and set up a camp. A very thorough investigation program was commenced. Two hundred craters were found in the forest, the larger ones being very reminiscent of the Tunguska damage. Trees were uprooted and the force of the explosion had laid them so that they pointed outwards from the crater. Some of the craters had been formed in solid rock and some in swampy areas.

The scientists were intent on obtaining as much of the original meteorite material as possible, and each crater presented its own special problem. In some craters the mass of iron had apparently exploded, for fragments of iron were found interspersed amongst the rubble in the crater walls. In some craters the mass of iron had sunk as deep as eighteen feet into the soft ground, and considerable sweat was spent in extracting the object. Smaller fragments were found scattered throughout the forest, being picked up from the ground or bed of leaves on which they had fallen. Altogether two hundred craters were located, the largest being nearly one hundred feet in diameter, and twenty-three tons of meteorite material were collected, to be distributed amongst the scientists of the world for further study. With great forethought and a little modesty the Russian team erected wooden structures over nineteen of the craters, not disturbing them at all. As science progresses, new theories and new instruments will appear, and I am sure scientists of future generations will be grateful to have these nineteen carefully preserved craters to work with.

People who were in eastern Siberia during the time of the fall have given us several eyewitness accounts. The accounts are quite similar to those of the Tunguska fall. An object as bright as the sun moved across the sky and crashed to earth leaving behind a column of smoke. A local artist made a painting of what he saw and has provided us with one of the few records that we have of the fall of a large meteorite. This painting is reproduced on the envelopes used by the committee on Meteorites of the Academy of Sciences of the USSR, and one of the envelopes is shown in the illustration. The stamps are also a treasure for the astronomical philatelist; one shows again the Sikhote-Alin fall, the other is a painting of the Tunguska fall with a portrait of the pioneering explorer Kulik.

Both the Siberian meteorites are classified as "falls," because there is indisputable evidence that an object came down from out of the sky. Sometimes, when a meteorite is extremely old or when nobody was around when it fell, we classify it as a "find." A find can be turned up by a plow, unearthed during excavations, or seen resting on the surface by an explorer or conquistadors entering virgin territory. Scientists can examine a find and tell whether or not it has come down to earth from the space between the planets by carrying out chemical tests. Some meteorites are stony, with a blackened crust caused by heating as it passed through the atmosphere. Others are metallic, being composed of a peculiar iron and nickel alloy. The irons are in fact a nickel steel, which has never been found occurring naturally on the earth and which has never been imitated in a steel foundry.

Meteorite finds have usually been on earth for several hundred years and have had many adventures during their stay. H. H. Nininger has unearthed several fine meteorite speciments from the graves of American Indians. The meteorites certainly did not fall into the graves; they must have been valuable possessions that were buried with the owner. A lump of thirty-four tons of iron fell at Cape York, Greenland, in the distant past and during the course of centuries chunks were broken off by Eskimos to make knives and harpoon tips. It was finally rescued by the American polar explorer, Peary, who loaded it on his boat—or rather, supervised the struggles of his crew as they levered and pushed and hauled. New Yorkers can see this "Ahnighito" meteorite, for it is owned by the American Museum of Natural History and is usually on display at the Hayden Planetarium. In the Holy Kaaba in Mecca there is a stone in the wall which scientists believe to be a meteorite, but no scientist, either infidel or Moslem, has been permitted to make the detailed examination to verify its origin.

Who owns a meteorite? The law varies between countries, and in the United States from state to state. Usually a meteorite belongs to the person who owns the land on which it is found. This point was established by the Supreme Court of Oregon in a suit concerning the Willamette meteorite, now safely housed in the Hayden Planetarium in New York. A huge mass of iron, weighing fourteen tons, was discovered accidently in the forests of Oregon. The discoverer, Ellis Hughes, was a farmer, but he realized the value of the object. He also realized that it was several hundred yards over the boundary on the property of the Oregon Iron and Steel Company. Ellis, with horse and sled, sweat and perseverance, dragged the mass through the forest across the line onto his own property. A trail was cut for three-quarters of a mile through the forest, and a wooden roadbed was laid over swampy regions. Finally he put it on display and charged admission. Everyone was impressed with Oregon's celestial visitor, and several people chipped off a piece in their enthusiasm. As Ellis proudly exhibited it, the steel company prepared their brief and filed a suit to regain possession. Whatever the legal arguments, one can't help feeling that Mr. Hughes should have had some reward for his labors and for bringing to the attention of scientists a most valuable specimen. Without his efforts the Willamette iron would certainly have rusted away in the damp forest for several more years. But three different courts each ruled in favor of Oregon Steel and Mr. Hughes lost his prize. The specimen is now on view in the Hayden Planetarium from 9.00 A.M. to 5.00 P.M. for a modest admission charge.

Arizona's meteor crater is also in the category of a find. Some ten or twenty thousand years ago, nobody knows exactly when, an enormous mass of iron hurtled through the air and blasted a hole nearly one mile across in the desert. At the turn of the century not many scientists believed that holes so large could be made by a meteorite. The entire crater, with surrounding territory, was purchased from the United States Government by Daniel Moreau Barringer who set about to prove to the world that the crater had a cosmic cause. He had an altruistic interest in astronomy, but was also intent on extracting the millions of tons of iron that he was convinced lay buried beneath the surface. A quick calculation showed that at ten cents a pound he might soon become a millionaire. Many stories have been written about Moreau Barringer which undoubtedly have become embellished as time has passed. Barringer certainly cut a number of deep drill holes in the center of the crater and on the rim to try to find the meteorite. He did not get a fortune out of the crater, indeed he poured a fortune in. Today the general opinion of scientists is that the original meteorite almost completely exploded on impact with the earth and that none of the original mass lies buried below the crater floor.

The drilling of Barringer revealed some surprising results. For hundreds of feet the drill cut through pulverized and shattered rock containing small metallic particles, and then dug into an undisturbed layer of red sandstone. The impact had clearly shattered the rock to a great depth below the present crater floor, turning much of the rock to a fine powder called "rock flour." The subterranean explosion forced up the surrounding rim of the crater into an escarpment rising some 160 feet above the surrounding countryside. Huge boulders were hurled out of the crater and now lie in a jumbled mass where they fell around the rim. Intense heat was generated, because some of the sandstone was fused instantaneously into a glassy foam and molten droplets of iron were scattered for miles around. Very little of the original meteorite survived the explosion. The largest piece of iron found weighed about a ton, and other smaller pieces have been picked out of the surrounding desert. Small souvenirs can still be picked up by the keen-eyed prospector, but year by year it becomes more and more difficult. I was unlucky and had to join the line and pass my dollar over the museum counter when I dropped by to look at the crater.

Dr. John S. Rinehart has made one of the most thorough studies of the meteorite dust in Arizona. He led an expedition from the Smithsonian Astrophysical Observatory one summer. While the Smithsonian flag fluttered at the expedition headquarters, 324 holes were dug at half-mile intervals around the crater. Magnets were used to sift out the meteorite dust, and from his survey Rinehart calculated that 12,000 tons of iron dust lay scattered in the desert topsoil. He concluded the iron droplets had cooled from the intensely heated cloud that must have hung over the disaster area.

Since the work of Barringer, other craters have been discovered in Australia and the northern wastes of Canada. The Deep Bay Crater in northern Canada is six miles across and must be at least fifty million years old. In New Quebec we have the Ungava crater that was discovered when somebody was looking over an aerial photograph. Ungava is three-quarters of a mile across and is now filled with a lake. The region in New Quebec where the crater is located is very difficult to get to. The lake does not thaw out until the end of May and begins to freeze over again in September. Nevertheless, one or two brave scientists have made the journey to measure the depth, look for meteorite fragments, and study the effects of the prehistoric blast. A few fish have made their home in the lake, but the crater is not a very choice spot. The upturned rim prevents any surface drainage from pouring into the lake. Thus the normal food supply is cut off. As a consequence, the fish living in this unnatural lake are undernourished and peculiarly malformed.

I have gone through the accounts of witnessed falls during the last two centuries to try to see how many meteorites hit the Earth each year. On the average between three and four objects weighing twenty pounds or more come down during the course of a day. A meteorite weighing four thousand tons hits the Earth every century. Of course, many of these fall into the oceans, lakes, or the polar regions, and are never found. In fact, most of them get buried or eroded away, and are lost to science. If a meteorite is to finish up in the hands of a scientist it should fall in a flat cultivated region where many people live. Some of the best collecting areas are India, Europe, and the Great Plains of the United States.

A suitable collecting area is marked on the map of the United States and each dot represents the place where the meteorite was seen to fall. The Great Plains area has been uniformly peppered. Since the

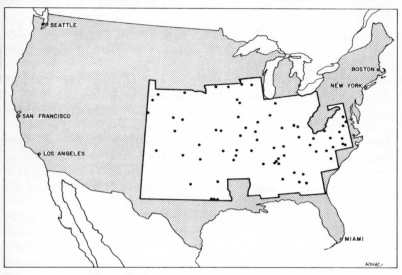

Fig. 30.    Meteorite falls in the United States

first settlements people have lived nearer the eastern seaboard, and this accounts for the apparent thinning out of the dots toward the West. There is a surprising connection between the number of meteorites seen to fall and the number of people living in a certain area of the country. As the population has increased, so has the number of recorded falls, but we seem to have reached a saturation point which corresponds to the figure of three or four meteorites falling on the entire surface of the Earth per day. The Earth has no doubt been collecting material at this rate since its creation. Over the last five billion years it has collected at least ten million million tons, sufficient to make a small planet about ten miles in diameter.

But despite this deluge no one need be alarmed. In the first place, if you are hit by a large meteorite then it is all over in a flash; in the second place the chance of being hit is quite small. Certainly the townspeople of Sodom and Gomorrah were smashed and incinerated by a meteorite, but there are very few accounts of people being hurt in modern times. From my youth I carry a vivid memory of having read about a monk who was pierced through the heart while resting in a field. He was having an easy time instead of staying at his devotions, and the horrible moral to the story was pointed out to succeeding generations at the monastery. However, I can find no confirmation of the story in present-day catalogues and it probably has little substance. According to E. F. F. Chladni, a meteorite killed a man and injured a woman in Oriang, India, in 1825, but Chladni was probably exaggerating a little, as no stone was produced and the evidence is not conclusive.

There is a very well-substantiated account of a dog that was killed in Alexandria, Egypt, in 1911. About forty stones fell, weighing in total some eighty pounds, and there was a flash in the sky, a detonation, and a cloud of dust. Then again a man was injured at Mhow, India, when one of a group of five stones hit him and one of the other stones broke a limb of a tree. In 1954 an iron meteorite crashed through the roof of a house forty miles south of Birmingham, Alabama. It injured a woman and a very revealing photograph of the bruise on her hip was carried in the newspapers.

Many people have had near misses, with a meteorite humming through the air to land at their feet, or crashing through the roof of a bedroom. Some have smashed into barns, bounced off the wall of a house, or landed in the middle of a road. One afternoon in August 1946 a large stone approached the town of Pena Blanca Spring in Texas. The meteorite fell very nicely into a swimming pool, making quite a splash since it weighed as much as a man. Fortunately, nobody was swimming in the pool at the time. The meteorite turned out to be of unusual composition, and parts of it are preserved in the United States National Museum in Washington, D. C.

There are two main classes of meteorites, the stones and the irons. A few specimens are hybrids, being partly stone and partly iron, but usually there is no difficulty in classifying a specimen. Most irons contain about 10 per cent of the metal nickel and the mixture has formed large eight-sided crystals. These crystals can be seen very easily if a flat slab is polished and etched slightly with acid. The process was developed by Dr. Widmanstätten and the crisscross pattern is called a Widmanstätten figure. Metallurgists are astounded at the size of the crystals, some of them are from ten to twelve inches long, and it would take thousands of years to grow them on the earth. We infer

17.  Surveyor and prospector on the moon

18.  The Pleiades or Seven Sisters

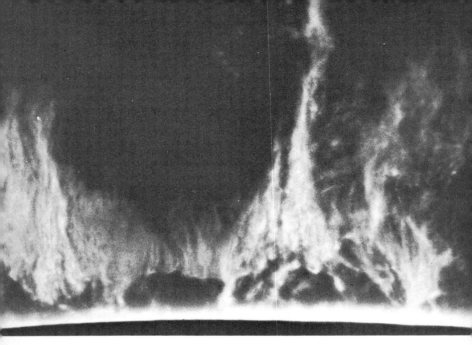

19. A hedgerow prominence hangs in the sun's corona

20. Looped prominences near an active sunspot

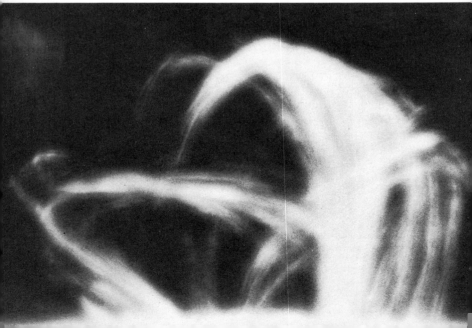

21. Planetary nebula, a glowing sphere in Aquarius

22. M 13, a globular star cluster in Hercules

23. The Crab nebula, a supernova explodes

24. Dust clouds in silhouette

25. Meteor dust through the electron microscope X50,000. Irregular fragments have been collected from the high atmosphere by the rounded mesh of the filter

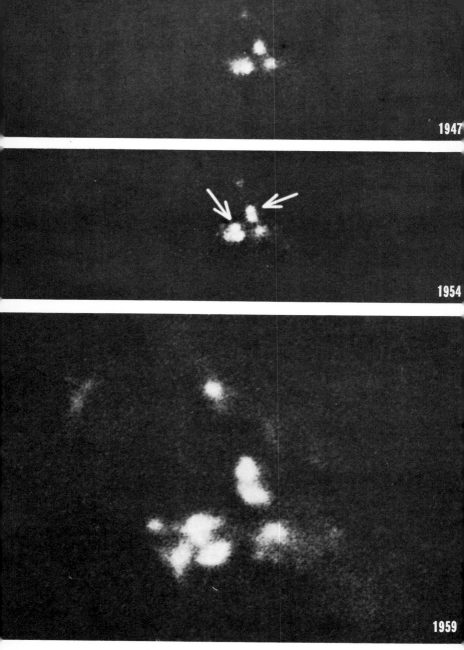

1947

1954

1959

26. New stars develop in Orion

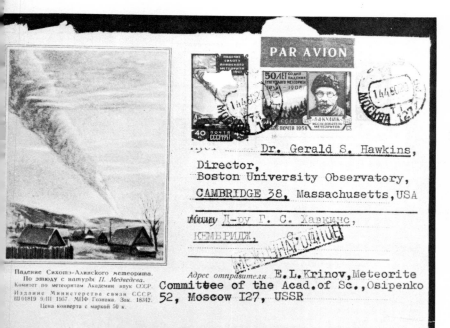

Падение Сихотэ-Алинского метеорита.
По этюду с натуры П. Медведева.
Комитет по метеоритам Академии наук СССР.
Ш 01819 9/III 1957 МТФ Госзнака. Зак. 18342.
Цена конверта с маркой 50 к.

PAR AVION

Dr. Gerald S. Hawkins,
Director,
Boston University Observatory,
CAMBRIDGE 38, Massachusetts, USA

Кому Д-ру Г. С. Хавкинс,
КЕМБРИДЖ,

Адрес отправителя E. L. Krinov, Meteorite
Committee of the Acad. of Sc., Osipenko
52, Moscow I27, USSR

27.  Commemoration of Siberian falls

28.  The gaping hole in Arizona

29. An iron meteorite with dark stony inclusions. The iron phase shows Widmanstätten figures. (Brenham, Kansas)

30. A meteorite composed of large iron crystals. (Sandia Mountains, New Mexico)

31. Pioneer V a few hours before launching

32. Cloud cover shown by Tiros 1.
    left: cyclone over Caspian Sea; right: cloud patterns over Pacific

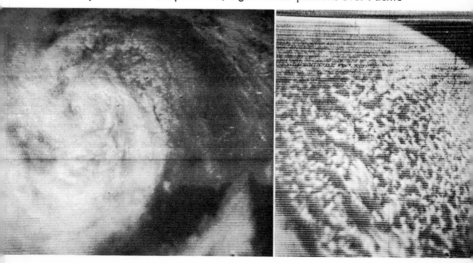

33. An elliptical galaxy resolved into stars, NGC 205

34. Galaxies in collision, MGC 4038 and 4039

35.  The great spiral galaxy in Andromeda, M 31

36. M 33, a galaxy of type S&

37. The 600-foot paraboloid
    the United States Navy
    Sugar Grove

that the meteorite formed part of a large mass that cooled and crystallized very slowly out in space. The fragments of iron from the Arizona meteor crater contain diamonds. There are about ten small diamonds per pound of meteorite, but they are not of gem quality. The diamonds tell us that the Arizona meteorite at least must have solidified under very high pressure.

The stones are very difficult to understand. Although they contain the same chemicals and some of the minerals that we find on the Earth, the stones are a very unusual mixture. Somehow in the past the various crystals of feldspar, olivine, and other minerals have been splintered and crushed and then packed together again. Thus through a microscope a stony meteorite looks like a very complicated piece of terrazzo cement, or an ultramodernistic tile pattern. But instead of one or two minerals being cemented together the meteorite contains many. To make matters worse, embedded in the mass we find almost spherical pebbles called chondrules and tiny flecks and veins of metal.

Dr. Fred L. Whipple and I have suggested that the stones were formed during violent collisions in space. We think that two asteroids a little larger than Mars collided, breaking up into millions of fragments, some large, some small. With more fragments, more collisions would take place, the larger objects holding together a little longer than the smaller. Thus a large fragment would continue to collect debris which would be cemented together in a hodgepodge fashion until the growing fragment itself was shattered by a further collision. The irons do not show much evidence of this mixing process and are the remains of the shattered core of the original asteroids.

Did life ever exist on this planet before the collision? Surprisingly enough the answer seems to be "Yes." After years of work American scientists have managed to coax strange bacteria out of the stony meteorite that fell in Murray, Kentucky, in 1950. Dr. Frederick D. Sisler and Dr. Walter Newton sterilized the surface of the stone with ultraviolet light, hydrogen peroxide, and bichloride of mercury. Then the specimen was crushed in a germ-free laboratory and placed in a nutrient culture. After a few months the liquid became cloudy and a microscope revealed millions of elongated bacteria, unlike strains found on Earth.

In the same year (1961) scientists at Fordham University, New York, made a careful analysis of a meteorite that fell in Orgueil, France, in 1864. They found chemicals which are normally regarded as organic—long hydrocarbon chains similar to cholesterol and fats. They concluded that the chemicals were the remains of some low form of life which once existed on the planet before it was shattered into the meteorite fragments. Clearly we must expect to find primitive life, bacteria, single cells, germs, under extreme conditions—in the cold, airless prison of a solid rock, on Mars, and in the dust of the moon. Yet we still hold to the view that higher forms of life, man, or at least a body capable of thought, can survive within only a narrow range of conditions.

In talking about visitors from space it is difficult to decide whether or not to include tektites. It is still undecided whether these glassy fragments found strewn over the world have indeed fallen from the sky. Certainly, like meteorites, they have long been valued in certain sections of the world as supernatural objects. In the East Indies they are called Agni Mani or "fire pearl," and a tribal war was fought in Java for the possession of a set of magic tektites. Geologists could find no explanation for them since the glass was scattered indiscriminately over all sorts of rocks and strata. They concluded that the tektites must have been scattered over the Earth from outside and the problem was handed over to the astronomers.

The United States has at least two areas where tektites are found. At Boston University we joined in the treasure hunt when we sent an expedition down to Georgia and Texas. Of course we were not just idly looking for specimens, we were taking note of the terrain and looking for clues as to how the tektites found their way to Texas. We saw what other scientists had reported; the tektites were embedded in a narrow layer of sandstone called the Jackson formation. The Jackson formation stretches as a thin line through Texas and the southern states to Georgia—in fact it is named after Jackson, the capital of Mississippi. The line marks an old shore of the Gulf of Mexico when the sea encroached inland about forty million years ago. The best tektite area is in a canyon near Bedias, Texas. My assistant was dismayed to discover a lake filling this choice location; a dam had been erected and the area flooded. It was high summer and the ticks and bugs were taking great samples of northern blood. The expedition might have faltered right at that point if the local people had not given encouragement to continue. They showed us the exact strata as it occurred in other gullies, and helped us collect over thirty specimens for further study. We also took samples of the soil in which the tektites were found, and later, in Boston, melted the soil in a solar furnace. We noticed that intense heat produced a glass, similar to but not quite as dark as tektites. This and other considerations led us to believe that tektites might be produced on the Earth by intense heat, and it would then be up to geologists to find out exactly how the glass was formed.

If a tektite is ever seen to fall—and none has yet—then it is undoubtedly a problem for the astronomers. Unfortunately, it is just as difficult for an astronomer to account for glass being made in interplanetary space as it is for a geologist to account for its occurrence on the Earth. Admittedly some tektites, particularly those in Australia, showed teardrop shapes and flanges which were presumed to be produced by the passage of the object through the Earth's atmosphere, but it is really unfair to pass the problem over to astronomers with such a slim piece of evidence. Astronomers fight back, pointing out that meteorites usually form a conical nose-cone shape as they pass through the atmosphere, and flanges could hardly form this way. They argue that the chemical composition of tektites is very similar to the rocks on the Earth and that sudden heating of earthly rocks could probably form a tektite. Maybe they were caused by a prehistoric meteorite that fused the soil, maybe they were ejected as molten magma from a violent volcanic upheaval—maybe they are a problem for the geologist after all.

# A STREAK IN THE SKY

IT IS NOT TRUE TO SAY THAT EVERY TIME WE SEE A SHOOTING STAR a child is born or a person dies. The birth rate has never equaled the rate of arrival of shooting stars, nor is there any connection between mortal flesh and the tiny fragment of dust streaking through the upper atmosphere. Gradually the world population has increased, aided by the cultivation of food, the conquering of disease, and the basic biological law that one and one usually make much more than two, until the present birth rate is close to 150,000 per day.

Meteors are even more prolific. Edward K. L. Upton and I have estimated that ninety million meteors visible to the naked eye enter the Earth's atmosphere each day, and they have been arriving at this rate for many years, even before Homo sapiens emerged in recognizable form from the process of evolution. It is interesting to speculate on the state of the world if the old wives' tale were true. There would be one thousand billion Earthlings alive, packed with a density of twenty thousand per square mile, so that every portion of dry ground would be covered with a rather overcrowded suburbia. The resources of the Earth might possibly be stretched to support this population, and the virility of the human race is certainly sufficient to produce it, but I do not think we will ever reach the limit where a child is born every time a shooting star appears.

If a shooting star does not represent a human birth it certainly represents a cosmic death, for we are seeing the last brief second of existence of a particle that for millions of years has traveled on a lonely path between the planets. As the meteor flashes across the sky the path is recorded by cameras or by a radar system, and from the

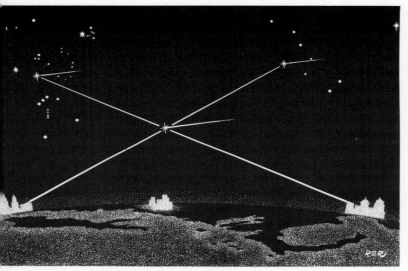

Fig. 31.    A meteor flashes over New England

record of its disintegration scientists are able to deduce the life history of the body. The particle is a fragile thing, crumbling as soon as it meets the resistance of the air. If we could cut a block of one cubic foot from a meteor and stand it on a table, the block would crumble under its own weight. It would be no stronger than cigarette ash. This explains why no meteors ever reach the surface of the Earth intact and why astronomers draw such a sharp distinction between meteors and meteorites. It is ironic that the most delicate material of the universe should be subjected to the fierce ordeal of entering a planetary atmosphere at a speed of thirty miles a second.

A considerable amount of research has gone into the problem of bringing a nose cone, or a man in a space capsule, safely through the atmosphere at a speed of five miles a second. With adequate protection, of course, a man can live through the hazards of re-entry, but a meteor has no hope. If it were not for Fred L. Whipple's theory of comets, it would be difficult for us to imagine how such peculiar material, something like a fluffy dust ball, could be formed in outer space, but we will see that meteors now give us an easy introduction to comets—objects that will be described in the next chapter.

Most professional astronomers avoid the study of meteors. They know that the streak in the sky is caused by atoms evaporating off the molten surface of the particle, and that the whole phenomenon is occurring not more than seventy miles above their heads. This is far too close to be called astronomy; in fact, even the moon and the planets are sometimes regarded as the "local backyard." The most interesting objects must surely be those that are beyond the boundaries of the solar system and on the very limit of visibility. Nevertheless many astronomers will admit that their interests began one night many years ago when they sat out under the stars to plot the track of meteors. A few of them, and I am among this number, have retained an interest and have tried to contribute to the growth of meteor astronomy.

It is still very rewarding to go fishing in the sky for meteors, especially if you choose a good time of the year and try to make a few notes of what you see. August is a very good month because meteors are plentiful and it is the summer in the Northern Hemisphere. Between August 8 and 12 the Perseids never fail to make an appearance; after midnight one can be sure of seeing about sixty meteors every hour. They move in rapid streaks away from the constellation of Perseus, the constellation named after the Greek legendary hero. Perseus, carrying the head of Queen Medusa, rises majestically from the northeast horizon in the late evening to climb slowly toward the zenith as dawn approaches. I have watched the Perseids on many occasions—from my home on the east coast of England when I was a member of a team of observers scattered over East Anglia, from a small sailboat bobbing off the coast of the Isle of Wight, from the White Sands Desert, and from the top of the Sacramento mountain range in New Mexico. I am always impressed by the event and look forward to the shower as an old friend.

The path of a meteor can be found quite accurately by two people if they are about fifty miles apart and if each one records the position of the meteor as he sees it in the sky. The diagram shows two observers, one in Boston and one in New York with a meteor passing between them, somewhere over New Haven. From Boston the streak of light is seen projected against the stars of the southern part of the sky, and from New York it appears over to the north in the Big Dipper. If the angles were accurately worked out from star charts, or were found by using a surveyor's theodolite, then our observers would find from a triangle drawn to scale that the meteor was over New Haven at a height of sixty miles. If the time of flight of the meteor were measured by one of the observers, then the speed could be calculated. A Perseid would be moving quite fast at about thirty-seven miles per second, while the slowest meteors come in at six or seven miles per second. Professional astronomers use the same method as our observers in Boston and New York, except that cameras replace the human eye and the speed of the meteor is measured by spinning a rotating shutter in front of the camera so that the light of the meteor is intermittently obscured.

The professional method of photographing meteors was pioneered by William L. Elkin while he was director of Yale Observatory. As early as 1893 he had set up two observation posts in Connecticut, each equipped with several cameras driven by clock work to follow the steady westward drift of the stars through the night. Some of these cameras looked at the sky through a rotating shutter which was ingeniously made from a bicycle wheel with the gaps between some of the spokes blacked out. We shall never know the reason that Elkin placed his observing sites only a few miles apart. Probably travel was difficult in those days and perhaps he had not planned the experiment as carefully as he should. The base line was certainly too short to give any worthwhile results since the parallactic displacement of the meteor trail as seen from each station was too small. The bulk of his results was never published, and many astronomers think that the plates obtained during his sixteen years of photography were never measured. After his death a search was made for the photographs in the hope that some benefit could be obtained by measuring what he had so laboriously obtained, but the plates were not found. It is conceivable that he destroyed them with his own hands when he realized that the chosen base line was too small.

Once or twice during the course of the last century meteors appeared in great numbers. Although the phenomenon lasts for only a few hours people are very impressed by the spectacle, talking and writing about it for many years after. The night of November 12-13, 1833 is regarded as the date of birth of meteor astronomy because the Earth plowed through a dense cloud containing billions of particles, and nineteenth century scientists saw a storm of meteors. The sky was alive with meteors. At least a hundred of them could be seen all the time, some brighter than the brightest stars and others faint on the limit of visibility. Many left glowing trains of light which twisted into contorted shapes as they faded from view and no part of the sky was free from the invasion of the shooting stars.

Astronomers around the world were startled by the phenomenon and very few of them recovered sufficiently from their amazement to make any scientific observations. For example, we have today no reliable estimates on the number of meteors that could be seen per hour. Estimates range from ten thousand to two hundred thousand meteors per hour visible to one observer. With numbers such as these even the most alert observer would lose count unless special precautions were taken to divide up the sky into small manageable sections. The statement that the "stars were falling as thick as snowflakes" is perhaps the most accurate description we will ever have of the Leonid shower of 1833.

The year 1833 was important for one single scientific discovery— several astronomers noticed independently that the meteors were apparently streaming from a point in the constellation of Leo, and no matter where the constellation was located in the sky the meteors still came from that point. The significance of a radiant point was immediately and correctly interpreted. The flash of light was produced by a particle dashing into the Earth's atmosphere, and since all the particles were traveling in parallel paths, these paths, when projected backwards, all intersected at one point. The meteor tracks were similar to the parallel lines of the walls of a room, or a system of parallel lines on a thruway, which appear to radiate from the perspective vanishing point. It was the discovery of the radiant that established the true nature of meteors to the scientists at that time and inaugurated meteor astronomy as a science. Little heed was given to the bright young students Heinrich Brandes and Johann Benzenberg at Göttingen University who, by observing the same meteors from two separate townships, had measured the height, direction, and velocity of meteors some thirty years before.

If the scientists were bewildered by the Leonid storm, we can easily imagine how the nonscientists felt. We do not know exactly how many deaths from heart failure and suicide could be directly attributed to the Leonids, but many people in the southern states were panic-stricken, thinking that the Day of Judgment had surely arrived. The print, drawn by a careful artist after the excitement was over, still contains the suggestion of the people's reaction. Some of the more nervous can be seen shielding their eyes, kneeling on the ground, or wringing their hands. Most of the adults are shown dressed in their best clothes complete with hat, but this is certainly an embellishment of the artist, for we are sure that most people must have rushed into the street in their nightshirts.

Scientists noted that the great explorer, Alexander von Humboldt, had watched a similar storm thirty-three years previously on November 12, 1799. The American astronomer, H. A. Newton, searched

Fig. 32.   Villagers react to the Leonid Storm of 1833

older records and found that a Leonid shower had been seen with a period of thirty-three years starting in A.D. 902. He made the prudent suggestion that the Leonids might return once again in 1866, and the prediction was verified with a beautiful shower of meteors radiating from the sickle of the constellation Leo. Once again the sky was alive with flashing meteors, but since there had been plenty of warning it did not cause widespread panic. The reputation of science was enhanced by the success of the prediction.

In the same year a comet passed close to the sun, in a long orbit with a period of thirty-three years. This comet was discovered by the political refugee, Wilhelm Temple, who was observing at the time at Marseilles. Like most comets it was an inconspicuous object, having just a small tail and being visible only in a telescope, but it was destined to become quite famous. Many scientists noted that the orbit of Temple's comet was almost identical with the orbit of the Leonid meteor swarm. In fact the swarm and comet were traveling around the sun together as companions, and scientists inferred that the meteor particles had been scattered as debris by the comet.

During the next thirty-three years the interest in meteors increased and a storm of them was confidently expected in November 1899. The Englishman John Couch Adams, who had already predicted by gravitational theory the existence of Neptune before it was seen by astronomers, turned his mind to the Leonids. His calculations showed that the swarm would pass close to the planet Jupiter in August 1898 and would be deflected sufficiently to miss the Earth. In spite of this warning, professional astronomers and most of the enlightened public braved the cold winter night to see the Leonids. Teams were organized by observatories, and Times Square was packed with hopeful stargazers. Everyone was disappointed; the celestial display did not occur. Charles P. Olivier, director of the American Meteor Society, said that by the time the empty night was ended by the dawn, astronomy had suffered a severe blow. Indeed almost forty years elapsed before professional interest could be rekindled in the streak in the sky.

Several small comets besides Temple's comet have become famous by producing a meteor storm. We are sure that every comet in the solar system is accompanied by a cloud of meteoric particles, but not every comet is able to produce a meteor shower. We see a shower only when the orbit of the comet crosses the orbit of the Earth, then the Earth is able to collide with the trail of debris. The comet Giacobini-Zinner, named after the two astronomers who discovered it, is another small comet with a privileged orbit. With a period of six and one-half years the comet has produced spectacular meteor swarms every thirteen years when the comet and the Earth were close together. Indeed, the comet passes uncomfortably close to the Earth and on one or two occasions has had a fair chance of collision.

Giacobinid meteors appeared in great numbers during the evening of October 9, 1933. By all accounts the storm was not as intense as the Leonids in the previous century but the event aroused a great deal of scientific interest. European observers were more fortunate than those in the United States because the shower was of maximum intensity for a period of less than an hour and the sun had not set over the United States when most meteors were to be seen. The best views were obtained by people in Belgium and Germany where the rate of meteors reached six thousand per hour. The British Isles, unfortunately, were clouded over, and there were many frustrated astronomers making rather earthy comments below the clouds.

The comet with its attendant swarm of meteors came close to Earth again on October 10, 1946, and on this return we had some astronomical justice, for the shower was visible both in Europe and in the United States. Many amateurs and professionals still have vivid memories of the event. Dr. Peter M. Millman was preparing to photograph the Giacobinids from the Dominion Observatory, Ottawa, when the weather gradually began to deteriorate until it was obvious that there would be no successful observations made from Ottawa that night. Following the traditions of travel and government support that had been established in the nineteenth century, Air Marshal Curtis placed at Millman's disposal a Dakota from the Transport Command of the Royal Canadian Air Force with permission to fly to any airport where the sky was clear. The cameras and observing party were loaded in the plane, a landing was made at North Bay, and within half an hour all the equipment was running and successfully photographing the meteor shower. These photographs proved to be the most valuable results obtained from the Giacobinids, because, like the Leonids, perturbed by Jupiter, they failed to appear in 1959, and there is little hope of seeing a Giacobinid storm again.

There were clouds over England on the evening of October 9, and the prospects for visual astronomy were not good. Only one observer persevered long enough through the night to see the Giacobinids. Mr. J. P. Manning Prentice, director of the meteor section of the British Astronomical Association, set his gaze on the clouds until there was a brief clearing around 4:00 A.M. which permitted a glimpse of the meteor storm. He was observing at his home in Stowmarket, Suffolk.

Meteors were appearing at a rate of five thousand an hour and as Prentice looked toward the constellation Draco he was impressed to see as many as seven meteors at the same time diverging from the radiant point like the spokes of a wheel.

Sixty miles to the south, in Surrey, a group of scientists under the direction of J. S. Hey had found a way of beating the English weather. They were using remnants of radar equipment left over after World War II, and of course the radar beam was able to penetrate through the clouds and fog. As a meteor plows through the air it leaves behind a trail of electrons and positive ions. This column of ionization is a good reflector of radio signals, producing an echo as an aircraft and missile will do. In fact, Dr. Hey was assigned the task of studying meteor echoes during the war because very little was known about them at that time, and the radar operators were confusing meteor echoes with echoes from the German V2 rockets. The Giacobinid echoes were recorded on film in such a way that the variation of distance with time could be seen. As the meteor came closer and closer to the radar station it traced out a parabolic track on the film from which its speed could be measured. Hey found that the speed of the meteors was twenty-three km. per second, which was exactly the speed to be expected if the particles were following in the orbit of comet Giacobini-Zinner.

Further north, at Jodrell Bank Experimental Station of the University of Manchester, Professor A. C. Bernard Lovell was leading a group of scientists who were also studying the Giacobinid shower by means of radar, using converted wartime equipment. The peak intensity of the storm was found to occur at 3:45 A.M. Greenwich mean time so around that time Dr. John A. Clegg pointed the antenna directly at the predicted radiant of the shower. Even though large numbers of meteors must have been appearing in the antenna beam above the clouds, the radar echoes dramatically disappeared. This was an important observation since it showed that meteors did not produce echoes when you looked at them head-on, and a successful method of radiant determination, used by Arnold Aspinall and myself, was later based upon this fact.

Both the Leonid and the Giacobinid swarms were moved beyond the reach of the Earth by Jupiter, and it is unlikely that we will see them in great numbers again. They have become known as the lost meteor streams. The Andromedids are another stream in this category. The parent to the swarm was Biela's comet, a remarkable comet that split into two parts while astronomers were observing it and left behind no trace except the meteor debris. Two spectacular storms were seen in 1872 and 1885 and then the swarm disappeared, or so it was thought. From photographs taken with the powerful Super-Schmidt cameras in New Mexico, I found, with Richard B. Southworth and Francis M. Stienon, that even today there are a few straggling members of the great swarm to be seen. Throughout the month of November one or two meteors per night were photographed with the Harvard Super-Schmidt cameras, and we found them to be following closely in the path of the old swarm. Working backwards we were able to find out what had happened. The pull of Jupiter gradually lifted the swarm so that it now passes two and a half million miles above the Earth on November 3. At the same time the compact swarm was dispersed over a wide area and only the stragglers are seen today.

There is no need, however, to wait for a storm like the Leonids, or a stream like the Perseids, before you go out to look for meteors. On any night you choose you will see between five and ten meteors during the course of an hour. These meteors are not moving in a compact swarm or moving in a well-defined stream, nor do we have any definite knowledge of the comet that gave them birth. Technically we call them sporadic meteors; they are the waifs and strays of the solar system. One or two scientists have tried to find out more about these waifs and strays, and the work triggered off a number of controversies.

It took fifty years to decide whether sporadic meteors belonged to our solar system or whether they came from the space between the stars. It might at first sight appear to be a simple problem, because meteors coming to us from the stars would be traveling at a high speed, whereas meteors belonging to the solar system would enter the atmosphere more slowly. In fact if all the meteors belonged to the solar system we would never see one traveling with a velocity of more than 72 km/sec. Velocities greater than 72 km/sec would correspond to a hyperbolic orbit, and simply by measuring the speed of a meteor we should be able to decide whether or not interstellar meteors existed.

Unfortunately the measurement of velocity is not easy unless you have very special equipment. Visual observers tend to exaggerate the speed of a meteor; they say the path in the sky was a little longer than it actually was, or they say that it moved more quickly than it actually did. Thus visual work, notably the catalogue of bright fireballs by von Niessel and Hoffmeister, showed without doubt that the majority of sporadic meteors had hyperbolic orbits. A few astronomers disputed this result and a special expedition was sent to Arizona by

Harvard Observatory, to obtain more accurate data. Dr. Öpik designed an ingenious device to help the observers make a more precise measurement of the meteor speed. A mirror was made to wobble rapidly so that any meteor seen through the mirror would make a spiral track. By counting the loops the speed could be measured. No one has ever understood exactly why, but the rocking mirror played peculiar tricks on the observer, with the result that a few of the loops were missed and the analysis showed very definitely that the meteors were coming from between the stars.

Once again a few astronomers were not convinced, and Öpik and Hoffmeister tackled the problem from a different angle. If meteors are not moving at very great speeds across the Earth's orbit, they argued, then the Earth should sweep them up like insects on an automobile windshield. If the meteors are moving at great speeds, and are interstellar in origin, then we should pick up quite a few on the back window as well. The Earth is moving in its orbit toward a point called the apex, and a person looking south faces the apex at dawn. Hoffmeister made a journey to the clear skies of Africa, observing every available night for two years. Both Hoffmeister and Öpik found that about three times as many meteors were seen at dawn as were seen in the evening hours. But if the meteors were moving slowly, they would have expected to find at least ten times as many at dawn. They believed that this was further proof for interstellar meteors. Unfortunately, as we shall see, sporadic meteors are swirling in a gigantic cloud in the same direction as the Earth. This increases the number of meteors falling on the Earth in the evening hours and invalidates the conclusion of Hoffmeister.

Hyperbolic velocities were also found with the new and more accurate observing methods. One meteor photographed with the Super-Schmidt cameras seemed to be definitely in this category, but it turned out that two meteors had appeared in the sky while the photograph was being taken. One meteor had been seen by the man operating the camera, but the photographed meteor had escaped his attention. After the muddle had been sorted out, the photographed meteor was found to be a well-behaved member of our own solar system. Then again a radar meteor from Manchester, England, was found with a very definite hyperbolic orbit. Although the tedious calculations had been checked three times, Dr. Lovell thought it prudent to repeat the work once more before publishing the result. It was found that the three scientists, working independently, had each made the same rather unusual mistake and that the meteor had not come from between the stars after all. Nowadays a meteor astronomer is liable to show an odd reaction if you ask him about hyperbolic meteors. With such a long history of troubles, anyone wishing to talk about interstellar meteors must produce indisputable evidence.

Modern methods have disclosed a gigantic cloud of particles stretching out beyond the orbit of Jupiter in a flattened cloud. Each particle moves in a separate orbit and constitutes a sporadic meteor. The whole system is rotating around the sun just like the Earth, Mars, and the other planets. At first sight the orbits of sporadic meteors seem to be hopelessly jumbled and intertwined, but gradually by careful observation you can pick out some important details. In the first place the orbits congregate in the plane of the ecliptic and the shape of the orbits are quite like those of the short period comets. So as a first guess one would say that the waifs and strays also began their life in a comet. The Andromedids, for example, were classed as sporadic meteors until a careful study of their orbit showed that they were the vestigial remains of the great swarm of 1872. We think that swarms and streams are gradually dispersed by perturbations and that the cloud of sporadic meteors represents the remnants of the imposing swarms of the past. The cloud can be seen out there in space as a hazy band called the zodiacal light. Sunlight scattered from the particles causes the glow. To see it best in the Northern Hemisphere one should look some spring evening toward the constellation of Aries and Taurus in a place where you are free from the city lights.

A meteor is not finished when it disintegrates so catastrophically in the upper atmosphere. Dust and fine particles are left behind and these slowly sink earthward. Sometimes the sun's rays can still shine on the high-flying dust, making it glow like a pearly cloud after sunset. The best conditions for seeing this phenomenon occur in northern Sweden during the summer months, and the clouds have become known as "noctilucent clouds." Gradually the dust floats downward— we estimate that several thousand tons fall to the ground per day. Some of the dust is caught in the filters of high-altitude rockets and experimental aircraft to be taken to laboratories for further study. Some of it is collected on sticky plates and once again finishes up under the microscope of a scientist. Dr. Curtis L. Hemenway, the director of Dudley Observatory at Albany, New York, thinks that some of the particles examined with the electron microscope are fragile and might be similar to the fluffy dust ball material already suspected from photographic measurements. Other particles are solid nickel iron fragments that have undoubtedly been produced by the evaporation of a meteorite.

Dr. E. G. Bowen of Sidney, Australia, has made a suggestion which, if true, greatly affects the lives of us all. His research shows that thirty days after a meteor stream has appeared there is sometimes a sudden increase in heavy rainfall over the world. The time taken for a small dust particle to fall from a height of sixty miles can be worked out and it comes quite close to thirty days. Therefore it is sensible to postulate that the meteor dust is influencing the weather, and Dr. Bowen feels that the meteor particles act as condensation nuclei in clouds. Although the meteor dust may not actually be responsible for the bad weather, if there is a storm brewing the dust can make the storm more intense, just as the thunderclouds over Australia were made to drop rain by seeding them with dry ice. Many arguments have been raised against Bowen's suggestion; in particular Whipple and I asked why heavy rainfall was not caused by sporadic meteors since they bring in as much material as do the streams. We also pointed out that several of the streams referred to by Bowen were weak and almost nonexistent. For example, one suspected rain producer was the lost Leonid swarm. The question is still under debate. Meanwhile with the dust from shooting stars falling relentlessly down toward the Earth's surface, this is perhaps an appropriate time to leave meteors and talk about their parents, the comets.

CHAPTER **25**

# COMETS

MOVING BETWEEN THE PLANETS ON LONG ORBITS WE FIND THE comets. The orbits are ellipses with the sun at one focus, and the speed of the comet depends upon its distance from the sun. Comets are perfect examples for showing the truth of Kepler's laws of planetary motion. It is surprising to find that Kepler himself, although working for years with observations of the planets, disregarded comets completely. In fact Kepler lived and died with the impression that comets did not fit into his scheme of the solar system, but moved steadily along straight lines with a complete disregard for the controlling influence of the sun.

At the time of Kepler, of course, comets were still regarded as supernatural bodies which came along to warn the world of some impending disaster. The importance of a king or emperor was easily checked by his subjects who only had to look in the sky at the time of his death to see whether or not a fiery comet appeared. Plutarch describes how the mourning of Caesar was accompanied by the visitation of a brilliant comet, even though Caesar himself was assassinated and did not die at his natural time. The psychological use of a comet by William the Conqueror is now a legend. Just before his invasion of England in 1066 a comet hung in the sky. King Harold's army, opposing William, interpreted the comet as a bad omen, as was normal in the Middle Ages. The same feelings spread among the Frenchmen, but William announced that this comet was different and had been sent as a sign of victory. William won the battle, of course, but it is difficult to say exactly how much his manipulation of current superstitions helped him.

Comets are divided into two groups, those of "long period" and those of "short period." Long period comets follow orbits that are

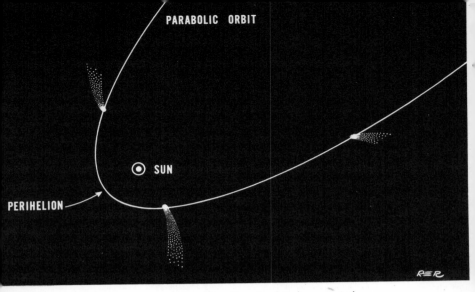

Fig. 33. Comet orbit, long period

almost in the shape of a parabola, and they pass close to the sun at a point called perihelion. Another name for a member of this group is "parabolic comet."

It may sound rather odd, but astronomers are sure that parabolic comets are not moving exactly in parabolic orbits. In a parabolic orbit a comet would make one and only one approach to the sun, but we are sure that each comet has visited the sun several times before. The orbits are therefore very long ellipses and it is impossible for the astronomer, even with present-day accuracy, to tell the difference between the long ellipse and the parabola.

The second group, the short-period comets, are quite different. Here the orbit is short enough for the astronomer to measure quite well. Most of the ellipses go no further away from the sun than the planet Jupiter so that the comet has a period of six years. We see the short-period comets repeatedly as they return to the sun, Encke's comet, for example, has been seen on more than forty occasions when it has passed around the sun at perihelion.

There is quite a difference between long- and short-period comets. Parabolic comets come into the sun at all angles and show no regard at all for the plane of the ecliptic in which the planets are located. The short-period comets are very well ordered, moving around the sun in the same direction that the planets revolve and keeping fairly close to the plane of the ecliptic.

The existence of a third group of comets moving in hyperbolic

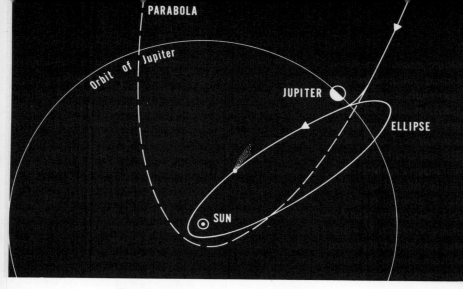

**Fig. 34.  Comet orbit, short period**

orbits was suspected at the beginning of the century. From what was said about hyperbolic meteor orbits, you will realize that a hyperbolic comet, if it existed, must surely have visited the sun from the space between the stars. As with meteors an interstellar origin for comets has finally been disproved, although it was not an easy question to settle. The Danish astronomer E. Strömgren and others have examined the orbits of more than two dozen comets which, according to observations, were definitely hyperbolic. For each comet they found that when it was traced far enough through the solar system the orbit changed back to a parabola or a long ellipse. It seems that gravitational disturbances from the planet Jupiter had forced these comets to change their orbits. Some of the comets may be disturbed sufficiently to be thrown out of the solar system entirely, never to return again, but every comet seen in the history of astronomy is definitely a member of the solar system, and was formed when the solar system was born. As with meteors we are still hoping one of these days to find a truly hyperbolic orbit, since it would give us some contact with the stars and alleviate the feeling of isolation.

We can talk of a comet's anatomy, for it has a hairy head and tail. The head is a large cloud of gas glowing in the sunlight and is sometimes over a million miles in diameter. Sometimes the head shows a bearded or hairy appearance which leads to the scientific term for the head, "coma." Gases streaming away from the coma make the comet's tail, which can be many million miles in length. We sometimes see a small, shining, starlike point of light embedded in the coma, and this is called the nucleus.

We now know, from the work of Dr. Fred L. Whipple, that the nucleus of the comet is a conglomeration of ice and dust, something like a dirty snowball. Nobody has ever seen the details of the nucleus because the comets are so far away from the Earth. Through the most powerful telescopes the nucleus always appears as a minute point of light. We can, however, determine the size of the nucleus from the amount of sunlight reflected from its surface. The measurements show a small snowball, usually less than half a mile across. Even in the largest comets it is seldom more than a mile in diameter. As the mass of ice moves in toward perihelion, the heat from the sun vaporizes the ice, and jets of gas are blown out to form the coma and the tail. The light rays from the sun ionize the gas in the coma and force it back by light pressure so that the tail of the comet always points away from the sun. As it approaches the sun the dirty ball of ice is transformed into a majestic figure. About one astronomical unit from the sun the tail begins to grow until it forms an enormous plume that sometimes extends halfway across the sky. The coma puffs up, new jets of gas appear, and the comet shows us a variety of shapes that are different from night to night. At perihelion the intense sunlight causes the coma to shrink and the comet loses a little of its dignity. It is forced to scurry away from the sun, tail first, because the pressure of light and charged particles from the sun continue to blow away the gaseous material in a relentless wind.

The ice in the nucleus is not entirely frozen water. Frozen ammonia, methane, and carbon dioxide are mixed with the ordinary ice. We are certain that these compounds are in the nucleus because the gases in the coma and tail could only be produced by vaporization of these ices. A spectroscopic analysis of the light from the coma shows the presence of carbon monoxide, CO, which is produced from the dry ice, solid $CO_2$. Solid methane produces molecules formed from carbon and hydrogen such as CH and $CH_2$. Chemists call these carbon-hydrogen molecules "free radicals," because they are the root of the complete molecule of methane, $CH_4$—one carbon atom combined with four hydrogen atoms. Free radicals are of great interest to chemists, because the incomplete molecule is always striving to become a complete molecule of methane. The desire is so strong that an explosion is likely to result. The molecules in the coma are well separated and cannot cause an explosion. If there are any free radicals contained in the icy nucleus, then an explosion could quite well take place as the comet is warmed in the rays of the sun. Indeed, as we shall see, several comets have exploded and their disintegration might well be due to the presence of free radicals.

The dirty snowball model was not proposed until 1950, but already the model accounts for much of the behavior of comets. Previous to 1950 a comet was thought of as a cloud of solid meteorite fragments moving like a flying gravel bank through space, and the gas of the coma and tail came out from the rocks like steam from the earth after a summer rainstorm. But the solid meteorites could not produce sufficient gas to form the coma and tail, and for this and other reasons the idea was dropped in favor of the icy model. We now know that meteorites are not related in any way to comets. Meteorites are the solid fragments produced by collision of two small planets between the orbits of Mars and Jupiter, and comets come from an icy breeding ground, out beyond the orbit of Pluto. Comets are, to be sure, related to shooting stars, or meteors, as we saw in the previous chapter, but both comets and meteors are quite distinct from meteorites.

The fluffy fragments that produce a streak in the sky follow the comet through space like the pilot fish around a shark. The comet is not a clean snowball, it is dirty and contains solid dust particles. As the ice evaporates the solid debris drops off and is scattered rather untidily around the comet. It is now easy to see why meteor particles are so fragile; they are a loose dust ball left over after the ice has evaporated out—they are the skeleton of the comet.

All comets are doomed, none can escape the continual attrition. If one wanted to preserve a comet, the best storage space would be an icebox rather than an orbit exposed to the glare of the sun. Many comets have evaporated completely before our eyes, and we think that even the biggest comets cannot make more than fifty or a hundred visits to the sun before being completely destroyed. Ultimately all the ice will be vaporized and there will be nothing left except the solid dust particles moving along the old orbit of the comet. We have no hope of seeing the dust particles out there in space because they are small and do not scatter much light. We can see the comet so long as it contains ice to form the enormous clouds of gas. When the ice is vaporized, we see nothing. There must be a large number of cometary skeletons in orbit around the sun, but while we are restricted to the Earth we will not be able to find them. If the Earth happens to pass through the swarm of the particles, however, then a meteor shower is produced. Showers such as the Geminids of December and the Quadrantids of January, although they are not now associated with a comet, must represent the remains of a large comet that had its heyday in the past.

We have shown how shooting stars are made from the debris of a comet, but of course we have not accounted for the comets themselves. It will never be possible for a scientist to account for the ultimate origin of everything in the universe, but he will always try to get as close to the answer as he can. The orbits of comets give us a partial clue to their origin. The parabolic comets move in tremendously long orbits and have not visited the sun more than ten or twenty times since the Earth solidified and the solar system formed. From Kepler's law of areas we know that parabolic comets spend most of their time at the furthermost extremity of the orbit. The aphelion must be almost one hundred thousand astronomical units away from the sun, halfway to the nearest stars, and if we could view the solar system from outside we would see it surrounded by a cloud of millions of icy comets. At such large distances from the sun the ice would not vaporize and the comet would not suffer a loss of material; in fact interstellar gas may even condense on the ice out there to make the comet grow. The comets are moving very slowly around the orbit at aphelion, but at the appointed time will make a rapid dash toward the sun, passing close to the planets and returning once more to the storage shell. This theory, suggested by the Dutch astronomer, Oort, explains very well the long-period comets which approach the sun at all angles without warning. It also explains how the delicate ice can be protected from the scorching rays of the sun, but can it explain the peculiar family which form the short-period comets?

Calculations show that some of the parabolic comets will pass close to Jupiter as they approach the sun. Jupiter, by the pull of gravity, can deflect the comet from the parabolic orbit to an elliptical orbit with a period of about six years. Other planets can also deflect a comet, but since they are smaller than Jupiter they do not produce such a big deflection. Over the course of the centuries Jupiter has captured several hundred comets, and those that have survived the ravages of sunlight are seen today as the short-period comets. Once a comet has been trapped into an orbit with a six-year period its revolutions are numbered. It will quickly disappear leaving behind only the solid meteor debris.

Jupiter can trap a parabolic comet during a single encounter, and the comet will follow a path shown in Figure 34. Calculations show that it is more likely for the capture to take place during a series of repeated encounters. We know of some comets that are now in the process of being snared. Comet Wolf I has been thrown around for the past hundred years and so has comet Pons-Winnecke. It is interesting to watch the drastic changes in orbit each time the comet approaches Jupiter, for the comet always has a sporting chance of surviving. There is about a fifty-fifty chance that the comet will be thrown back to the reservoir, or into a hyperbolic orbit that allows it to escape from the solar system and travel on a path between the stars. If Jupiter wins, another comet is removed from deep freeze to amuse us Earthlings in its demise.

Comet hunting is a rewarding sport, for comets are named in honor of their discoverer. Every year about a dozen comets come within range of our telescopes. Prior to World War II Harvard Observatory patrolled the sky every night by taking photographs, and many comets were discovered. Since the war, professional astronomers have left the work to amateurs who sweep the sky at dusk and dawn with telescopes. A comet is usually discovered as a hazy patch of light, without a tail, in a region of the sky near the sun. It is a very laborious task to sweep the telescope systematically over a large area of the sky night after night, always expecting to see a comet and perhaps never finding one. The search is made more difficult by nebulae which look very much like a comet but are, in reality, distant clusters of stars or remnants of supernovae. The French comet hunter, Charles Messier, was tricked so many times by nebulae that he made a catalogue of their positions. Future comet hunters would then not be misled as he was. Ironically he has become more famous for his catalogue than he has for the discovery of comets. The Messier catalogue is still used as a guide to the most prominent clusters, galaxies, and planetary nebulae visible from the Northern Hemisphere. There is not one short-period comet that today bears his name.

The position and brightness of a new comet must be sent immediately by telegram to the proper authorities. The International Astronomical Union has chosen Harvard College Observatory as the data center for the United States and Pacific, and Copenhagen Observatory for Europe and Asia. Trouble develops if this procedure is not followed. Peter Cherbak, an American, discovered a bright comet on July 31, 1957, but sent a report to the Griffith Observatory, California, where the announcement was delayed. Mr. Cherbak had a grandstand view of the comet because he was an airline pilot, and watched the comet from his cockpit. Meanwhile the veteran comet hunter of Czechoslovakia, A. Mrkos, who was sweeping the sky, picked up the comet on August 2 and sent a telegram immediately to Copenhagen.

The comet was officially named after Mrkos before the sad story of the airline pilot came through. During the next few days eleven more telegrams came to Harvard from people who had independently discovered the comet, and to add to the confusion a local newspaper stated erroneously that it had really been discovered by "Mr. Kos." After the turmoil the official designation still held, "Comet Mrkos 1957 d."

Two comets were reported on the Harvard announcement cards in August 1959 which carried the same name, Alcock. At first astronomers thought they were reading about the same comet. Gradually they realized that someone had broken a record, and discovered two new comets within a week. I was very pleased because Mr. G. E. D. Alcock was originally a member of our observing team in England when we plotted the movement of meteors over East Anglia. Geda (he was always known by his initials) had left the meteor group to devote his life to comet hunting. If anybody feels that Alcock was unusually lucky, they should remember that the discoveries were made after more than 560 nights of searching, and that to help his work Geda had memorized the position of nearly 10,000 telescopic stars.

A comet is given a provisional letter immediately it is discovered. For example, the second and third comets discovered in 1960 were 1960 b and 1960 c. Later the comets are renumbered in the order in which they pass the sun, and the second and third comets to pass the sun in 1960 were 1960 II and 1960 III. The order a, b, c, does not always correspond to the order I, II, III. Finally, if the comet is a new discovery it takes the discoverer's name. If it is a comet that had been discovered many years previously but subsequently lost, or if two or more people discover the same comet, then hyphenated names are used in recognition of each discoverer. Comet Honda-Mrkos-Pajdusakova was discovered independently by the three observers after whom it is named. By general agreement a comet is never loaded with more than three names.

Although the professional astronomer does not spend his time actually looking for comets, he discovers them nevertheless. Many blemishes on routine survey plates later turn out to be the hazy coma of a comet. High-powered cameras can detect comets much fainter than the amateur can see with his telescopes, and with a carefully planned program the professional could easily put the amateur out of business. Already professionals are discovering more comets by accident than the amateur finds by sweeping the sky. But there are many other things in the sky that demand the attention of the astronomer, and for many years to come astronomers will be glad to rely on the amateurs for the lonely and time-consuming vigil. Of course as soon as any new arrival is spotted, the large instruments of the professional can be brought to bear for studying the spectrum, determining the path in the sky, and photographing the tenuous details of the tail and coma.

You always hope that a comet named after you will put on a good performance as it dances in the sunlight. One or two comets have become famous. Halley's comet impressed everybody who saw it in 1910. With an average period of seventy-seven years it was visible the year Mark Twain was born and, as he predicted, he died when it returned.

Halley's comet breaks the rules. It has come to the sun regularly throughout recorded history and nobody knows the name of the first discoverer. Nor is it a parabolic or short-period comet, because the orbit stretches from Venus to Pluto. The capture process is incomplete and perhaps one day Halley's comet will be thrown into a short-period orbit where we can see it more often. Using the gravitational theory of Isaac Newton, Sir Edmund Halley calculated the orbit of the bright comets of 1682, 1607, 1531. The orbits were the same and Sir Edmund realized he was dealing with a single body moving regularly around an orbit. Comets which had hitherto been thought of as supernatural were now shown to obey the simple laws of nature and, in proof of his work, Halley expected the comet to return the end of 1758. His comet reappeared Christmas Day 1758, seen first by the eager Messier, and was a wonderful sight during the spring of 1759. Halley did not live to see his comet return. He died in 1742, but a romantic French painting shows an angel raising Halley from the grave to gaze at his comet. One should not conclude that Halley was a modest man. Scientific prestige was a sore point for England in the middle of the eighteenth century, and in making the prediction Halley wrote "Wherefore if it should return . . . about the year 1758, candid posterity will not refuse to acknowledge that this was first discovered by an Englishman."

Encke's comet is the comet without a tail. Like comet Halley, it is named after the mathematician who first noticed that a series of cometary discoveries between 1786 and 1818 were the appearances of the same comet. Encke's comet goes around the sun once every three and a third years, the shortest period known. It has made fifty visits to the sun since 1786 and is now only a shadow of the great comet that it must have been long ago. Most of the ice has vaporized and its surface must be crusted over with meteroic dust. It responds to the warming rays of the sun by throwing out a feeble coma, but never manages to grow a tail. There are some cracks in the dusty outer shell through which gas leaks. The jets act on the comet like the thrust of a rocket and have caused comet Encke to accelerate measurably over the last hundred years.

Comet Morehouse, 1908 III, was the comet that lost its tail. The tail twisted in the solar wind and several pieces became detached, moving rapidly out into space. Disturbances like this have been seen more recently on comet Arend-Roland, 1956 h, and also on Halley's comet. Light pressure alone could not cause such violent disruption. Additional forces must be produced by the charged particles that occasionally stream outward from the sun.

The small comet discovered by Montagne in 1772 and rediscovered by von Biela in 1826 was destined for the Hall of Fame. When the calculations were finished, some astronomers were alarmed to find that the orbit of the Earth and the orbit of the comet intersected. There was a possibility of collision. Fortunately, the comet missed the Earth on each return; in 1846 it split in two. Night by night the parent and offspring separated from each other in the spawning process. In 1852 the twins returned to the sun, but that was the last time they were seen. Some violence, probably a free radical explosion, had split the icy nucleus in two. Subsequent grilling by the sun completed the destruction. When the earth finally collided with the comet in 1872, 1885 and 1892, there was nothing left except a cloud of dust. The cometary skeleton produced the meteoric storm known as the Andromedids.

Biela is the classic example of disruption, but it goes on today. We know of at least forty-three short-period comets that have become lost. Some of them may have been overlooked as they returned to the sun, because they were too far away or because they were obscured by the glare of the sun. Comets lost through the fault of the astronomer may some day be rediscovered. Stefan's comet of 1867 was lost in 1905 but recovered again in 1942 by Miss Oterma of Finland. Comet Wolf was lost for three returns after 1925, but was finally recovered in 1951. Perturbation by Jupiter had disturbed the orbit, and the astronomers were not looking in exactly the right position. Many comets, however, are lost because they really have disappeared. They have been turned to gas and blown away from the solar system. The destruction will continue so long as the sun is shining. On the average one comet succumbs each year, leaving its frail skeleton in the zodiacal cloud.

CHAPTER **26**

# MAN-MADE MOONS

No LONGER CAN WE REGARD SPACE AS SACROSANCT, NOR CAN WE, AS Aristotle did, view the moon and planets as ethereal objects, mysterious and unattainable. Space has been conquered. The space age began on October 4, 1957, with the launching of Sputnik I from a secret pad in Russia, probably close to the shores of the Caspian Sea. With a thousand-ton kick, a small metal sphere was ejected into a circular orbit around the Earth to become an artificial moon. Sputnik I was a faint speck, almost invisible from the ground. The object that people stared at moving across the cold twilight of the dawn was the empty casing of the huge carrier rocket. Russia had achieved a significant "first" which awed the world.

Sputnik II followed within a month, carrying into orbit the dog "Laika" with two radios to transmit the heartbeat, respiration rate, and other medical data. The "beep" signals were tape-recorded by amateurs and sent to the scientists in Moscow for analysis. By choosing the regular "ham bands" at 20 and 40 megacycles, the Russians were sure of worldwide reception of the signals at no cost to themselves. From a few press releases we obtained an accurate account of the last seven days in the life of Laika. At take-off the dog struggled a little until it was pinned to the side of the capsule by the force of the acceleration. Its heartbeat quickened, racing at three times the normal speed. Breathing was also difficult; the dog panted rapidly without completely filling its lungs. The action of the heart and lungs returned to normal during the first few revolutions around the Earth, when the dog and the container were moving according to Kepler's three laws of orbital motion. According to an article in *Pravda*, "The first appraisal of the results obtained shows most clearly that an animal endures the conditions of cosmic flight well."

In 1959 three space craft were sent to the moon. Lunik I passed within five thousand miles of the moon to enter a nearly circular orbit between the Earth and Mars. Lunik II followed a very precise trajectory, crashing on the surface of the moon in Mare Imbrium near the Appenine mountain chain. A cloud of sodium was emitted during the flight when the rocket was between the Earth and the moon. This cloud spread to a diameter of 360 miles in 4 minutes thus marking the position of the rocket. The instrument capsule contained cosmic ray detectors and magnetometers which operated up to the moment of impact. Preliminary results showed that the moon, as expected, did not possess a large magnetic field. As a by-product of the shot, a large number of metal plates were distributed over the surface of the moon bearing the insignia of Soviet Russia.

A complete photographic studio was packed aboard Lunik III. There was a 35 mm. camera with two interchangeable lenses—one for wide-angle shots, the other for telephoto work. There was a tank for developing and fixing the film, a dryer, and compartment for storing the film after development. On command from the Earth, automatic arms pointed the camera at the moon and about a hundred pictures were taken. An exposure meter measured the brightness of the scene so that the aperture and shutter speed could be adjusted in much the same way as we do on the Earth when we take an ordinary snapshot. When Lunik III returned to the vicinity of the Earth the film was unwound from its container. The photographs were examined by a scanning device to be transmitted by television down to Earth. For the first time in the history of mankind we were permitted to look at the mountains, plains, and craters on the far side of the moon. In November 1960 the Russians released a detailed map of the hidden side and this map is reproduced here.

The United States has also achieved several "firsts" in the space age. These include the establishment of an orbit passing from pole to pole and the recovery of a capsule from outer space. On August 11, 1960, on the thirteenth attempt of Project Discoverer, a retro-rocket was fired enabling a capsule to burn its way through the atmosphere. But, of course, in the exploration of space the primary aim is not to be first, nor do we wish to compete with other countries in gross spectacularity. There are scientific explorations to be made; there are benefits to be culled in the development of artificial satellites. These considerations inevitably lead to a long-term program. The question of who was first will become less and less important when viewed in historical perspective. Ultimate leadership will rest with the country that is most successful in developing space science and space technology.

Russia did not really anticipate the propaganda value of Sputnik I. Russian scientists were proud of their achievement but did not feel

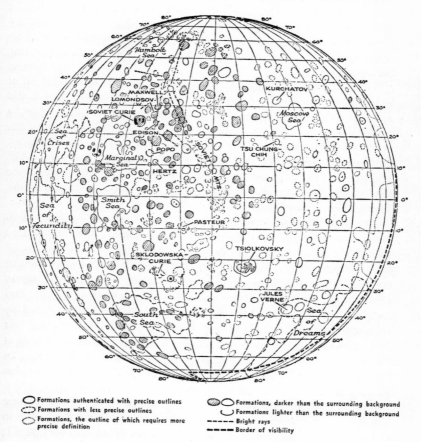

Fig. 35. Russian map showing back of the moon

superior. Dr. A. I. Berg said on Radio Moscow: "The palm of priority in launching the Earth's first artificial satellite will always belong to the USSR. Hardly any one in the USSR, however, thinks that American scientists and engineers are, therefore, less talented than Soviet Space Flight Experts."

Truculence developed later when the United States satellites were ridiculed for their small size. In May 1958, a press statement said: "It is the opinion of prominent scientists that only Sputniks of great weight can promote the rapid solution of the problem of space flight, which cannot be solved with the aid of small satellites having very limited possibilities for scientific research." Yet, despite their small size, our satellites have had considerable success. Most of the important discoveries have been made by American scientists. Russian scientists, although possessing similar data, have seemed to miss the opportunities.

The first American satellite, Explorer I, was put together in a rush, in less than four months. It was launched by strapping together rockets already available in the armory. The rockets were of low power, designed for short-range work and so the satellite contained only eighteen pounds of instruments. Yet Dr. James A. Van Allen of the University of Iowa obtained with this meager equipment the first indications of a dense cloud of electrons surrounding the Earth. The discovery of the Van Allen belt was one of the most significant results of the International Geophysical Year.

The launching of Vanguard I, a six-inch sphere weighing three pounds, was also a great achievement. In its high orbit, Vanguard I will still be circling the Earth in the year 3000 A.D. A miniature transmitter, powered by solar energy, has given good service and will continue to send signals indefinitely. The satellite can be followed by means of the transmitter and can also be photographed with the special high-powered cameras of the Smithsonian Astrophysical Observatory. Although diminutive, Vanguard I shows irregularities in its long orbit due to a distortion of the Earth. From the motion of the satellite we conclude that the Southern Hemisphere is slightly warped, and the North Polar Sea is raised some thirty feet. The Earth, already bulging at the equator, shows an extra "pear-shaped" distortion, due perhaps to the stirring of material deep below the crust. A six-inch satellite did the work of many survey teams.

Our interest has turned from pure science to the use of satellites for the benefit of mankind. Accurate weather forecasting is essential for modern life since the weather affects travel, communications, and most of our activities. Meteorologists working on the ground have always been hampered by lack of data. A large storm, covering an area one thousand miles across, is traced by plotting a large number of reports from meteorologists, air pilots, and navigators at sea. This was a slow, laborious process and not always a reliable one. But a camera in orbit becomes a weather eye, showing the entire storm in a single exposure. Although we do not expect 100 per cent accuracy from satellite forecasts, the pictures of cloud cover will be very helpful and we will gain a deeper insight into the workings of the lower atmosphere.

The concept of a weather eye is a credit to the United States. Tiros I was launched for its epic flight from Cape Canaveral on April 1, 1960. Like Lunik III, the space craft carried a wide-angle and telephoto camera, but instead of using ordinary film with developing tanks the picture was printed on magnetic tape. As Tiros I passed over Fort Monmouth, New Jersey, scientists radioed a command which instructed the satellite where and when to take a picture. A sequence of 32 was taken, each picture being converted into electrical signals and recorded on video tape. After a successful run the satellite was interrogated. A scientist at Hawaii or Fort Monmouth radioed a command which caused the video tape to play back the pictures. Then the tape was erased, rewound, and was ready for the next command.

With this system there was no limit; so long as Tiros was not damaged and sufficient power was available it would respond to ground commands. Batteries were placed aboard to run the electronic equipment, and the charge was maintained by 9,200 solar cells fixed to the outside of the satellite, giving it the appearance of a ceramic tile table. Powered from the sun, the satellite could have lasted many years. Unfortunately one of the switches on board failed after a period of 78 days and the television transmitter could not be turned off. The solar batteries could not take the heavy load for long; the power supply for the satellite failed within half an hour. Nevertheless, Tiros I had responded to command more than 700 times during its active life, giving the meteorologists 22,950 pictures. Nimbus, Aeros and other weather eyes may surpass Tiros I in efficiency, but we will always have affection for the prototype of the series.

Weather satellites have given scientists some pleasant surprises; discoveries have been made which were completely unexpected. For example the TV pictures showed smudges in the St. Lawrence River which turned out to be ice floes. With one picture the satellite has the potential of showing dangerous ice areas over six hundred thousand square miles of ocean. White streaks were identified as vapor trails along the jet route from Miami to New York. Under favorable conditions the satellites might therefore give information on the movement of jet aircraft. The contour lines in isolated regions such as the

Himalaya Mountains could be accurately surveyed in an unusual fashion. The snow line, which separates the bare ground from the white cap of a mountain, follows a contour of almost constant height. Thus the pattern of the snow field shows at a glance information that would be difficult to obtain from the ground. At a height of four hundred miles the reflection of the sun in the calm sea makes a bright spot about fifty miles in diameter. However, when the sea is rough the bright glint expands to cover one hundred or even two hundred miles. This simple physical property gives a potential method of assessing the roughness of the sea.

Echo I will also find a place in the pages of history as the forerunner of our communication satellites. This satellite was a hundred foot balloon, plastic with an aluminum coating. The balloon was packed into a nose cone to be inflated when the thousand-mile orbit was reached. During the summer of 1960 it made a fine sight glistening like a first-magnitude star in the twilight sky. I remember Echo I for rather unscientific reasons. I first saw the satellite when I was preparing the fire for a summer beach party. Two hours later it was again passing overhead. Echo I had traveled once around the world while we sat beside the glowing barbecue.

The coated balloon forms a mirror in the sky, and from its surface radio signals can be flashed from one side of the continent to the other. It is a passive device; we do not have to rely upon the response of electronic equipment carried aboard the space craft. This means that the number of channels is unlimited. If a million people wish to bounce a signal all at the same time, they may do so—the mirror will reflect each signal. Echo I successfully passed coded signals from California to New Jersey. Ordinary speech and music followed, and it also bounced a letter in a flash from one post office to another by means of television.

There are great prospects for these mirrors in the sky, in fact a chain of reflectors is contemplated by NASA (National Aeronautics and Space Administration) in Operation Rebound. A large number of balloons will be in orbit at the same time, thus providing a mirror for every location. To use these reflectors, however, one needs a high-power transmitter and a large antenna. This can be avoided only by using an active satellite containing a receiver and a transmitter to relay the message. Orbital telephone exchanges, as they may someday be called, like this are being developed in the Courier sequence.

Satellites are also an aid to navigators; Transit I was the forerunner of such instruments. These artificial moons are orbital beacons, and we may look upon them as lighthouses in the sky. Just as the navigator of a ship can find his position by taking a bearing from two landmarks, so can he use the transit satellites. It is not necessary to find the position of the satellite by pointing a radio antenna toward

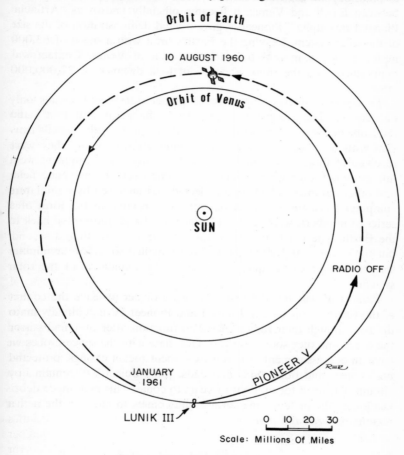

Fig. 36. The path of Pioneer V

it. The navigator has only to record the tone of the signal from Transit, which is sufficient to tell him the instant when he is closest to the satellite as it passes by. Two or three sightings like this will give him a fix which is accurate to a fraction of a mile. Needless to say the system works through fog and cloud with equal accuracy and can be used in regions of the Earth that are poorly marked, such as the Pacific Ocean and the Polar regions.

Pioneer V was a paddle-wheel satellite which passed, according to plan, beyond the Earth-moon system. As it entered the long orbit between Earth and Venus, it became officially known as "Artificial Planet 1960 alpha." Pioneer V gave a vivid demonstration of the size of the solar system. Leaving the Earth's orbit with a speed of 63,000 mph., it took 6 months to reach the orbit of Venus. Contact was maintained with the robot aboard out to a distance of 22,000,000 miles.

To conserve energy, the artificial planet transmitted signals only on request. The request was sent from the giant 250 foot radio telescope at Jodrell Bank in England. Although the radio signals traveled with the speed of light, two minutes elapsed before they were received at Pioneer V. On reception, the automatic equipment went into action. Information concerning cosmic rays, the magnetic field, and other parameters had been collected and analyzed by a miniature computer since the last interrogation. The results, in the form of a series of numbers, were released from storage and transmitted back to the Earth. The reaction time of the satellite was less than a second, but the scientist at Jodrell Bank was compelled to wait four minutes for the answer to his question, such is the immensity of the solar system.

Pioneer V was not the first man-made object to leave the control of the Earth-moon system. Lunik I and Pioneer IV had already made the trip, though their radios ceased to function after they had passed the moon and they soon were lost. Out there with the space probes we have an odd assortment of hardware—spent rocket casings, protective nose cones, and other odds and ends. Each object will remain in a circumsolar orbit for millions of years to come. This man-made debris has joined the meteors, meteorites, and comets to move in the nether regions *between the planets*.

PART VI

# FAR HORIZONS

The great spiral galaxy in Andromeda as seen through the 72-inch telescope of Lord Rosse. From a nineteenth century print. (*General Astronomy*, C. A. Young, Ginn and Company)

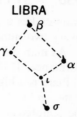

LIBRA

CHAPTER **27**

# ISLAND UNIVERSES

THE DEVELOPMENT OF MAN'S UNDERSTANDING OF THE UNIVERSE has taken place very slowly. Like a child he has faltered on the way, for the lesson has been difficult to learn. With a strong ego, he placed himself in the center of a tiny world, and was reluctant to admit his true position. The Earth was the center of a universe created entirely for him. The sun and moon provided light, while the jeweled firmament turned each day to do him homage. As well as being a thing of beauty, the sky, with its constellations and planets, was also there to be of service to mankind. The changes in the celestial panorama showed him when to plant his crops, and told him of future events in his life as planned by the gods.

Although Copernicus downgraded the Earth, people found solace in the belief that the sun was the true hub of the universe. Then Galileo's little telescope resolved the Milky Way into stars, and our sun became just one member of a large organization. William Herschel could find no end to the stars as he probed to fainter and fainter magnitudes. The Dutch astronomer, J. C. Kapteyn, repeated Herschel's work at the beginning of this century by counting the number of stars in each direction in the sky. After years of work, he produced a model of the universe which encouraged the old egoism. In the Kapteyn universe the number of stars decreased as one moved away from the sun. The sun, and with it the Earth, held a privileged position. The words of Thomas Digges, some three hundred years before, rang true; "The sun like a king in the middest of al raigneth and geeveth lawes of motion to ye rest." Unfortunately Kapteyn was wrong. The American, Harlow Shapley, shook the complacency by discovering the true center of the galaxy in the constellation of Sagittarius. The sun is near the edge of a flattened cloud of stars, and like other

249

stars makes a circular journey around the nucleus of the galaxy once every two hundred million years.

As man gropes his way toward the truth he shows a very poor performance. If there is a fork in the road, he takes the wrong turning; if there is a high wall, he tries to climb it instead of going through the gate, and if there is a pit in the road, he tumbles in. A pessimist would be tempted to formulate a *law of progress,* "If a mistake is possible, mankind will make it."

A fine example of this is the recognition of the galaxies outside our own. For a hundred years or more astronomers had seen hazy patches of light through their telescopes, the nebulae. Very few people were willing to recognize the nebulae as island universes in space, like our own. The argument reached a climax at a meeting of the National Academy of Sciences in Washington, D. C. At this time Harlow Shapley and Heber D. Curtis took opposing viewpoints. Shapley had just announced the correct position of the sun in the Milky Way, but he chose the wrong side of the argument during the debate on nebulae. Curtis pointed out how the light from some of the distant nebulae was exactly like the light from stars, and the spectrum must be produced by a large aggregation of stars. Curtis also discussed the peculiar effect known for some time as the "zone of avoidance." Very few nebulae were found in the direction of the Milky Way; they seem to avoid the plane of our galaxy. Curtis said that the nebulae were distributed uniformly through space, but were obscured near the plane of the Milky Way by clouds of interstellar dust.

Shapley, on the other hand, thought that the zone of avoidance was real, and that there was no other galaxy comparable in size to our own. In his viewpoint, the nebulae were small clouds of gas scattered around the galaxy, and as the galaxy moved through space, like a flying saucer, the nebulae were pushed aside by some unknown force so as to avoid the central plane. Within three years, the viewpoint defended by Shapley was proved wrong. Edwin P. Hubble, using the new 100-inch telescope on Mt. Wilson, resolved the great nebula in Andromeda into stars. It was a galaxy, a gigantic cloud of stars like our own Milky Way system. Shapley quickly recognized the discovery, changed his viewpoint, and devoted his long career to the study of galactic systems.

One of the difficulties in the study of galaxies is how to determine their distance. Without a measure of distance, a faint hazy patch can be a small nearby object or a large remote one. But distances are not easy to obtain, for the parallax is infinitesimal. Sometimes a nova appears in a distant galaxy, as a white dwarf star momentarily flares up. Novae in our own galaxy usually reach an absolute magnitude of $-7$, and it is reasonable to suppose that they do so in other galaxies as well. Of course, the distant nova will appear much fainter than $-7$, and the measurement of its faintness tells us the distance. Another type of star that gives away its distance is the Cepheid variable. We saw in an earlier chapter how the Cepheid star pulsates rhythmically, and how the time between the oscillations depends upon the average brightness of the star. There is a definite relation between the period and luminosity of the star. If the period is 6 days, like delta Cephei, the absolute magnitude is $-3$; if the period is 50 days, the magnitude is $-5$, and so on. This relationship has been found for Cepheids in our own galaxy, and we again presume the relationship to hold in distant galaxies.

Unfortunately there is a pitfall in the method, and astronomers fell into it. There are two relationships, one for stars of Population I, and another for II. The Population I Cepheids are about four times brighter than the corresponding Cepheids in Population II. Astronomers thought that there was just one type of Cepheid, and by some mischance were using the period luminosity relation for Population II stars. Now the Cepheids that we see in distant galaxies all belong to Population I. They are the brighter stars set within the spiral arms. Population II Cepheids are fainter by one and a half magnitudes, and as luck would have it, are just below the limit of the 200-inch telescope. If we had possessed a larger telescope, the two period luminosity relationships would have been seen easily, and the error found. The error in the distance scale was suspected for many years, but it could only be uncovered at the time by an indirect approach. The mistake, however, became painfully obvious when Walter Baade discovered the two populations of stars in 1944. When the distance scale was corrected, the galaxies turned out to be twice as far away as we had previously believed. The announcement caused some rather unfair murmurs from the press about the capricious astronomers who had overnight doubled the scale of the universe.

A galaxy contains about one hundred billion stars, and the galaxies themselves seem to be never-ending. When Hubble pointed the 100-inch telescope away from the dust in the Milky Way, he saw thousands of galaxies. Long-exposure photographs with the 200-inch telescope on Mt. Palomar penetrate to a magnitude of $+23$. These photographs show 5,000 galaxies in a one-degree square. The "O" on this page is about one-half degree across, and if you were to hold it up to the

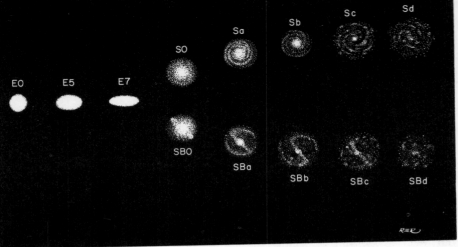

Fig. 37.  Hubble's classification of galaxies

sky ten inches from your eyes it would cover 1,000 galaxies. Even the period (.) would cover up 10 galaxies, there are so many of them in the universe. A 400-inch telescope would show galaxies as faint as magnitude +25, and this, as we will see later, would take us almost to the limit of the universe. If the numbers increase at the same rate as they have done with the 100- and 200-inch telescopes, then we expect to be able to photograph 1 billion galaxies. The membership of the universe must be even greater than this, for many galaxies are obscured by dust clouds which lie within the Milky Way. If you wanted to count the galaxies, like grains of sand, "1, 2, 3, etc. . . . ," it would take you a hundred years to reach the figure of a billion, working seven days a week, eight hours a day. Astronomers, of course, have not been able to count every galaxy, but their estimate of numbers is made from a survey of small selected regions of the sky.

It was a relief to find order among the multitudes of stars. The galaxies also can be placed in few well-defined classes. Dr. Hubble first recognized the different types of galaxies and placed them in a logical sequence. He recognized three distinct types: spirals, barred spirals, and elliptical galaxies. The three main types were then subdivided according to the sequence shown in the diagram. In the original diagram Hubble omitted with "d" spirals and the SO and SBO galaxies, adding them at a later date. There is also a choice in the arrangement of the sequence of elliptials; in the original diagram the sequence was reversed.

The elliptical galaxies take their name from their shape. They resemble huge globular clusters that have been distorted from the spherical shape, and the numeral gives a measure of the flattening. EO galaxies appear exactly circular in outline, while E7 galaxies are extremely flattened ellipses. There are, of course, intermediate types from E1 through E6. Plate 41 showns an E5 galaxy taken with the 200-inch telescope. It has been resolved into individual stars on its outer fringes, but the nucleus is still a hazy nebula.

There is a pitfall to be avoided with elliptical galaxies. Even though we see different shaped galaxies in the sky, we cannot assume that these different shapes actually exist. It is quite possible for all the shapes from EO to E7 to be produced by just one form, a flattened disk. Thus, when we viewed the disk edge-on we would see Type E7, when we looked from above we would see the circular outline of an EO. The intermediate types could be produced by different angles of tilt. A very careful investigation was needed to avoid this pitfall. Hubble worked out how many EO galaxies we would expect if just one shape of galaxy were involved. In theory there should be fewer round shapes than elliptical in the sky, but by observation Hubble found more EO galaxies than E7. He concluded that spherical galaxies really did exist, and that there were true differences in the shape of ellipticals. A refinement of the method shows equal numbers in each of the classes from EO to E7.

Ellipticals resemble the globular clusters in another way. They contain Population II stars, the old, first-generation stars. No young stars are seen, and presumably new stars are not forming at the present time. Interstellar dust is absent in ellipticals, and they seem to be a closed system, doomed to extinction.

Elliptical galaxies are in the minority; three galaxies out of four are spirals. The spirals are split into two groups, the normal spirals, S, and the spirals with a bar, SB. Apart from the bar, there is very little difference between the S and SB spirals. We will follow the sequence of the normal spirals, and what we say about them will also apply to the barred spirals.

All spirals have a bright nucleus at the center of a disk of stars. The nucleus is composed of Population II stars, and this region, at least in our own galaxy, seems to be devoid of dust and gas. The disk surrounding the nucleus is composed of Population I stars, and is permeated by thick clouds of dust from which the young stars are forming. As we move along the sequence, the nucleus becomes smaller and smaller, until at Type Sd it has disappeared. The spiral arms surrounding the nucleus become more open and well-developed as we move along the sequence. Thus an Sb has tightly wound arms, while an Sc is more open. The Andromeda galaxy is an Sb spiral, and we think the Milky Way is the same. When we look at a photograph of a spiral we must allow for the effects of tilt, because we see some spirals face-on, and others at an angle. We view some galaxies exactly from the side, and then it is impossible to see any detail of the spiral arms. In the edgewise view, the spiral structure is indicated by the dark lanes of dust which are embedded within the arms in the central plane of the galaxy.

The SO spirals show no sign of an arm, and were it not for the large nucleus it would be difficult to separate them from the elliptical galaxies. If the SO galaxies are related to spirals, then we would expect the disk to be composed of Population I stars and the nucleus Population II. At the time of writing this has not been checked observationally, and we must wait to see whether the speculation is correct. The SO's very frequently show an outer ring, and so do the barred spirals. In fact a ring of stellar material can occur in any of the spiral types. The French astronomer, Dr. Gerard de Vaucouleurs, proposes to add a suffix (r) when a spiral contains a ring. At the end of the sequence we find the Sd spirals, an amorphous collection of stars showing very little indication of spiral structure and containing no nucleus. Among the spirals the most frequent types are Sc and SO. Type Sd is the least frequent. Not more than four spirals in a hundred fall in this category.

Galaxies vary in size. There are giants and dwarfs in each class, but we can talk about an average size. The ellipticals are, in general, smaller than the spirals. The ellipticals are ten thousand light years in diameter, and are three thousand light years thick. The average Sb spiral is fifty thousand light years in diameter and about eight thousand thick. The Sa and Sc spirals are somewhat smaller than the Sb's. Their average size is thirty thousand light years.

Because of the error in the distance scale, and because of the neglect of interstellar absorption, our galaxy for a long time was considered to be the largest in the universe. Careful measurements have now reduced our estimates of its size to proper proportions. A diameter of but eighty thousand light years seems to be close to the truth. In contrast, our estimates of other galaxies have been increased by the recent doubling of the distance scale; they are all twice as large as we originally thought. Because of this revision the Andromeda spiral was reappraised at a diameter of eighty thousand light years instead of forty thousand. In fact, some measurements show the Andromeda galaxy to be a little larger than our own.

Our superiority complex has been shaken over the years until we are led to contemplate a *law of mediocrity;* "The Earth is an ordinary planet; the sun is an ordinary star, the Milky Way is an ordinary galaxy . . ." One fact, however, saves our pride; both Messier 31 and our own Milky Way system seem to be in the upper class of the Sb spirals. They are both thirty thousand light years larger than the average. We may be wrong though. We can see more detail in the nearby galaxies, and we may tend to overestimate the size of M 31 and the Milky Way. Also a further revision in the distance scale might force us to admit that all distant galaxies were larger than we think at present. Then our galaxy would be reduced from an upper-class giant to an average spiral, or perhaps even a mediocre dwarf.

Each galaxy is rotating about an axis like a flying saucer spinning in the air. The spirals rotate so that the arms are trailing or winding up. This simple statement is the result of years of work, for the sense of rotation presented another stumbling block. With a spectroscope astronomers can certainly tell which side of a galaxy is approaching and which side is receding, but this does not tell the direction of rotation, because it is very difficult to tell how the galaxy is tilted. If the top of the galaxy is tilted toward us or away from us it will appear the same in a photograph. This presents an ambiguity, for if the spiral arms are trailing when we assume a galaxy is tilted forward, then the arms will do the reverse if we assume the galaxy is tilted backward. Thus we were provided with substance for a debate where the proposer and the opposer had an equal chance. The argument, sometimes heated, continued for more than twenty years, but gradually evidence accumulated to show that the arms of all galaxies were trailing. The most concerted opposition to this viewpoint came from Swedish astronomers led by Professor B. Lindblad. The conclusive evidence came from an investigation of the Milky Way system, when radio astronomers mapped out the arms. Our galaxy is rotating clockwise when viewed from the north galactic pole, and under these conditions the arms are trailing. One or two Swedes, however, remain unconvinced.

When Hubble set the galaxies in a sequence, it was very tempting to ask about evolution. Did the galaxy begin as an elliptical and proceed through the SO stage to become a degenerate spiral, or did a loose collection of stars collect, spinning faster and faster until they formed an elliptical galaxy? As in the main sequence of the stars, the galaxies in their evolution probably move into the sequence from the side, and do not proceed from one type to the other. There are many speculations, of which I will describe just one, the suggestion of Dr. Jan H. Oort of Holland. According to him, each galaxy developed from a huge cloud of gas, from which formed proto-stars. The life history of a galaxy is controlled entirely by the rotation of the original cloud. If it rotates slowly, the condensation of stars is very efficient, and almost all of the material is used up. Under these conditions an elliptical galaxy would form—a slowly rotating cloud of stars, all of the same age, with no rebirth. If the original cloud were rotating rapidly, then a flattened disk of gas would be ejected from the spinning nucleus. The nucleus would then condense completely, forming a homogeneous cloud of Population II stars. Star formation would be impeded in the disk by the rarefaction of the gas and by the stirring action of the rotation. Thus not all the material would be used up in the initial star formation process, and the residue would over the years slowly collect together to form new stars, the stars of Population I. It is difficult to explain the spiral arms by Oort's theory, however. Not only does his theory fail to explain how the spiral arms formed in the beginning, but it does not account for their present motion. The arms near the nucleus revolve at twice the speed of the outer edge. Thus the arms are continually trying to wrap themselves up, and if the process continued a galaxy would rapidly evolve from an Sc to a Sb and then finally an Sa. If this process did occur, the Sc spirals would rapidly disappear, and yet they are the most numerous of all the spirals found in space.

All theories have their difficulties in the early stages, and if the objections can be overcome the theory is strengthened. Astronomers do not have sufficient knowledge at present to continue their speculation about the evolution of galaxies, but with better instruments and more powerful mathematical methods the answer may not be far away.

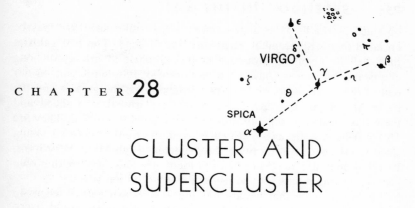

# CHAPTER 28

# CLUSTER AND SUPERCLUSTER

WE HAVE SEEN IN PART IV THAT THERE IS A HIERARCHY OF STARS; twins, triplets, multiplets, and then the complex system of a galaxy. There is also a hierarchy among the galaxies themselves. Field galaxies exist in isolation; others occur in pairs. NGC 5426 and 5427 of the *New General Catalog* are a good example of a double system where the galaxies are clearly separated. There is a faint bridge of light between the two objects, where the spiral arms of each galaxy have been distorted. The galaxies are revolving around each other as a binary system, but it will take millions of years of observation to measure an accurate orbit. We do not know whether the galaxies will swing around each other and then separate along parabolic orbits, or whether the orbits are ellipses and the galaxies form a permanent binary system. The pair, NGC 4038 and 4039, are even closer and the distortion is more pronounced. Here the galaxies are close enough to make contact with each other, a collision is in progress. We can also see multiplets such as the group of five galaxies close together in the constellation Pegasus known as Stephan's Quintet. These galaxies are acting upon each other with gravitational forces which tend to hold the group together.

Our own galaxy and M 31 form a double system, but there are at least fifteen other galaxies involved, and the complex is called the "local group." We, in the Milky Way system, are at one end of the group, and M 31 is at the other with a separation of 1.5 million light years. The Andromeda galaxy, M 31, is approaching us at a speed of 160 miles per second. This speed is only the line of sight velocity obtained by the Doppler displacement of spectral lines; there may be an additional displacement across the line of sight. The two galaxies may well be revolving around a common center of gravity on long elliptical orbits but we have no direct proof of this at present. At our end of the local group we have two companions, the greater and the lesser Magellanic Clouds. These clouds are irregular in shape and their classification is difficult, but they may be of Type SBd. They are 150,000 light years away, which is quite close cosmically speaking, since the distance is only twice the diameter of the Milky Way itself. In all probability the Magellanic Clouds are satellites to our own galaxy, making a pass around us once every 3 billion years.

We can imagine that we are looking at our own galaxy when we look at the great spiral in Andromeda. We cannot see much detail within the Milky Way, because we are set inside, but we recognize the main features such as the nucleus and outer arms. Like our galaxy, M 31 has a retinue of globular clusters set in a spherical halo around the nucleus. The spiral arms are marked by the giant stars of Population I which have been formed recently from the thick clouds of dust. We can also see planetary nebulae and clouds of hydrogen illuminated in the intense ultraviolet light of the young stars. In addition to the galactic clusters which occur in profusion along the length of the arms, there are also stellar associations and irregular nebulae similar to the Orion nebula in our own galaxy.

M 31 has more companions than has the Milky Way. Two dwarf galaxies which are very close to the great spiral are undoubtedly satellites. You can see M 32 in Plate 40, a small round elliptical, and NGC 205, a larger and more distant E5. Three other ellipticals and one irregular galaxy are also in this region, but are not included in the area of the photograph. Close by Andromeda we find M 33 in the constellation of Triangulum. It is 500,000 light years away from the Andromeda spiral. M 33 is a fine example of an open spiral of Type Sc. It is average in size, some 30,000 light years across, and is typical of its class in every respect. It has a small nucleus and four well-developed spiral arms. The 200-inch telescope shows us many details. Population II stars are found in the center and the giant stars of Population I can be seen in the arms. Individual clusters of stars can be resolved and there is also a large amount of interstellar dust.

The local group pales to insignificance when compared with the clusters. A cluster of galaxies contains on the average about 150 galaxies of all types from giant spirals to dwarf ellipticals, crowded into a volume of space not much bigger than the local group. Whereas

M 31 is 1.5 million light years away from us in the local group, it would be less than 1 million light years away if we were in a typical cluster. As the survey proceeds, more and more galaxies are found to be associated with some cluster or other, and astronomers are beginning to suggest that a completely isolated galaxy is a rarity. There must be millions of clusters in space awaiting discovery by the 200-inch telescope.

Our local group is a mediocre collection of galaxies, and hardly qualifies to be called a cluster. At the other extreme there are clusters with thousands of members. One of these giant clusters is in the constellation of Coma Berenices, a constellation that passes almost overhead in the southern part of the United States. The galaxies in the giant cluster tend to collect together in the shape of a ball. If the galaxies could be replaced by stars they would look very much like the globular star clusters, with a high concentration at the center and a gradual thinning out toward the edge. In the Coma cluster, 10,724 individual galaxies have been photographed so far, and there may be many dwarf galaxies that have escaped detection. Doppler measurements reveal an agitation among the members of the cluster, which constantly swarm like a cloud of gnats. This movement maintains the shape of the cluster, for if the velocities were reduced to zero the cluster would collapse under the action of gravity. Each galaxy has a sufficient motion to prevent the collapse of the cluster, but very few of them have a high enough velocity to escape completely from the cluster.

The giant clusters with 10,000 members or more are very homogeneous in make-up. Usually they contain SO and elliptical galaxies but no well-developed spiral galaxies. This segregation is a mystery. Did all the members in a particular cluster of galaxies form at the same time, and are we to presume, from the predominence of ellipticals, that only Population II stars are to be found throughout the cluster? Since some astronomers have found evidence for dust and gas between the galaxies in the Coma cluster, we would be surprised to find no Population I stars there amongst the intergalactic material. Perhaps the members of the cluster are too close together for the extensive spiral arms to form. In the Coma cluster, for example, the individual galaxies are no more than 50,000 light years apart. If any of these galaxies were originally spirals, then the spiral arms would touch. Perhaps during the course of history collisions have taken place between the galaxies in which the spiral arms have been stripped off, and only the nucleus survived. If this suggestion is correct, all we see now are the nuclei made of Population II stars, and the debris from the spiral arms has been scattered through the intervening space.

There is another giant cluster in the constellation of Virgo. Here one thousand galaxies or more are crowded together in a spherical group, but the crowding is not as great as in the Coma cluster. Many spiral galaxies are to be found mixed in with the ellipticals. Perhaps, since the cluster is more open, collisions do not occur and the spiral arms can survive.

This cluster in Virgo at a distance of 30 million light years has caused much speculation. Stretching upward from Virgo toward the constellation of Ursa Major there is a concentration of galaxies which forms an irregular band. Curtis called this the "canopy of galaxies." It is very tempting to imagine another Milky Way made up of galaxies instead of stars. Indeed a careful study shows a disk-shaped system with its center in the Virgo cluster and with a diameter of about 100 million years. The sun is set near the edge of the Milky Way, and likewise our galaxy is set near the edge of this super-system. It contains at least 10,000 galaxies, has the shape of a flattened disk, and shows signs of a slow rotation centered about the Virgo cluster. Yet we hesitate to talk of a "super galaxy" where the members are galaxies instead of stars. It has been given various names such as "hyper galaxy," and "inner meta galaxy," but perhaps the best name for it is "supercluster." We do not believe, nor do we wish to infer, that the Virgo system is the hub of the universe, and that we are located in a privileged cluster. On the other hand, it does appear to be unusually large and it certainly dwarfs in size the clusters like the one in Coma Berenices. Presumably there are other superclusters besides our own for at least one other has been found in the skies of the Southern Hemisphere. Perhaps superclusters, with a diameter of 100 million light years, and a membership of 10,000 galaxies or more, form the ultimate building block of the universe. Certainly it is hard to imagine anything more extensive or majestic than these super-clusters.

CHAPTER **29**

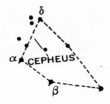

# THE REDSHIFT

HUBBLE'S EXPLORATIONS MOVED FORWARD BY GIANT STEPS AFTER he had found the distance to the great nebula in Andromeda. He relied heavily on the concept of brightness and the inverse square law, which states that a tenfold increase in distance produces a hundredfold decrease in brightness. Galaxies 10 million light years away should appear five magnitudes fainter than galaxies 1 million light years away. A further step out to a distance of 100 million light years should again produce a decrease of five magnitudes.

As we increase the size of our step we ultimately reach a distance where even the brightest objects are just a ghostly glow when examined through the telescope. Then the galaxy is at the limiting magnitude of the instrument, and further galaxies cannot be seen at all. With long-exposure photographs the range of a telescope can be extended by two or three magnitudes. At the limit, we are dealing with a sprinkling of silver grains in the emulsion, representing a galaxy that the eyes of man have never seen. The limiting magnitude of the 200-inch telescope is +23. This is a practical value applying to average conditions of atmospheric seeing and night-sky glow. On exceptional nights with extreme care the range of the instrument can be extended another magnitude, but for routine work the limit is +23. Cepheid

### TABLE 4. RANGE OF 200-INCH TELESCOPE

| Object | Absolute Magnitude | Distance (light years) |
|---|---|---|
| Cepheid type I | −3 | 5 million |
| Super giant I | −6 | 21 million |
| Nova | −7 | 32 million |
| Globular cluster | −9 | 82 million |
| Supernova | −15 | 1 billion |
| Giant spiral | −19.5 | 10 billion |

variables have an absolute magnitude of $-3$, which is the brightness they would have at a distance of 33 light years. The Cepheids in the arms of the Andromeda spiral appear on photographs with a magnitude of $+21$. Because of the apparent faintness of the Cepheids we know that the Andromeda spiral is at a distance of 1.5 million light years. If M 31 were at a distance of 5 million light years, the individual Cepheids would be below the limit of detection. Cepheids, because of the period luminosity relation, are one of our best indicators of distance, yet we cannot use them to full advantage. They enable us to measure the distance of M 31, the spiral in Triangulum and other members of the local group, but beyond that they are useless.

When the Cepheids fail us we turn to the next brightest objects on the list, the super giants of Population I. These are the very brightest objects in the spiral arms, and by using them we can explore out to a distance of 21 million light years. We cannot place too much reliance on them, however. Hubble himself was mistaken several times. What he took to be super giants turned out to be emission nebulae. The star itself was embedded in a region of hydrogen gas, and a large volume was made to glow by ultraviolet stimulation. The combined brightness of the nebula and star was about four times as bright as the star itself, and Hubble obtained erroneous distance measurements.

The globular clusters take us another step into space, out to a distance of 82 million light years. As far as earthly standards go this is a tremendous step, nearly 500 billion billion miles, but by astronomical standards this is not enough. The globular clusters become useless as a distance marker before we have left the confines of the supercluster. A supernova will extend our range with a step more than ten times as large as the one we make with the globular clusters. But supernovae occur only once every five hundred years or so in a galaxy, shining at maximum brightness for not more than two weeks. It is entirely a matter of luck when one is caught on the photographs.

When all our better known objects are exhausted, we are forced to use the brightness of a galaxy itself. The total magnitude of M 31, a giant Sb, is $-19.5$, while M 33, a normal Sc, is $-17.2$. We use the total brightness of a galaxy only as a last resort, for by its use we are flirting dangerously around the brink of abysmal errors. When a galaxy is showing as a featureless collection of silver grains we have no way of telling whether it is a giant, a normal galaxy, or a dwarf. In assuming an absolute brightness, we can easily make an error of five magnitudes, and with it a tenfold error in distance. On the average, though, if we study a large number of galaxies, we have a fair chance of being right. Until a better method of distance measurement is found, astronomers have no choice. They prefer to take the risk, and probe deeply into space, rather than confine themselves to the more secure foreground.

The drive to reach for the far horizon comes partly from man's yearning to touch the inaccessible, and partly from the discovery of a puzzling phenomenon, the redshift. Each galaxy shows a smeared-out spectrum of a multitude of stars; so with the spectroscope astronomers can find definite absorption and emission lines. The pattern of the wave lengths can be clearly seen, and the light from various atoms can be compared with the light from similar atoms on the Earth. The light from distant galaxies becomes extremely reddened, the wave length is longer and the frequency is higher than it should be. All the spectral lines are displaced toward the red end of the spectrum.

When this displacement occurs in starlight we invoke the Doppler effect and infer that the star is receding from us. Now the displacement in starlight is so small, that the eye cannot detect the slight change in color of a line and one would assume that the corresponding velocity would be only a few miles per second. But the displacement in the light from galaxies is much larger; lines which are normally blue are displaced the entire length of the spectrum to become red. If the displacement is due to the Doppler effect, then the speed of the galaxy is enormous, many thousands of miles per second.

There is a lingering doubt in the minds of astronomers concerning the displacement of the lines. Hubble, who devoted his life to the study of galaxies, called the effect the "redshift" instead of the "recession of the galaxies," because although the displacement to the red was an undeniable phenomenon its interpretation was open to doubt. Over the last thirty years, however, cosmologists have shown that a general expansion of the universe is possible, and that we may, in the absence of an alternative explanation, assume that the displacement is a true Doppler effect. The observations are therefore measured and described in terms of a velocity of recession, but the whole phenomena is still conservatively called the redshift.

The redshift does not show up in the local group, but it appears and increases as we look farther into space. In the diagram we show the results of a survey by the American astronomers, Humason, Mayall and Sandage. Black spots represent individual field galaxies, and the circles are results obtained from clusters of galaxies. Instead of arranging the points according to distance, we have plotted them according to their brightness. Presumably the faint galaxies are at great distances from us, and it is these galaxies that have the large recession velocities. Galaxies in the Virgo cluster have an average

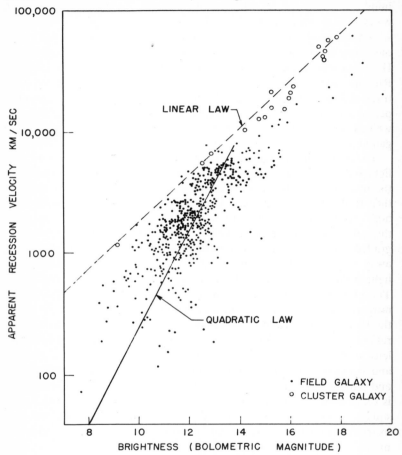

Fig. 38.  The redshift of distant galaxies

speed away from us of 700 miles per second, while the galaxies in the Coma cluster, some six times farther away, have a velocity of 4,800 miles per second.

There is a rough proportionality between speed and distance. The speed increases by 20 miles per second for every step of a million light years into space. The relentless increase is very puzzling, for it surely cannot go on indefinitely. The theory of relativity predicts a speed limit in the universe of 186,000 miles per second, the speed of light. Nothing can crash through the light barrier, for all masses become infinite at the speed of light. Yet if the redshift continues to increase we will very soon reach the point where the galaxies are receding with this speed. Already William Baum has measured the displacement in the energy curve for a galaxy of the twentieth magnitude. He finds the velocity of recession to be 75,000 miles a second. Rudolph Minkowski of Mt. Wilson and Palomar Observatories has tracked down a faint galaxy in Boötes, with a velocity of 90,000 miles per second. Perhaps with careful work, using the 200-inch telescope, we can make a further step into space and reach the point where the galaxies are almost at the speed limit.

There are many difficulties in measuring extreme redshifts. The light from the galaxy is enfeebled by distance and is also reduced by the redshift itself. If a photon of light suffers a decrease in frequency, then it also loses energy, and is more difficult to detect. We have no hope of seeing a galaxy at the speed limit, because the energy from the galaxy will never reach us. The photons will be completely degraded, or if we look at it another way, the galaxy will be moving away faster than the beam of light is coming toward us. The feeble light from the galaxy must be carefully collected and used efficiently. The photons are collected by reflection from an accurately polished mirror, such as the 200-inch, and brought to a focus. At the focus the light is concentrated further by means of a fast lens with a large ratio of aperture to focal length; the f-number of the spectroscope lens at Palomar is 0.6. The light is passed through the spectroscope and concentrated on a photographic plate. The plates are sensitive and panchromatic to record the redness of the light. The spectroscope is very compact, and the plates themselves are no bigger than ½ inch square, being cut specially for the instrument. Even with the best instruments in the world at his disposal, the astronomer must still make a long exposure of several hours to record the redshift from a far distant galaxy.

In talking about light years we bring out another interesting fact about the universe. The light from the Andromeda galaxy has taken 1.5 million years to reach us, thus we see it today as it was in prehistoric times before man roamed the Earth. The message of starlight cannot reach us instantaneously, so as we look further into the distance we are also looking backward in time. Galaxies at a distance of 3 billion light years are within our present range, and we see them as they were at the early dawn when the Earth was being formed. With extra care, and perhaps with a 400-inch telescope, we can use nature's time machine to look back to the time when the sun itself was being formed. Surprisingly enough, as we look backward in time we see no signs of youth. Our 1.5 million-year flashback finds the Andromeda galaxy looking very much as the Milky Way does today. The Virgo cluster, 30 million years back, seems to contain typical, well-formed spirals. The energy curve of a galaxy near the limit of our telescopes seems, after correcting for the redshift, to be identical with the energy curve from nearby and, therefore, older galaxies. The redshift astronomer has an awesome prospect as he reaches outward to the limit of the universe and backward to the beginning of time.

C H A P T E R **30**

# A RADIO VIEW

FOR MANY YEARS THE ASTRONOMER, WITH MODEST PRIDE, HAS FELT that he could count with certainty the number of bright stars in the sky. For years he has been in error. Even the shepherds of old, marveling at the beauties of the constellations, only saw one-half of the picture. In the dark spaces between the stars, so long thought to be empty, there are objects shining with radio waves, invisible to the human eye. Energy can be sent out on many different wave lengths, and when we add all the components together we have a spectrum. The light that we can see has a short wave length; fifty waves of yellow light would fit into one-thousandth of an inch. Heat rays have a longer wave length and are invisible. Radio waves are also invisible, having a wave length of several yards. If an object sends out radio waves alone, then we need a special instrument to find it, for if we stare like the shepherds of old we will not see it, no matter how long we look. We call the newly found objects "radio stars," but we do this in ignorance of their true nature, just as the shepherds called Venus the star of the evening and the star of the morning.

Our view of the hidden sky came as a result of the Second World War. It is strange to see a new science growing from a field of destruction, unfolding fresh branches as it reaches toward the sky. Radio engineers made great advances during the war when, under pressure of conflict, all their energy was turned toward the production of ingenious radio systems. When the conflict was over, the armed forces found themselves with a surplus of valuable radio equipment. Some of it was given to scientists in universities who used the receivers and antennas to explore the radio sky. At first the steps were rather unsure, and there was a vagueness in the exploration program, but then they stumbled across the threshold of the radio universe, seeing objects which, since Adam first walked the Earth, had been invisible.

To find a radio star you need a radio telescope and a sensitive receiver. A radio telescope is similar to the reflector designed by Sir Isaac Newton. A metal mirror, shaped like a paraboloid, brings the radio waves to a focus where a radio image is formed. This image is picked up by a small antenna, and a signal is carried down a cable to the laboratory. Here the signal is amplified several million times in the receiver, and then it is ready to be looked at by the radio astronomer. The signal can be fed to a television tube, and the radio telescope can be scanned backwards and forwards to form a visible picture of the radio star. This is seldom done, however, because at a fast scanning rate the picture would not be clear. The scientist prefers to have a permanent record by feeding the signal to the pen of a recording chart. The signals can be heard by playing them through a loud-speaker. The voice of the cosmos is sometimes loud and sometimes soft, but it is always a steady hiss. One of the largest radio telescopes in the world is at Jodrell Bank, England, where Professor Sir Bernard Lovell of Manchester University has pioneered the science of radio astronomy. In the United States, a mammoth radio telescope has been under construction for several years now. It will stand on a half-mile slab of solid rock at Sugar Grove, West Virginia. The mirror is six hundred feet across, and the total height of the telescope will be comparable to the Empire State Building in New York City.

More than one thousand radio stars have been found, and their positions marked on a star chart. Radio astronomers do not connect them up to form invisible constellations in the sky. They choose to follow the historic constellations of the shepherds. The most intense radio star in the constellation of Cygnus is called Cygnus A, the second brightest is called Cygnus B. Here we see the influence of the new on the old. Classic scholars would have insisted on the Latin genitive, A Cygni, but the system introduced by the radio engineers is eloquent enough. When a professorial chair was created at Manchester University for the new science, objections were voiced concerning its title. "The word radio comes from a Latin root, and astronomy from the Greek; it would be inappropriate to couple the two words together." Nevertheless Manchester University now has a chair of radio astronomy.

If we had radio-eyes, the brightest star in the sky would be Cassiopeia A, yet with ordinary eyes there is nothing to be seen. Astronomers have not paid much attention to this black part of the sky. It had been photographed, of course, in routine surveys, but had never been closely scrutinized. For a long while astronomers were sure there was nothing there. Then with long-exposure photography, straining the telescopes to the limit, a faint wispy cloud was found. Without the radio signals this nebulous object would have been overlooked. After several years of study we still do not know what the object is. We know the gas out there is in rapid motion, because the spectral lines are displaced, but apart from this fact, we have no clues to break the mystery. Are we looking at a bright object obscured by a dark cloud of dust; is it a violent explosion, or is it a star in the making?

Astronomers also had trouble in finding Cygnus A, the second brightest radio star. Part of the trouble was caused by a disagreement over the exact position of the star. Radio astronomers in Cambridge, England, said it was in the middle of the triangle formed by the stars gamma, delta and eta Cygni, but radio astronomers in Sydney, Australia, said it was slightly displaced. Each group checked and rechecked their measurements, and gradually the two positions came together, until there was complete agreement on the position of Cygnus A. The error in the measurement was one minute of arc, about the size of a period on this page. Walter Baade and Rudolph Minkowski at Palomar turned the 200-inch telescope to the predicted position and took a photograph. The circle of error, one minute of arc, in diameter, was filled with nearly one hundred faint stars and galaxies. This was no surprise to the astronomers. Wherever they point the telescope they expect to find many objects within the area of a period. The richness of the field containing the radio star was indeed a problem. How could the astronomer identify the source of radio waves from so many objects? It must surely be something unusual, something not found in any other direction in the sky. Close to the center of the photograph was an irregular patch of light, which in outline looked like a butterfly with rounded wings. This was the radio star. Two galaxies, two huge systems of stars and gas, were involved in a collision.

The chance of a collision between two galaxies is quite small. We know of only a few such events in the entire universe, and Cygnus A is the best example. When two galaxies collide, the stars are not affected. The space between the stars is large when compared with a star's diameter and we can regard the system as an open skeleton. Very few of the stars collide during the impact. The majority pass on their way undisturbed. Thus the two galaxies pass through each other, each system of stars emerging from the encounter unscathed. But the gas between the stars is not so fortunate. Atoms within the gaseous clouds are more tightly packed than the stars, and atomic collisions are inevitable. As the gas clouds rush together at hundreds of miles per second, tremendous heat is generated. Atoms become ionized and raised to high levels of excitation by the tremendous temperatures. The agitation of the electrified particles generates strong radio signals. The radio signals are several million times stronger than the light from the stars, and a radio astronomer observes with ease an object that is almost on the limit of sensitivity for the optical astronomer.

When the spectrum was photographed it showed the usual displacement of lines toward the red. The velocity of recession was found to be 10,450 miles per second, indicating a distance of some 200 million light years. A measurement of distance was also found by assuming the galaxies to be of average brightness and average size. From the apparent brightness and size on the photographs, two other values of the distance were obtained, and these values agreed with the figure of 200 million light years previously given by the redshift. Each galaxy is a large object, and although the galaxies are colliding with a speed of several hundred miles per second a million years must elapse before the two galaxies have passed through each other. Now the light by which we see the collision started on its journey 200 million years ago, so the whole collision process ended 199 million years ago, and the two galaxies are now moving along their separate course through space. The actual disengagement, however, will not be seen by astronomers on the Earth until 1 million years have passed by.

Another radio star coincides with Messier 87, a peculiar galaxy in Virgo. The radio signals almost certainly come from some part of this galaxy. M 87 is not like other galaxies, for it has a long jet of glowing material which rises from the nucleus. The radio noise must be caused in some way by the jet, but we do not know exactly what is taking place out there. Another radio star corresponds in position with Messier 31, the great spiral in Andromeda. Here we are certain that the radio noise is coming from every part of the galaxy, because the area of radio emission fits around the outline of the spiral arms as they appear in photographs. The total emission is quite feeble, but we are able to see it because the Andromeda galaxy is our closest neighbor. If distant galaxies radiate no more than M 31, then the signal would be too faint for us to detect here on the Earth.

The third brightest radio star in the sky is near zeta Tauri, at the tip of the lower horn of Taurus the bull. A good telescope will show a faint hazy patch in the position of the radio star. This is the Crab nebula, the remnants of a supernova explosion. Once again we have a link between the old and the new. In the year 1054 A.D. the chief astrologer to the Imperial Emperor of the Sung Dynasty prepared a careful account of a guest star in the constellation Taurus. Admittedly his main concern was whether the brilliant star was a good omen or a bad omen for his Emperor, yet the record tells us very clearly the time, place, and brightness of the explosion. Photographs taken in the present century show us that the glowing cloud of gas is still expanding, and that the explosion is still continuing as the remnants disperse. Now the strong radio signals give us one further piece of evidence. The radio waves are generated by fast-moving clouds of electrons rushing outwards from the central portions of the nebula. The electrons move in spiral paths along magnetic lines of force. The magnetic lines of force thread their way through the filaments of the nebula like an untidy head of hair. In this radio star both the visible light and the radio waves come from the same source. The electrons as they spiral around the lines of force send out a continuous spectrum ranging from the short light waves to the longer radio waves. This type of radiation is well known to the physicist in his laboratory. Its existence was predicted by theoretical physicists, but to produce synchrotron radiation in the laboratory was difficult because of the high energies involved. Physicists were therefore pleased, but not surprised, to find a natural synchrotron in the universe, energized by the explosion of a star.

The three brightest radio stars have turned out to be surprising objects—a galactic collision, a natural synchrotron, and a mysterious wisp of gas. The other radio stars, and there are hundreds of them, have not been identified. Their positions are not known accurately enough for an astronomer to begin a search with his telescope, nor do we know their distances. We do not know whether the radio stars are set among the distant galaxies, or whether they are nearby, among the stars of the Milky Way. Two other supernova have been seen since the explosion that formed the Crab Nebula. Tycho Brahe saw one in the constellation of Cassiopeia and Johannes Kepler recorded one in Ophiucus. In both positions a faint radio star is detected today, and emission is probably caused by streams of fast-moving electrons as in the Crab nebula. But we do not expect to find a large number of supernova remnants in our own galaxy, and it would be wrong to suppose that all the hundreds of radio stars are nearby supernovae. There may be a place beyond the red end of the main sequence where a star sends out most of its energy at radio wave lengths. An object such as this could not be photographed by an astronomer, nor could he see it. It would be a new class of star, a true radio star. There is indeed a radio Milky Way in the sky. The faint radio glow follows the main course of the Milky Way and shines brightly in the constellation of Sagittarius where we are looking toward the center of our galaxy. The radio Milky Way could be the unresolved glow of thousands of radio stars, or it could be produced by the cloud of protons and electrons in which the stars are embedded.

We know for sure that some of the radiation comes from gas. The hydrogen atom sends out a very weak signal when the proton at the nucleus changes its spin. The signal is sent out at a definite wave length, 21 centimeters, which forms a line in the radio spectrum. If the hydrogen cloud is moving toward us, then the wave length is slightly less than 21 centimeters, and if the hydrogen is moving away from us the wave length is slightly greater. By measuring the exact wave length we can, therefore, measure the velocity of the gas. Now velocity depends upon distance from the galactic center, this we know from studies of the stars in the spiral arms. Thus a radio astronomer can find the exact position of the hydrogen cloud in our galaxy. His measurements are not limited in any way by dust and other obscuration in space, for the radio waves pass through. With this advantage he has been more successful than the optical astronomer in exploring the far reaches of the Milky Way.

The hydrogen line has been studied with the combined efforts of radio astronomers in Holland, Great Britain, the United States, and Australia. Piece by piece we are obtaining a complete picture of our galaxy. The hydrogen follows closely the lanes of the spiral arms in which the stars are found. About a dozen spiral arms have been traced, showing that we live in a tightly wound system. It is a little early to classify our own galaxy. With a single photograph we can obtain a picture of other island universes and classify them almost at a glance. Observing the galaxy from the inside, however, is more difficult. There is more detail to see and much more work to do before we can be sure. The preliminary results show that our tightly wound galaxy is probably an Sa or Sb galaxy on the Hubble system. It certainly has no bar stretching through the nucleus, nor is it widely dispersed like Messier 33. We think that our galaxy is almost a twin to the great Andromeda spiral, except that we are a little smaller.

When the hydrogen atom becomes ionized it does not send out a single wavelength at 21 centimeters, but emits a continuous spectrum.

By comparing the continuous spectrum and the hydrogen line, radio astronomers can trace out the clouds of ionized hydrogen as well as the hydrogen atoms. Gart Westerhout, in Holland, has studied the two forms of hydrogen near the center galaxy. He finds that our galaxy is behaving like a giant whirlpool, drawing hydrogen in toward the nucleus and then spinning it out along the spiral arms. The nucleus is the center of the whirlpool and is almost clear of gas. Right at the center are one or two bright radio stars surrounded by a thin halo of protons, but the surrounding space seems to be clear, like the eye of a hurricane. The galaxy is dynamic, a living cloud. Stars are born in the spiral arms to follow a course of evolution and ultimate decay. As the stars die, a fresh supply of hydrogen is drawn in from the surrounding space to supply more material for the new generation of stars. If Dr. Westerhout's conclusions are correct, then the galaxy will be perpetuated with new populations replacing the old. His results make it very difficult to answer the questions "How old is the galaxy?" and "How long will it exist?"

# CHAPTER 31

LUPUS

CENTAURU

# PRESENT-DAY VIEW
# OF THE UNIVERSE

COSMOLOGY IS A FIELD WHERE ASTRONOMERS FEAR TO TREAD. IT IS a field of study that covers the entire universe, from planets and stars to the billions of galaxies in the space around us. The universe was quite a puzzle to the Greek scholars. Although they concerned themselves only with the sun and its attendant planets, the growth of their understanding was slow. For thousands of years the ancient stargazers watched the planets moving around the ecliptic without inquiring into the cause of the movement. The high priests of Babylonia reached a plateau of empiricism; planetary movements were predicted year after year by rule of thumb with no insight into the true nature of the solar system. Then Ptolemy's system was introduced, giving greater accuracy in predictions even though the theoretical framework was erroneous. Another thousand years elapsed before Copernicus suggested that the Earth was not the center of the universe. His theory required the life's work of Tycho and the brilliant intuition of Kepler to substantiate it. Later, Newton showed that Kepler's three laws of planetary motion resulted from the gravitational field of the sun. However, a full understanding of the solar system could not be achieved until the laws of physics and modern science had been developed. In this century, infinitesimal deviations in the motion of the planet Mercury have been explained in terms of space· curvature in Einstein's theory of general relativity. Many new scientific laws were established from our inquiry into the workings of the universe in the limited region around the sun.

Now the horizon has expanded, and we are faced with a universe far more complex than the solar system. Within the last fifty years we have come to regard the sun as an ordinary star, one among the 100 billion of the local galaxy. The giant reflectors have shown a seemingly endless panorama of other galaxies; perhaps 10 billion or even 100 billion of them could be photographed if the dust of the Milky Way were removed. Light from distant galaxies is shifted toward the red, the wave length is longer and the frequency is lower than light generated on the Earth. If this is a Doppler effect then the galaxies are receding from us, and the universe is expanding. Cosmologists must now concern themselves with the multitude of galaxies and the matter between them. They must account for the formation, evolution, and decay of galaxies; the twins and multiplets; the clusters and the superclusters. In particular they must try to explain the remarkable phenomenon of the redshift.

There are three philosophical themes running through cosmology, each one being an aesthetic stipulation, plausible but unproven. They can be written down in terms of three principles. Each one seems reasonable by itself, but no theory has been produced that agrees with the principles to the satisfaction of all cosmologists.

*The principle of conformity* expresses our belief in some set of scientific laws which underlie the workings of the entire universe. We would expect all the laws of physics determined in the laboratories here on Earth to apply throughout the universe. We are not sympathetic toward any theory that suggests one set of laws for the galaxies and another set for the planets. For example, we expect a cosmological theory to follow the laws of Kepler (or more exactly, of Einstein) when applied to the small volume of space surrounding the sun. If the *principle of conformity* is not true, then the Earth is a unique place where unusual laws apply. Uniqueness, of course, swells our ego, but we avoid such an assumption since it has been proved many times in the past that the Earth is not in any way a special domain.

The *cosmological principle* stresses the uniformity of the universe. As well as obeying the same laws of physics, the material throughout the universe appears the same from any viewpoint. As we look from the Earth we expect to find the same number of galaxies and clusters of galaxies in every direction. There is no unique center to the universe, or, at least, if one exists we do not expect to see it. The universe has the same average density at every point. If a giant took an enormous drag net, he would scoop out the same number of galaxies wherever he dipped. The cosmological principle reduces the universe of galaxies to a cosmopolitan group. If we on the Earth do not have a unique position, then neither does anyone else. The principle is also a useful starting point since it is a simplifying assumption without which the mathematics of cosmology would be almost insoluble.

Recently H. Bondi and T. Gold in England enunciated the *perfect cosmological principle* in which the universe is supposed to be uniform in time as well as in space. From the Earth we see a certain number of galaxies uniformly scattered in the sky. This number will remain the same for eternity. Even though certain galaxies may disappear, others will develop to take their place. As with the first two principles, the reasons for accepting the *perfect cosmological principle* are aesthetic. It says there is nothing unique about the present time. The universe was not created at a particular instant in the past, nor will it disappear at any time in the future. This principle is objectionable to some minds; indeed, there are certain important cosmological theories that pay no regard to it.

Before turning to cosmology, astronomers have to think very carefully about space itself. For everyday purposes we can imagine space to have three dimensions—length, breadth, and height, which gives us a clear concept of distance and a straight line. But physicists know that this is not exactly true; space itself is a little more complicated. Gravitational fields produce a distortion which is exactly accounted for by Einstein's theory of *general relativity*. Einstein showed that we must deal with four dimensions instead of three, the fourth one being proportional to time. Space and time are inseparable quantities which form the space-time continuum. The distance between two points is defined by a new metric or measurement interval, one that includes time. Without the application of a force, an object moves through space-time along a geodesic line. This is regarded as a state of rest and embodies Newton's law of motion: "An object will move uniformly in a straight line unless acted on by a force." However, in the theory of general relativity, the straight lines are geodesics which become curved orbits in a gravitational field. Even a person resting in a chair is moving rapidly along the time axis in the space-time continuum with a speed approximately equal to $i/c$, the square root of $-1$ divided by the velocity of light.

Einstein set up general field equations which help us to calculate the space-time distortion produced by gravity. If we know the distribution of mass, then the field equations lead to the metric, which in turn describes the geodesic line and the motion of a free particle. The metric for a point mass was derived by the German astronomer Karl Schwarzschild at the beginning of the century. This solution was of great interest because it applied to the space around the sun. Space-time was found to be curved and the geodesic lines were approximately ellipses, conforming to Kepler's laws of planetary motion. The planet Mercury had for many years been discussed by astronomers because it did not exactly obey the laws of Kepler and Newton. Yet Mercury and all the other planets follow exactly along a geodesic line as given by the theory of general relativity. The discrepancy with Newtonian physics had been accounted for by the curvature of space-time in the region around the sun.

But how could general relativity be extended to describe the entire universe? It was a difficult mathematical problem to derive the metric in the solar system where only one massive object need be considered. How could the metric be made to take into account all the other stars and the multitude of galaxies? To do this, scientists have had to rely heavily on the *cosmological principle,* assuming the universe to be homogeneous when considered on a large enough scale. The innumerable galaxies are regarded as a collection of particles which, in the extreme viewpoint, can be treated as a continuous fluid. Even with this simplification there is no general agreement among scientists as to the correct metric for the description of space-time between the galaxies.

Dr. Albert Einstein turned to the problem in 1917, before the redshift had been discovered. It was natural that he should look for a static solution in which the universe behaved as a fluid at rest. Unfortunately the field equations of general relativity would not produce a static metric. Einstein was compelled to alter the field equations in a somewhat arbitrary manner. He added space-time coefficients multiplied by a certain number called the "cosmological constant." This constant was not needed to explain the motion of the planets around the sun and therefore its introduction violated the *principle of conformity.* However, Einstein supposed the cosmological constant to be so small that it would not produce any noticeable effects even if it were introduced into the equations of the solar system. As a result he produced the "Einstein universe."

The Einstein metric contained a space distortion but there was no distortion in the time dimension. With this system one would expect the galaxies to remain at rest or move at random through a static space like the molecules of a gas. But the metric had been obtained by the introduction of an arbitrary constant of doubtful validity. Einstein himself disregarded the constant in later years. Furthermore, Sir Arthur Eddington showed that the Einstein universe was unstable. If atoms were converted into radiation then the pressure would increase and the universe would begin to expand. The Einstein metric was finally abandoned when Edwin Hubble discovered the redshift, for in the static universe no redshift was to be expected.

In the same year, 1917, the Dutch astronomer W. de Sitter obtained a second solution to the field equations of general relativity. He derived a second type of metric which predicted distortion both in time and space. All subsequent cosmological theories have been based on metrics remarkably similar to the metric of the "de Sitter universe." The original work of de Sitter is therefore of fundamental importance. In particular the de Sitter universe predicts an expanding universe and, because of the expansion, a redshift in the light from distant galaxies.

In the original derivation, de Sitter encountered a term $p + \rho$, where p is the pressure and $\rho$ is the average density in the universe when regarded as a fluid. The universe could only be homogeneous, in accordance with the *cosmological principle,* if $p + \rho$ was equal to zero. Dr. de Sitter thought that a negative pressure was impossible. He was therefore compelled to assume that both the pressure and the density were equal to zero. Thus his metric described an empty universe, devoid of matter and pressureless.

The movement of galaxies in a de Sitter universe was most puzzling. Assuming the galaxies to move along geodesic lines, then each galaxy would move toward the Earth, rest momentarily, and then move outwards once again. This peculiar motion did not necessarily put the Earth in a unique position, for the same equations could be set up at any point in the universe with similar consequences. Perhaps the universe was contracting as a whole and then re-expanding. Each observer would notice the galaxies moving away from him but he would be unable to observe a center to the universe. Thus the *principle of conformity* and the *cosmological principle* would be honored. But the theory violates the more recent *perfect cosmological principle* in a decisive way. According to the theory, the separation of galaxies will continue without limit until each observer is left in splendid isolation. The sky, at present studded with galaxies, will ultimately become empty. In several billion years' time we expect an astronomer to see only the stars in the local galaxy. He would have no knowledge of the universe beyond.

Several cosmologists, including Sir Arthur S. Eddington, A. Friedmann, and G. Lemaître, adopted a new interpretation of the de Sitter metric. It was permissible to regard space-time itself as expanding, carrying with it the multitude of galaxies. Although it was difficult to imagine, space-time seemed to be drawn on the surface of a sphere in a multi-dimensioned space. The radius of this sphere increases with time; the space-time continuum expands and the galaxies become separated. A general contraction is also permitted by the equations, but if we interpret the redshift as a Doppler effect we are forced to adopt the expanding solution at the present epoch.

Lemaître continued the argument to its ultimate limit, producing what has become known colloquially as the "big bang" theory. In the beginning all the galaxies were contained in a primeval atom of extremely high density. This epoch corresponded to a singular point in time; we may regard it as the time at which the universe was created. With explosive violence the expansion began. From the gaseous debris the galaxies condensed and continued in the outward movement. According to the theory we look today on a universe in which galaxies are all of the same age and at the same stage of evolution. In the end the galaxies will be completely separated from each other, the stars will burn out, and matter will take up a uniform, lukewarm temperature. The universe will finish as a dark, changeless world, devoid of life, expanding into nothingness.

Although the big bang theory has been popular for many years, it is now falling into disfavor. It is an evolving universe, in violation of the *perfect cosmological principle*. The primeval atom, by definition, was at the center of the present-day universe, and we might expect to find a few remnants left behind at the seat of the explosion. It would conceivably be possible to find these remnants with a powerful telescope and hence find a unique center to the universe. Thus there is a possibility that the theory also disagrees with the *cosmological principle*. The uniform expansion is accounted for well enough by the expansion of the space-time continuum, but nevertheless, there are difficulties in understanding the actual physics of the explosion. If we restrict our argument to a small region in the vicinity of the primeval atom, then material must be ejected in such a manner that it will spread out uniformly. The debris must presumably be a gas of uniform density, otherwise galaxies would not condense from the medium equidistant from each other. Galaxies now distant from the center must have been ejected at a high velocity, others at a correspondingly lower velocity. If the primeval atom ever existed it was a physical monstrosity. The pressure and density were extremely high, comparable to or perhaps exceeding the pressure and density in the core of a white dwarf star. How remarkable to think that the entire object almost instantaneously was converted into a tenuous gas from which the galaxies later condensed. Surely one would expect a few dense fragments of the primeval atom to have survived the catastrophe, forming a number of freak galaxies, enlarged and overdense.

In 1948, the British astronomer Fred Hoyle introduced the "steady state" theory. Dr. Hoyle replaced the cosmological constant in the Einstein field equations with a tensor. With this step he was open to all the criticism that had been leveled at the earlier cosmologists when they introduced the cosmological constant. The field equations in the vicinity of the sun did not need an extra constant or an extra tensor, and the *principle of conformity* was in danger of violation. But, like Einstein's cosmological constant, Hoyle's tensor was so small that it would have no appreciable effect on the motion of the planets and there would be no need to revise the Einstein planetary laws. However, the tensor did imply a remarkable change in one of the fundamental laws of physics, the law of "conservation of matter." On this basis many physicists strongly object to the introduction of the new tensor.

Matter, if we interpret the tensor in a particular way, is continually being created throughout space. Hydrogen atoms, or perhaps neutrons, are appearing from nothingness at a regular rate. The process has been going on indefinitely and will continue into the infinite future. Einstein pointed out the equivalence of mass and energy, and the concept of matter may be extended to cover the sum total of these quantities. Physicists firmly believe that matter can be neither created nor destroyed. It is a scientific expression of the everyday viewpoint that "you cannot obtain something for nothing." Every experiment in physics verifies this postulate exactly. To placate the conservative scientist, the supporters of the new theory argue as follows. "Although the law of conservation of matter is violated by the creation process, the rate is so slow as to make no measurable differences in experiments carried out in the laboratories." At the moment, continuous creation can neither be proved nor disproved on the Earth and we must look to the larger laboratories, the galaxies, for further information.

The steady state theory leads to a de Sitter-type of metric with an expanding universe, but there is one important difference. During the expansion, the density of the universe remains constant. The galaxies will not separate from each other into the condition of splendid isolation. New galaxies will form from the newly created material. Although in billions of years' time the present galaxies will have moved out of sight, replacements will form to give the sky much the same appearance as it has now. Whereas the galaxies are of the same age in the big bang theory, in the steady state theory we must expect to find galaxies of all ages and in all stages of development. Because of the general expansion, however, there will be a tendency for nearby galaxies to be younger than distant galaxies. This provides a possibility of distinguishing between the two theories and several astronomers are at present searching for some evidence of age differences among the galaxies.

In 1959, at the Cleveland meeting of the Astronomical Society, I suggested that we look very closely at the de Sitter-type of metric with a view to explaining the redshift as something other than a Doppler effect. If the redshift can be explained without invoking motion, then the concept of a larger scale expansion would be erroneous. The universe would be non-expanding, or static. As early as 1929 the American astronomer F. Zwicky, for example, attempted to explain the redshift by the action of gravity on rays of light. Apart from the redshift there is no other evidence for expansion; in fact the existence of clusters of galaxies seems to argue against it. Professor Zwicky has always referred to the expansion as the "symbolic velocity of recession." Even Dr. Hubble was not completely convinced about the expansion interpretation. For that reason he always spoke of the "redshift" and not the "velocity of expansion."

If we go back to the original work of de Sitter and allow the pressure to be negative, then a solution of the Einstein equations is again possible. The universe has a distortion in both space and time but, unlike the original de Sitter universe, a finite density of material is allowed. The metric itself is very similar to the metric of the steady state theory, but it has been derived without the introduction of an arbitrary cosmological constant or a creation tensor. Thus the metric does not imply continuous creation of matter with the consequent change of one of the fundamental laws of physics.

Within the framework of the theory, a static solution is possible; the galaxies remain forever at the same distance from each other. Even though there is no large-scale expansion, the theory still predicts a wave-length shift toward the red. The redshift, however, is not produced by the Doppler effect. It is related to the distortion in the space-time continuum, and the constraint acting upon the galaxies.

In the static universe the galaxies are not moving along geodesic lines and the solution implies a radial field of force. The nature of this force is not yet understood. Is it virtual or is it real? Whatever its nature, this restraining field seems to be a necessary corollary to any static solution. When the static solution is applied to the region near the sun, then a radial field of force is still present. In this case, however, the force is familiar to physicists—the major component being the Newtonian force of gravity. There is an additional radial term, the general field of the universe, but it is so small that it produces a negligible distortion in the movement of the planets.

Apart from the avoidance of the concept of continuous creation, the static universe is very similar to the steady state one. We would expect to find galaxies at different stages of evolution. The universe itself did not appear spectacularly at some instant of creation. It has been here for a period close to eternity, and will remain for a long time to come. There is, however, one prediction which distinguishes the static universe from all other models. The expanding universe leads us to expect a linear redshift, where the displacement of the spectral lines is proportional to the distance of the galaxy. In a static universe, however, we expect a quadratic redshift, where the displacement is proportional to the square of the distance. Even with such a marked difference the observations do not give conclusive evidence one way or the other. The result of thirty years work is summarized in the redshift diagram of Chapter 29. There is a large scatter among the points, and the galaxies which belonged to clusters seem to show results which differ from those of isolated field galaxies. The linear law of the expansion theory seems to fit the cluster galaxies, yet the quadratic law of the static universe seems to fit the points which represent the field galaxies.

There are, of course, many uncertainties in the observations which cannot be removed at the present time. For example, we tacitly assume that each galaxy on the average is as bright as its neighbor. A systematic change, a progressive increase or decrease in brightness in galaxies with distance, will affect the diagram. We do not entertain this as a possibility at the moment because it is at variance with the *cosmological principle*. There is also the possibility that light is absorbed by dust and obscuring matter in the space between the galaxies. Such obscuration would seriously affect the results. It would tend to deviate the quadratic lines in the diagram, making it become more parallel to the line through the cluster data. But here both theory and observations are lost in uncertainty and all progress seems to be barred. Dr. Otto Struve, an American astronomer with years of practical experience, has a very solid outlook. He regards cosmological theories as "bubbles of pure thought." Perhaps he is right, but so long as the mind of man is active I am sure there will always be someone curious enough to let his thoughts wander out to the mysterious regions of the *far horizons*.

# SUGGESTIONS FOR
# FURTHER READING

For general reading in astronomy I recommend:

*Frontiers of Astronomy,* by Fred Hoyle. Harper & Brothers, New York, 1955.

*Larousse Encyclopedia of Astronomy,* by L. Rudaux and G. de Vaucouleurs. G. P. Putnam's Sons, New York, 1959.

*Source Book in Astronomy,* by Harlow Shapley and H. E. Howarth. McGraw-Hill Book Co., New York, 1929.

*Source Book in Astronomy, 1900-1950,* by Harlow Shapley. Harvard University Press, Cambridge, Mass. In preparation.

*The Individual and the Universe,* by A. C. B. Lovell. Oxford University Press, London, England, 1959.

Articles of current interest are carried in several magazines such as:

*Sky and Telescope* (Monthly), Sky Publishing Corporation, Cambridge, Mass.

*Scientific American* (Monthly), New York.

For astronomy in ancient times the reader should refer to:

*The History of Astronomy,* by J. L. E. Dreyer, which gives an authoritative account up to the Renaissance. Dover Publications, Inc., New York, 1953.

*The Exact Sciences in Antiquity,* by O. Neugebauer, is a scholarly book which pinpoints our knowledge, or rather our lack of knowledge, concerning astronomy in antiquity. Princeton University Press, Princeton, N. J., 1952.

*Copernicus,* by Angus Armitage, contains an excellent account of Copernicus and the details of his famous book. Thomas Yoseloff, Inc., New York, 1957.

*Kepler,* by Max Caspar. This new biography gives a revealing description of Kepler and his work. Abelard-Schuman, Limited, New York, 1959.

*The Discoveries and Opinions of Galileo,* by Stillman Drake, is a direct translation of some of Galileo's work and provides a background from which to judge his scientific achievements. Anchor Books, Doubleday & Company, Inc., New York, 1957.

*The Crime of Galileo,* by Giorgio de Santillana, describes in detail the manner in which he clashed with the Church. University of Chicago Press, Chicago, Ill., 1955.

Astrology was a part of the way of life in medieval times when the wizards and witches seemed to take an unfair advantage of the credulous public. One gets a glimpse of this power in medieval diaries such as:

*The Travels of Marco Polo,* by Marco Polo. The Orion Press, Inc., New York, 1960.

For further information on the planets, I recommend:

*Earth, Moon and Planets,* by Fred L. Whipple. Grosset and Dunlap, Inc., New York, 1958.

*The Planet Venus,* by Patrick Moore. Faber and Faber Limited, London, England, 1959.

*The Planet Jupiter,* by Bertrand M. Peek. Faber and Faber Limited, London, England, 1958.

*The Face of the Moon,* by Ralph G. Baldwin, is a book in which the author adopts the viewpoint that the surface features of the moon are almost entirely produced by meteorite bombardment. University of Chicago Press, Chicago, Ill., 1958.

*The Moon,* by Zdenek Kopal, is a recently published book for the general reader which is less biased than the book by Baldwin and discusses both the volcanic and meteoric origin of lunar features. Chapman & Hall Ltd., London, England, 1960.

*The History of the Telescope,* by H. C. King, gives an excellent and accurate account of the development of the telescope from early times to the present day. Sky Publishing Corporation, Cambridge, Mass., 1955.

For more information concerning the oceans of the Earth, three excellent books are available:

*Frontiers of the Sea,* by Robert C. Cowen. Doubleday & Company, Inc., Garden City, New York, 1960.

*The Sea Around Us,* by Rachel L. Carson. Mentor Books, New American Library of World Literature, Inc., New York, 1954.

*Book of the Seven Seas,* by Peter Freuchen. Julian Messner, Inc., New York, 1957.

For a description of meteors, comets, and asteroids, I recommend:

*Between the Planets,* by Fletcher G. Watson. Harvard University Press, Cambridge, Mass., 1956.

For a comprehensive account of the sun as a star, I recommend:

*Our Sun,* by Donald H. Menzel, Harvard University Press, Cambridge, Mass., 1959.

For a discussion of the stars in general:

*Stars in the Making,* by Cecilia Payne Gaposchikin. Harvard University Press, Cambridge, Mass., 1952.

For a very readable account of the various theories of cosmology:

*The Unity of the Universe,* by D. W. Sciama. Doubleday & Company, Inc., Garden City, New York, 1960.

# INDEX

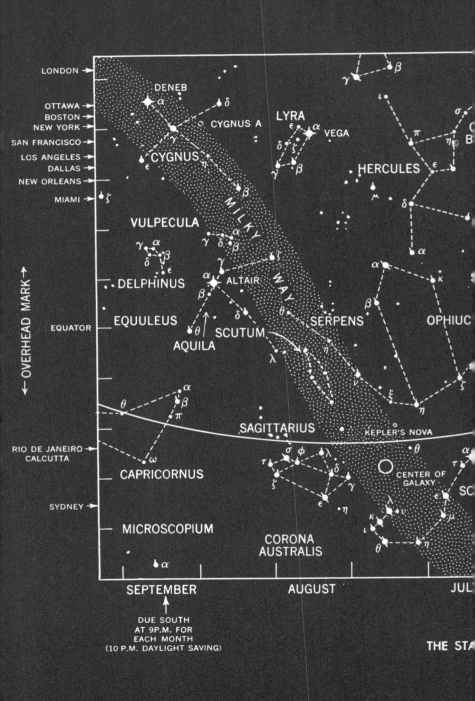

LONDON →

OTTAWA →
BOSTON →
NEW YORK →

SAN FRANCISCO →

LOS ANGELES →
DALLAS →

NEW ORLEANS →

MIAMI →

ζ

← OVERHEAD MARK →

EQUATOR

RIO DE JANEIRO →
CALCUTTA →

SYDNEY →

DENEB

α

CYGNUS A

γ

CYGNUS

ε

β

VULPECULA

γ α

δ β

ε

DELPHINUS

EQUULEUS

θ

AQUILA

α

ALTAIR

β

δ

θ

δ

γ

SCUTUM

λ

α β

θ

π

ω

CAPRICORNUS

MICROSCOPIUM

α

LYRA

ε

δ κ ζ

γ β

α VEGA

HERCULES

μ

δ

α

SERPENS

θ

η

ν

ξ

η

SAGITTARIUS

σ φ λ

τ

δ

ζ

ε

η

γ

CORONA
AUSTRALIS

KEPLER'S NOVA

θ

CENTER OF
GALAXY

λ

κ υ

ι ι μ

θ

η

α

ι

π

η

σ

δ

α

κ

β

OPHIUC

τ

α

ε ι

SC

SEPTEMBER

AUGUST

JUL

DUE SOUTH
AT 9 P.M. FOR
EACH MONTH
(10 P.M. DAYLIGHT SAVING)

THE STA